IMAGES
of America

AFRICAN AMERICANS OF HOUSTON

On the Cover: During this country's Reconstruction era, the Buffalo Soldiers served with distinction in the American West. Black rodeos in Houston and other Southern cities honor the memory of those men that contributed so much at a time when blacks were relegated to second-class citizenship in this nation. Likewise, the African American community in Houston has contributed to the city's development as an international city and key energy center in the United States. Sadly, like those of the black soldiers of the 19th century, the contributions of Houston's black community have too often been overlooked or ignored altogether. While some wrongs, like the confinement of blacks behind chicken wire during the 1928 Democratic convention, can never be corrected, the acknowledgment of the contributions of Houston's black community to the city's overall development promotes the racial and social progress of one of the most diverse cities in the country.

IMAGES
of America

AFRICAN AMERICANS OF HOUSTON

Ronald E. Goodwin

ARCADIA
PUBLISHING

ISBN 978-0-7385-8487-4

Published by Arcadia Publishing
Charleston, South Carolina

Printed in the United States of America

Library of Congress Control Number: 2013933117

For all general information, please contact Arcadia Publishing:
Telephone 843-853-2070
Fax 843-853-0044
E-mail sales@arcadiapublishing.com
For customer service and orders:
Toll-Free 1-888-313-2665

Visit us on the Internet at www.arcadiapublishing.com

This book is dedicated to the many black men and women who suffered under Jim Crow racism, celebrated their blackness during the civil rights era, and finally exhaled in the age of Obama. These men and women forged a community out of the rubble of slavery and sacrificed all they knew so their children and their children's children would finally have access to everything this great country has to offer. To them is owed a debt that can never be repaid.

Contents

ACKNOWLEDGMENTS

All images appear courtesy of the Houston Public Library unless otherwise noted.

INTRODUCTION

The experiences of Houston's African American community mirror those of the larger black community found throughout the United States. Many blacks that initially settled in Houston were former slaves who found themselves restricted to certain areas of town. Houston's Freedman's Town was one of those areas, and it remains a reminder of the violence and segregation that once restricted the mobility and livelihoods of the city's black populace. The presence of black regiments and the ensuing riots in 1917 illustrated that Jim Crow was alive and well and that the lives of blacks were worth significantly less than those of whites. Jim Crow also encouraged state officials to create Texas Southern University (TSU) with the hope of avoiding the integration of the flagship institution—the University of Texas at Austin. Nonetheless, the Supreme Court's decision in *Brown v. Board of Education* lit the flame of civil rights throughout the country, and it burned in Houston as well. However, hoping to avoid destruction and chaos of other Southern cities, leaders integrated public places without fanfare or hysteria after coordinating with officials at Texas Southern University.

Today, many in Houston's black community have little understanding of the trials and tribulations of those who went before us. While the careers of Barbara Jordan and Mickey Leland receive accolades and recognition—and justifiably so—lesser-known individuals paved the way for today's generation of scholars and athletes. How many of Houston's black schoolchildren know of Heman Sweatt? These stories need to be told. These pioneers are our family; they are our aunts, uncles, "Nanas," and "Big Pappas." They prayed for a world where their children could live without fear, and those prayers live on today in each member of Houston's black community. It is time we honor them by looking at their contribution to today's fourth largest city in America.

One

HOUSTON'S PUBLIC SPACES

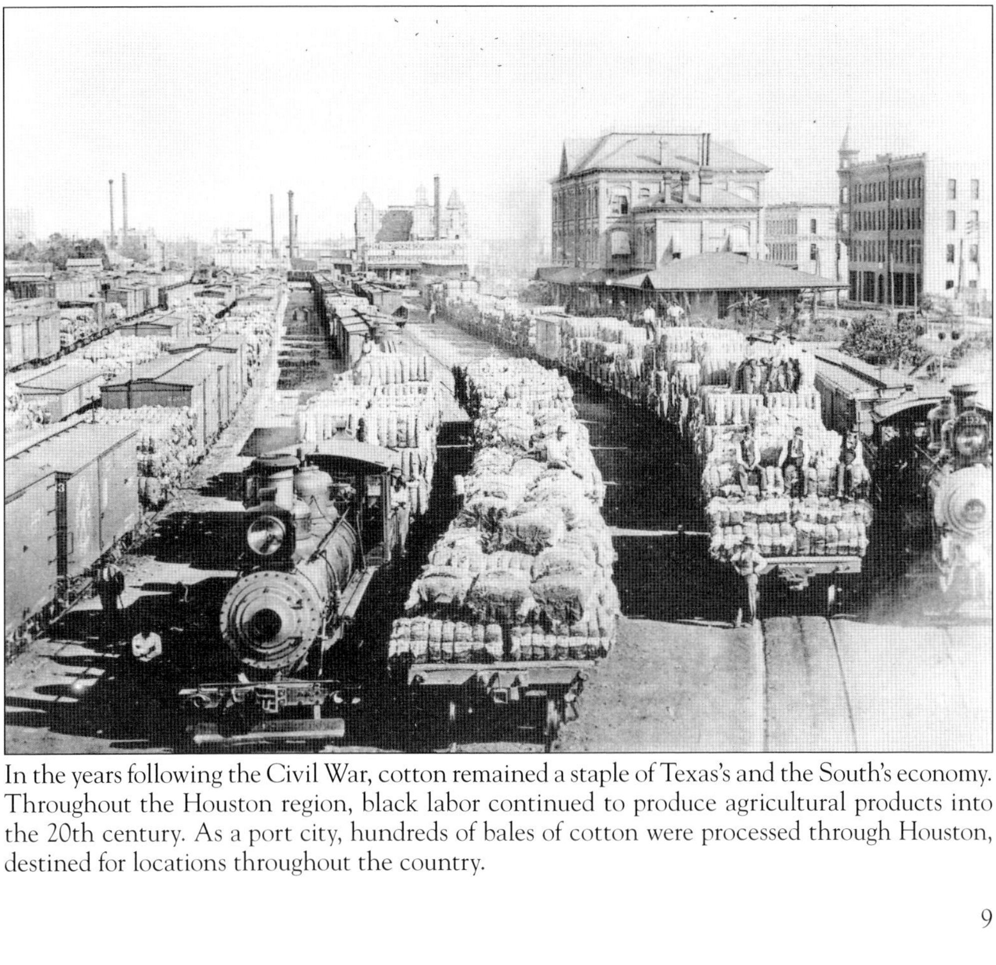

In the years following the Civil War, cotton remained a staple of Texas's and the South's economy. Throughout the Houston region, black labor continued to produce agricultural products into the 20th century. As a port city, hundreds of bales of cotton were processed through Houston, destined for locations throughout the country.

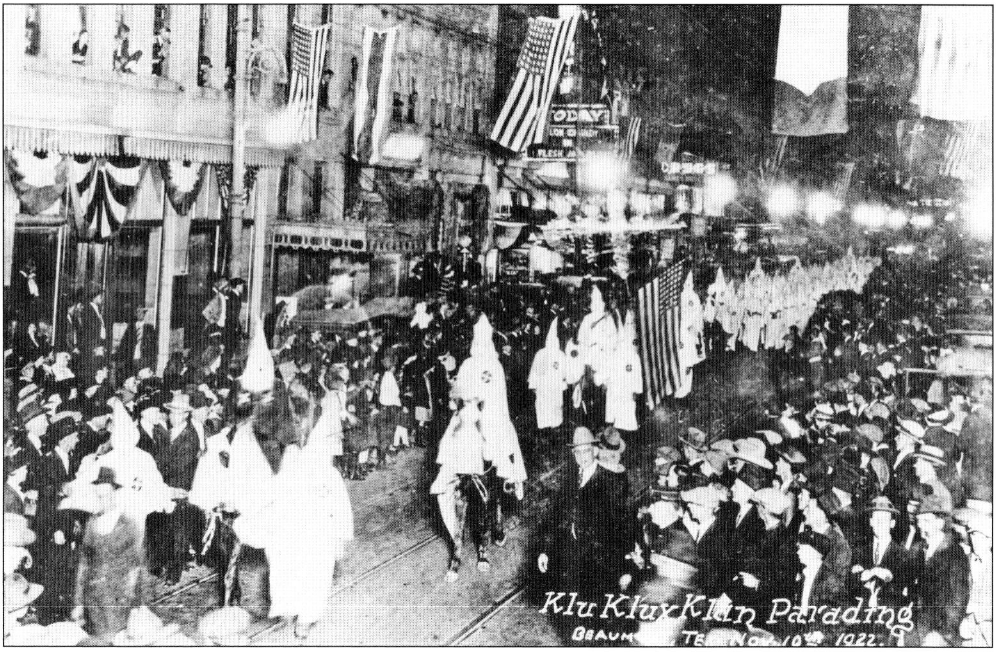

The Ku Klux Klan played a significant role in suppressing the rights of blacks throughout the South during the last quarter of the 19th century. While the organization was subdued during the Progressive Era, the Klan returned in the post–World War I years in demonstrations throughout the country. In Texas, the Klan made their presence known, effectively suppressing the rights of the city's black population.

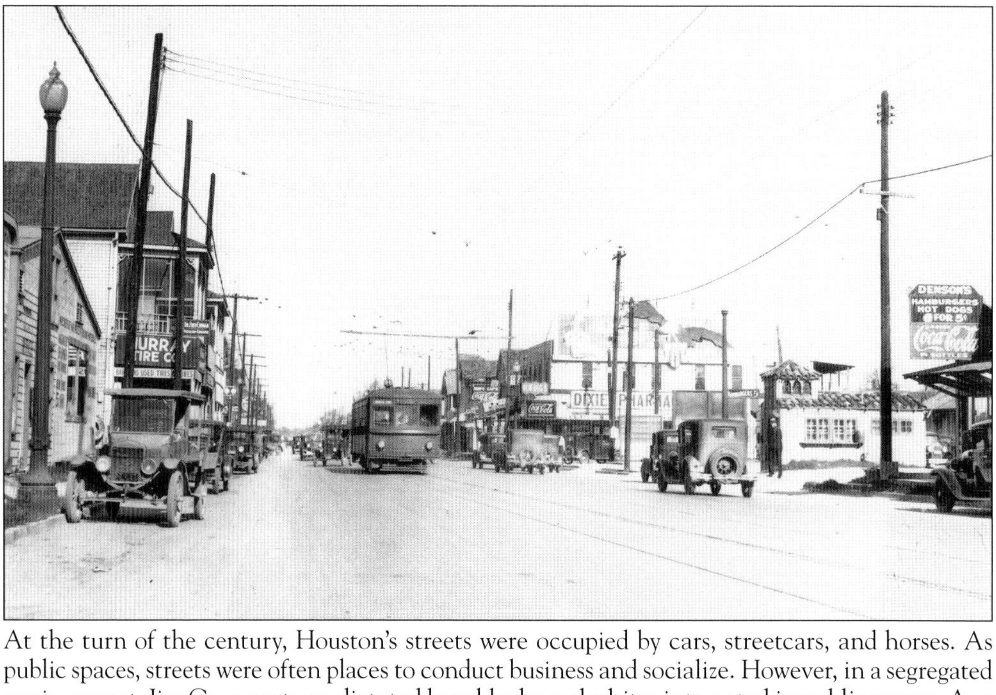

At the turn of the century, Houston's streets were occupied by cars, streetcars, and horses. As public spaces, streets were often places to conduct business and socialize. However, in a segregated environment, Jim Crow customs dictated how blacks and whites interacted in public spaces. Any violation of Jim Crow rules could result in dire consequences for the offender.

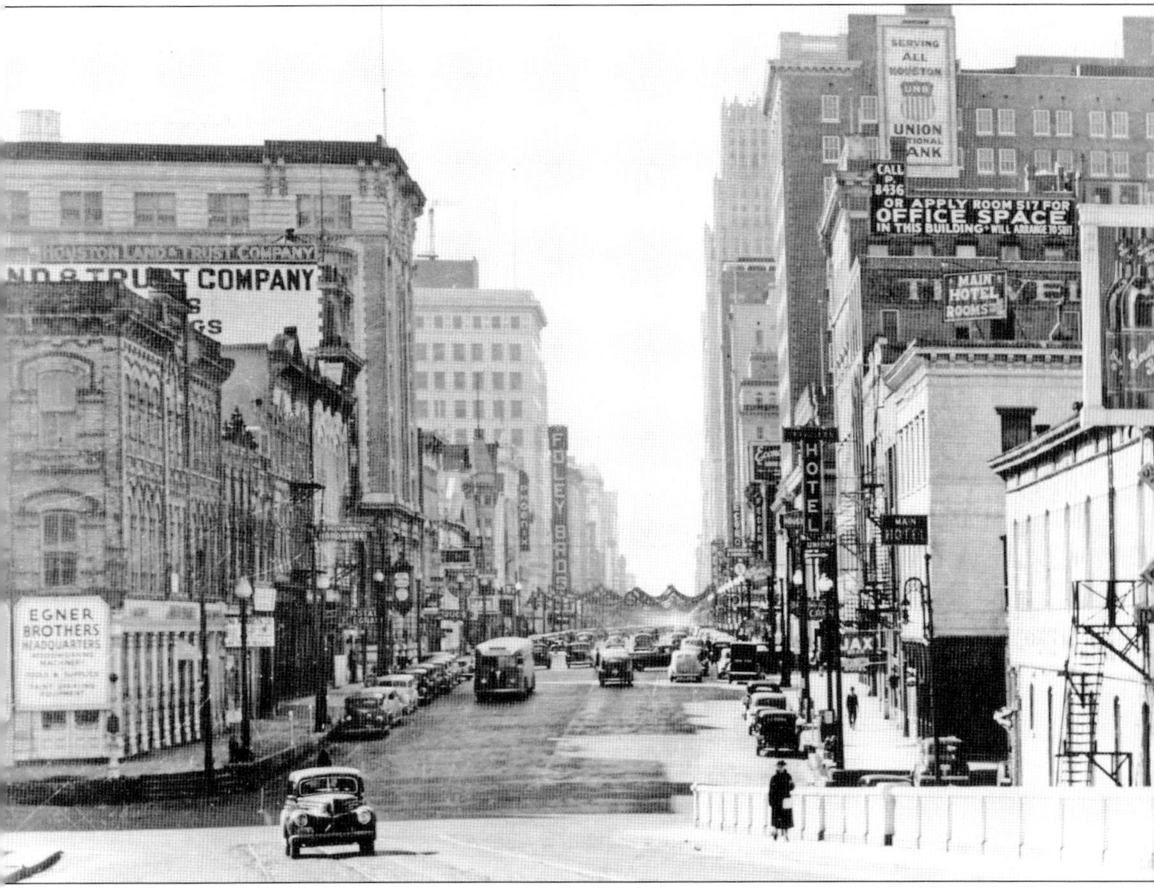

In the early 20th century, Houston's downtown skyline was already identifiable as scores of buildings were rising from the ground. Even though the city was segregated, racism was not overtly identified with its character. However, the residential areas, usually hidden from public view, were bastions of racism, as in other Southern cities. This street scene illustrates the modern character of 1920s Houston as buses and cars dominate the streets. The new transportation technologies moved people around the city, but even these conveyances were segregated by race, severely limiting access to the black population. Unfortunately, these segregated conveyances were often dilapidated and seldom complied with the essence of "separate but equal." As a result, Houston's black population moved around the city in vehicles that were uncomfortable and on schedules that were lesser than those provided the city's white commuters.

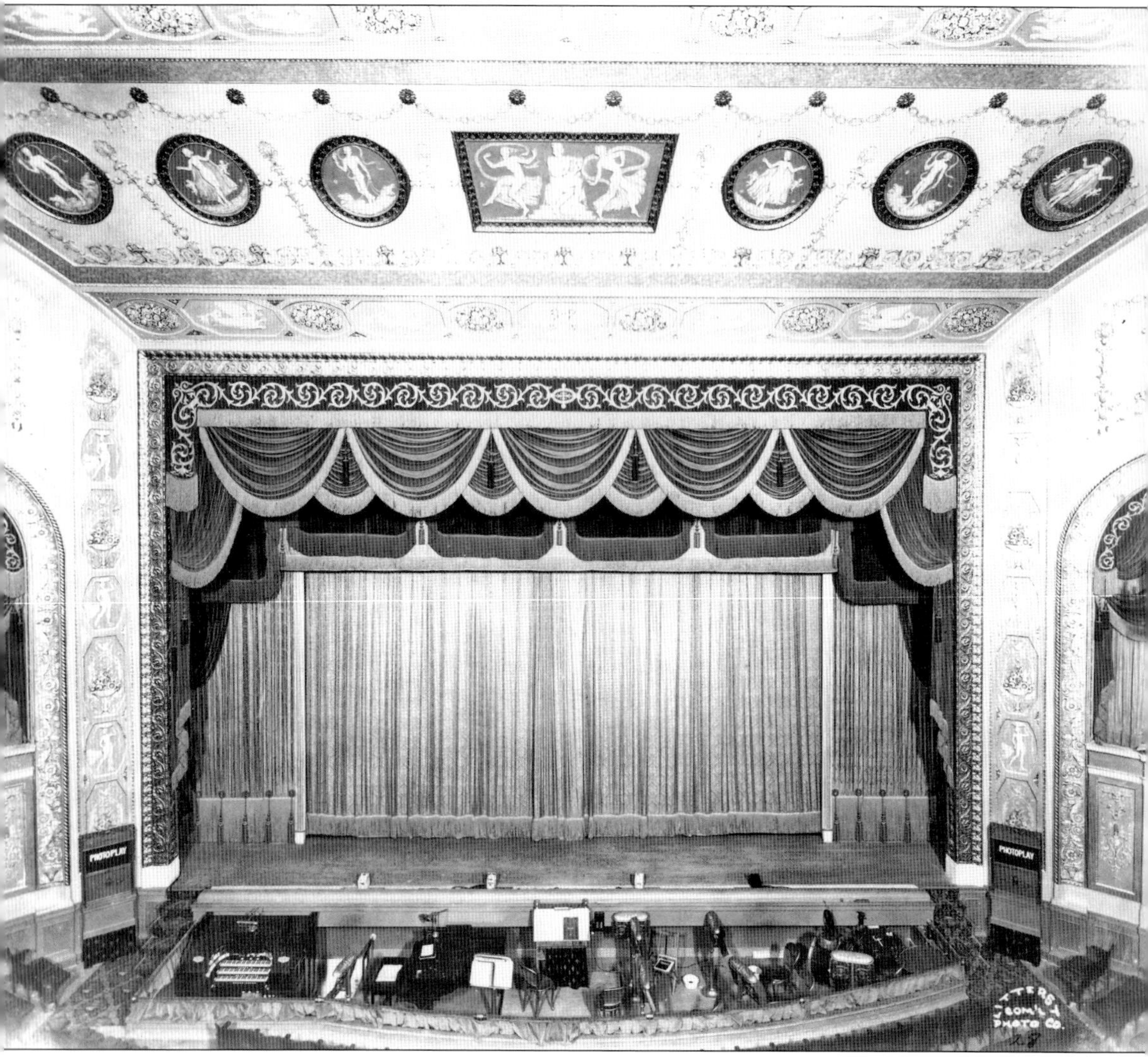

Pictured here is the stage of the Houston's Majestic Theatre. Created by famed architect John Eberson, it was one of three he designed in Texas (the other Majestic Theatres were in San Antonio and Dallas). The intricate designs reflected Eberson's European influences and brought an exquisite style and elegance to the 1920s Houston's cultural scene. Opening in 1923, Houston's Majestic Theatre was Eberson's first atmospheric design, featuring a vaunted ceiling meant to provide the illusion of an open sky. For those attending performances at the Majestic, the architecture would hopefully transport the audience to faraway lands and places where the economy was not a matter of concern. However, it would be the economy that limited the number of atmospheric theaters being built, as the cost was too expensive for a Depression-era facility. Sadly, Houston's black population had to enjoy the beauty of the Majestic Theatre from the outside unless they were employed as part of the cleaning crews.

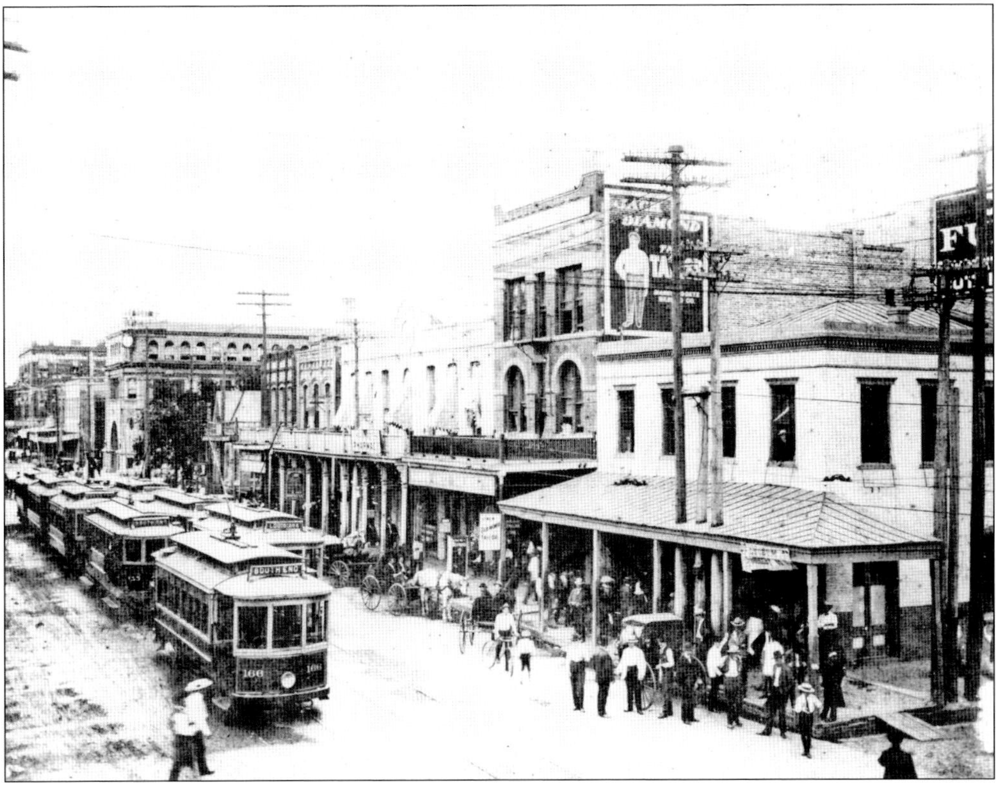

Electric streetcars were a common occurrence on Houston's downtown streets for almost three decades before eventually being replaced by the bus with its combustion engine. City leaders considered the streetcar too inflexible to adjust to the area's rapidly changing demographic profile. As a result, Houstonians would not see electric streetcars for the next 70 years.

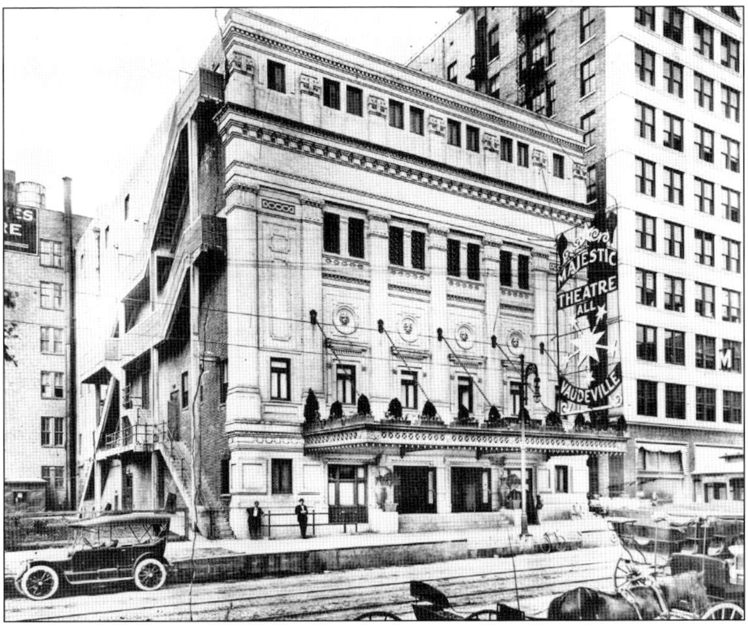

This outside street view of the Majestic Theatre dates to the 1920s. The scene is indicative of the image Houston wanted to portray of itself: clean streets, distinctive architecture, and blacks hidden from plain view. While there were no legal restrictions preventing the city's black population from public spaces, Southern custom dictated how they would behave in those places.

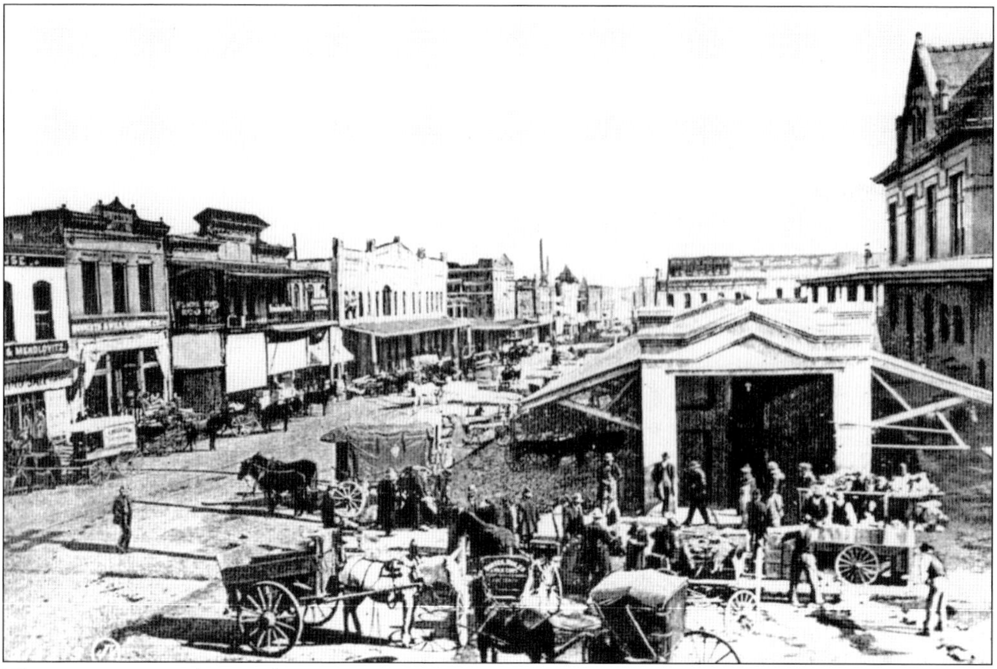

This c. 1910 image depicts the movement of goods on horse-drawn carriages. Goods were transported to the city via the newly expanded port and the city's extensive network of railroads. Those blacks that did not work in the peripheral farms found employment along the port or one of its staging areas.

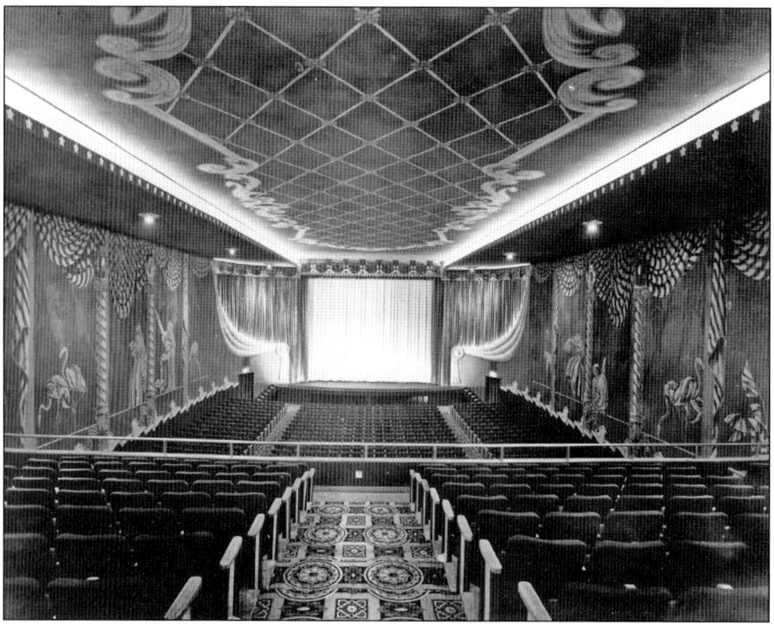

A view from the balcony of the Majestic Theatre illustrates the beauty that was a known trademark of John Eberson's designs. While the city's black community was restricted by Jim Crow from patronizing the theater, many African Americans were employed in service positions.

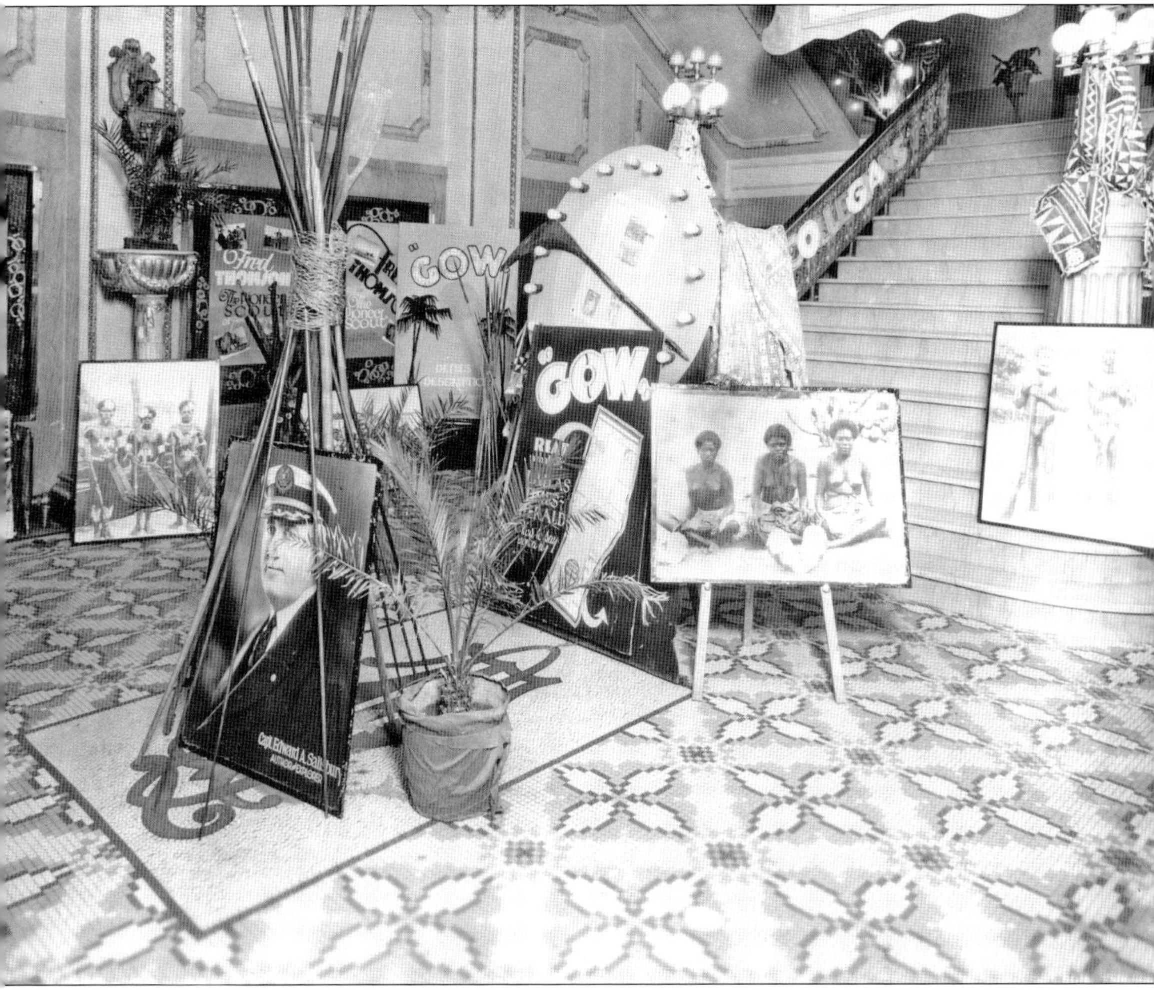

The lobby of the Majestic Theatre is seen here with the display of an African exhibit around the 1920s. Since many of Houston's white citizens had little day-to-day contact with blacks, these exhibitions served as their only insight into black culture. Unfortunately, the culture was of blacks in Africa and not blacks in the city's Fourth and Fifth Wards, where Jim Crow–induced poverty was endemic. These kinds of exhibits also reinforced the commonly held belief in the 19th and early 20th centuries that black Africans were barbaric and somehow less civilized than even the poorest whites in America. Such a negative stereotype was difficult to eradicate from the consciousness of most white Houstonians as blacks eventually began the concerted push for equal access to the city's facilities and services in the years following World War II. However, many blacks continued to support their own segregated facilities and institutions in the Third, Fourth, and Fifth Wards well into the latter years of the 20th century.

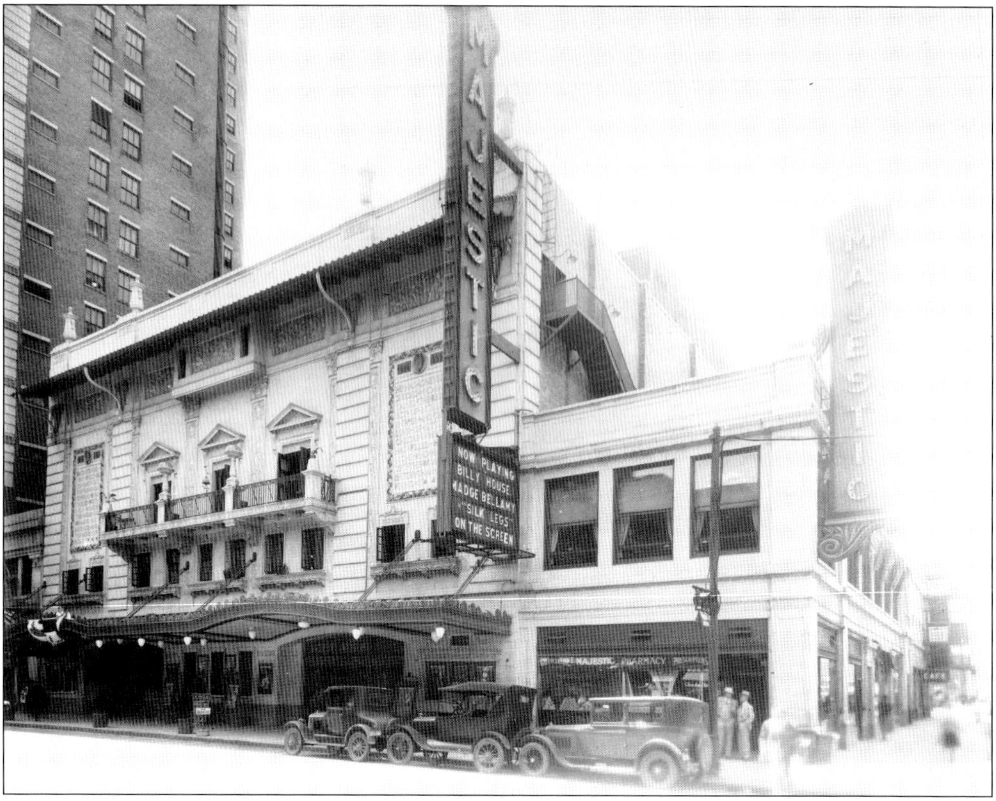

Thanks to political giants like Jesse Jones and John Nance Garner, Houston's skyline was beginning to take shape during the Great Depression. While money was being spent erecting skyscrapers near the Majestic, as seen in the background, city leaders showed little interest in providing even basic municipal services to its black communities. As a result, the divide between black and white Houston was not only social and political, but physical as well.

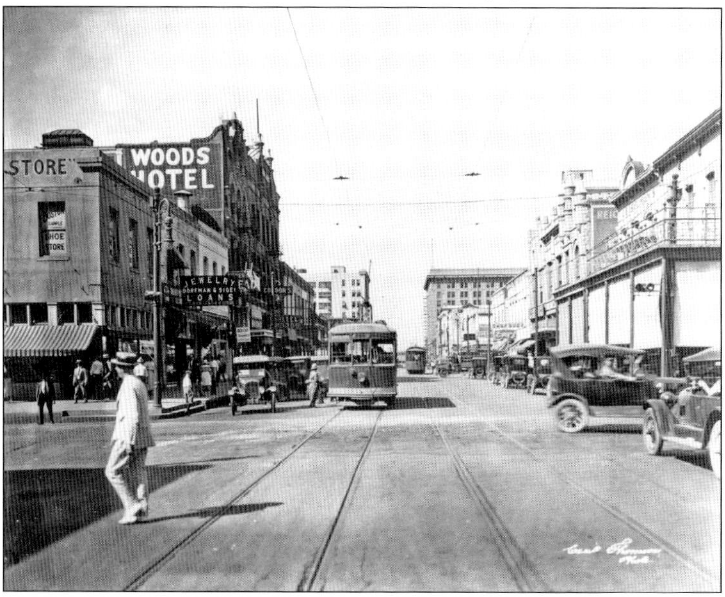

This downtown Houston street scene illustrates the confluence of streetcars and automobiles around the 1920s. As public spaces, streets were often the one place where Houstonians interacted with one another regardless of race and ethnicity. However, Jim Crow customs dictated how those public interactions would be conducted between the races.

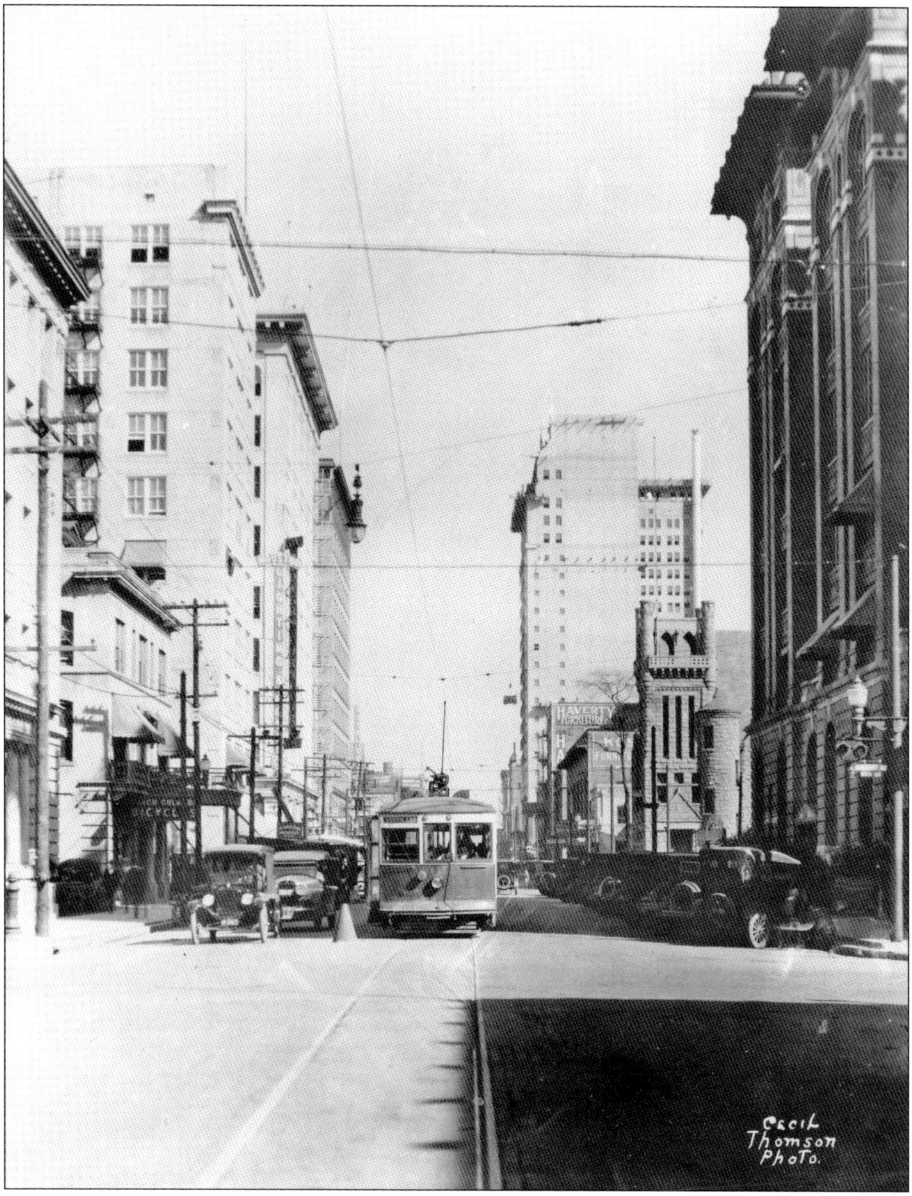

A minor street in downtown Houston again depicts the various forms of mobility available to Houstonians during the World War I era (around the 1920s). However, very few of those in Houston's black community owned cars, and segregation limited access to the city's streetcars. While there were streetcar lines serving Houston's black communities, they were the first to be sacrificed in the 1920s when the streetcar company experienced financial hardships. Bolstered by the editorials of the city's black newspapers, black Houstonians vocally expressed their displeasure at being treated with political and economic callousness more than 50 years after the end of slavery. The editorials reminded black Houstonians that the city's white establishment would always sacrifice their needs on the altar of social and technological advancement. By the time buses were introduced on Houston's streets, segregated black communities were well defined and often isolated from access to the city's power elite. As a result, Houston's black community often had inferior services and facilities when compared to white communities.

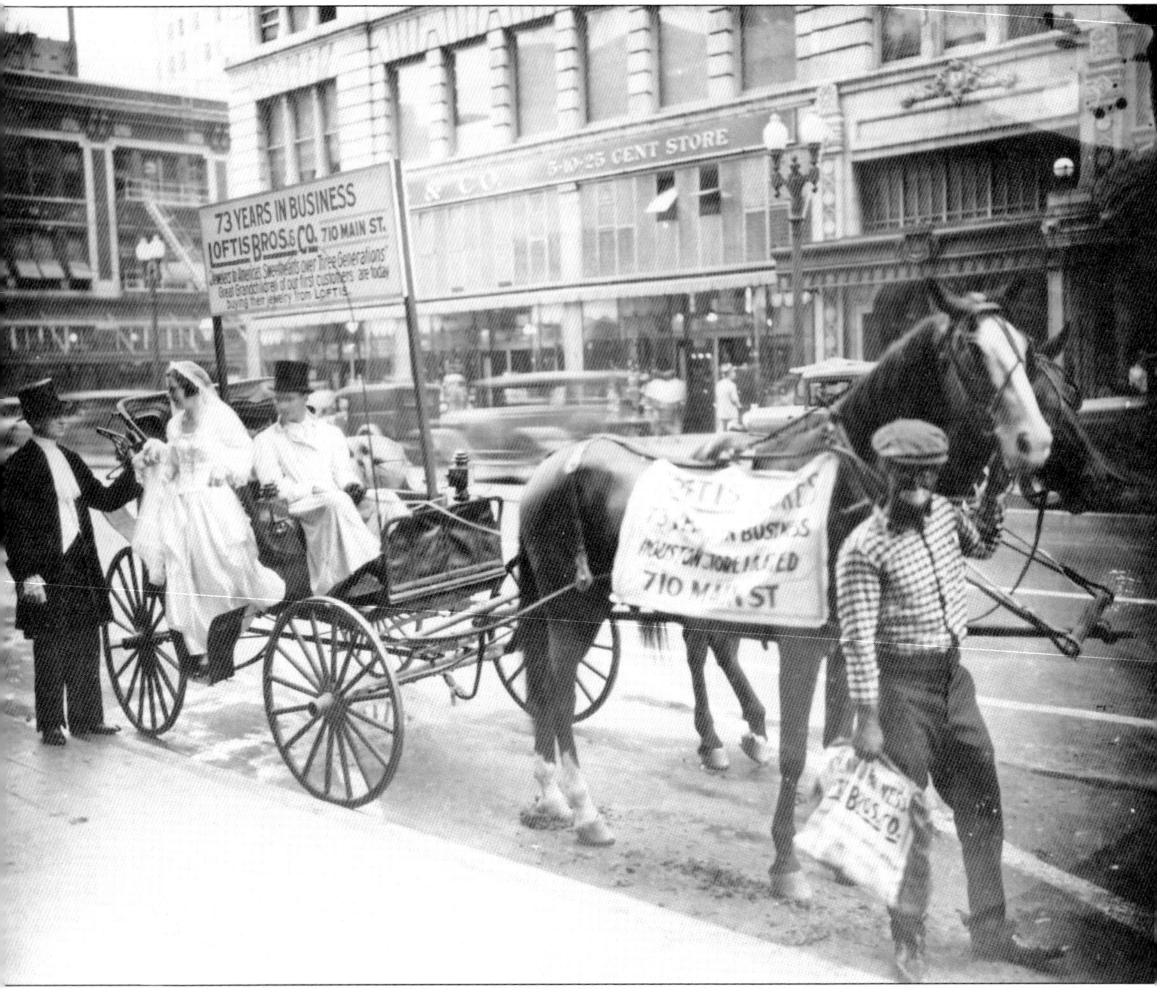

This image from around the time of World War I shows a couple using a horse-drawn carriage after a wedding. The operator of the carriage is in blackface. The practice of whites appearing in blackface was typically found in the performing arts with whites assuming the roles of black characters instead of hiring blacks for those roles. The custom originated in the 19th century and continued into the post–World War II era. Blacks found the practice of blackface degrading and humiliating. Those portraying black characters mimicked stereotypical black behaviors as well, including speaking in drawl-laden, broken English; acting nervous in the presence of whites; and the incessantly dragging their feet as they walked. Such mannerisms were embodied in the mythical Sambo, thought to represent the typical antebellum slave—dependent upon his supposedly benevolent owner. By the time of World War I, blacks across the country rejected this caricature of the black male and believed it only existed in the minds of whites who wanted to see blacks behave in such a nonthreatening manner.

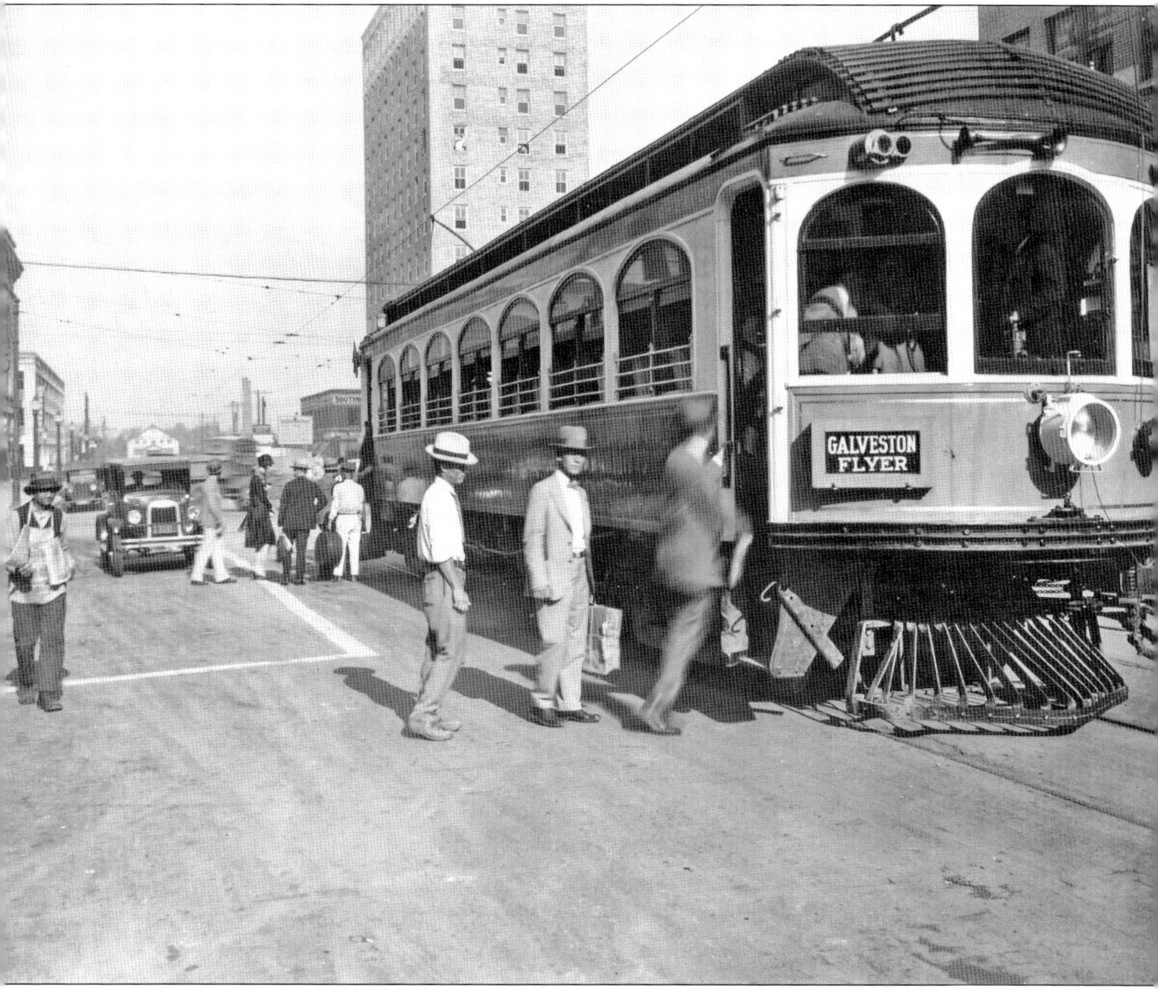

The island of Galveston was once the major city in Texas. However, after a natural disaster in the early years of the 20th century destroyed the city, Houston's business elite reconfigured the port between Houston and the Gulf of Mexico to allow the ingress of ships with deeper cargo holds. The financial investment in Houston's port ultimately led to the virtual ruin of Galveston's economy. Nonetheless, the Galveston Flyer provided access between Galveston and Houston for the region's commuters. Like Houston, Galveston was also mired in Jim Crow, and too often its black community encountered challenges in accessing the city's services. In the years after the decline of Galveston's economic fortunes, the city became a tourist attraction and eventually home to one of the state's medical teaching institutions. Decades after the demise of the Galveston Flyer, city officials reintroduced local streetcar services to provide accessibility to the medical facilities, the business district, and the local beaches.

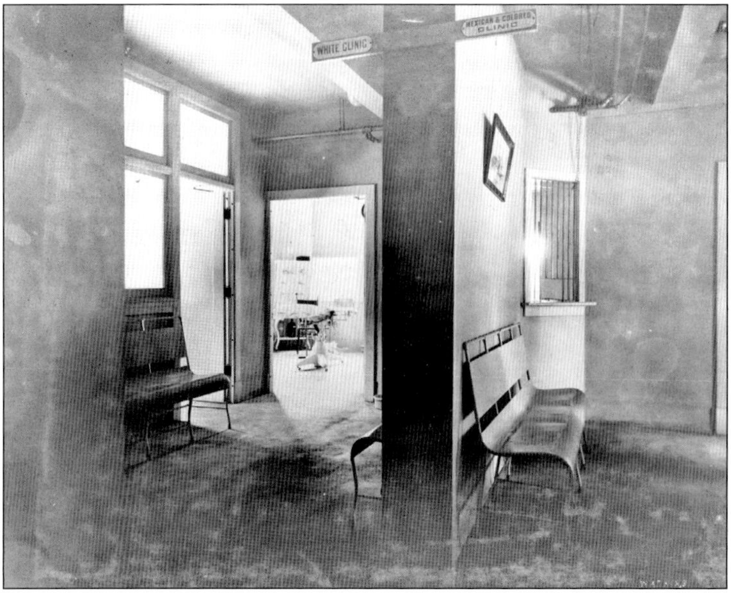

In the late 19th century, the US Supreme Court ruled that it was not a denial of constitutional rights for businesses to have separate facilities for blacks and whites, as long as those facilities were supposedly equal. As a result, perhaps the most recognizable forms of Jim Crow are the signs identifying facilities by race.

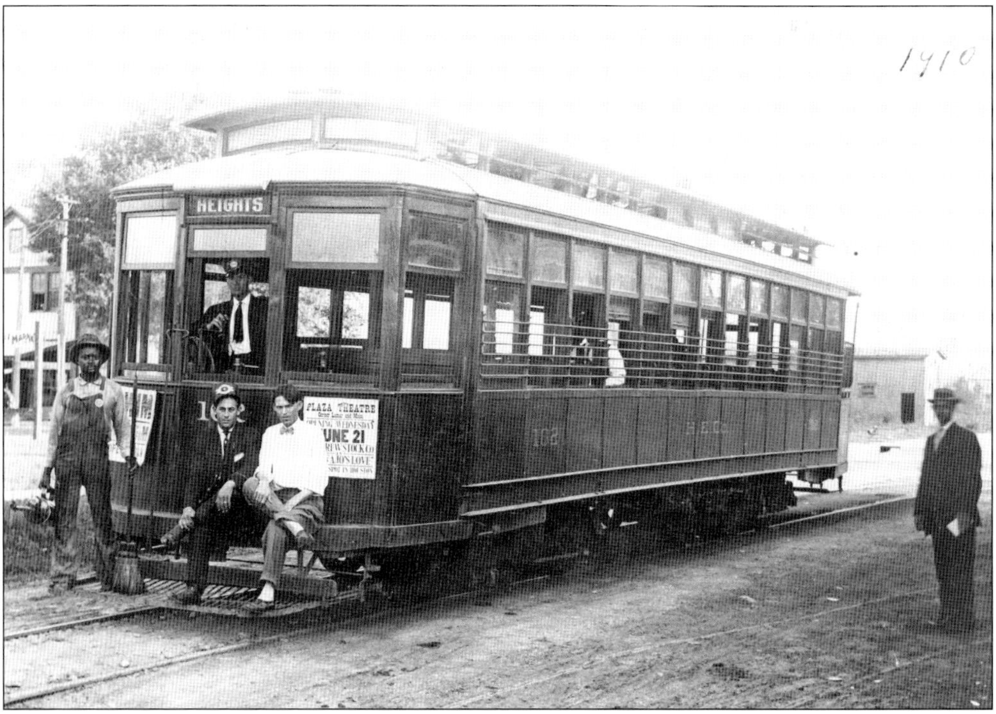

The Houston Electric Company operated streetcars throughout Houston in the first decades of the 20th century. As with most other public conveyances of the Progressive Era, strict Jim Crow laws prohibited blacks from utilizing many of those streetcar lines and designated where they could or could not sit on the streetcars that were accessible.

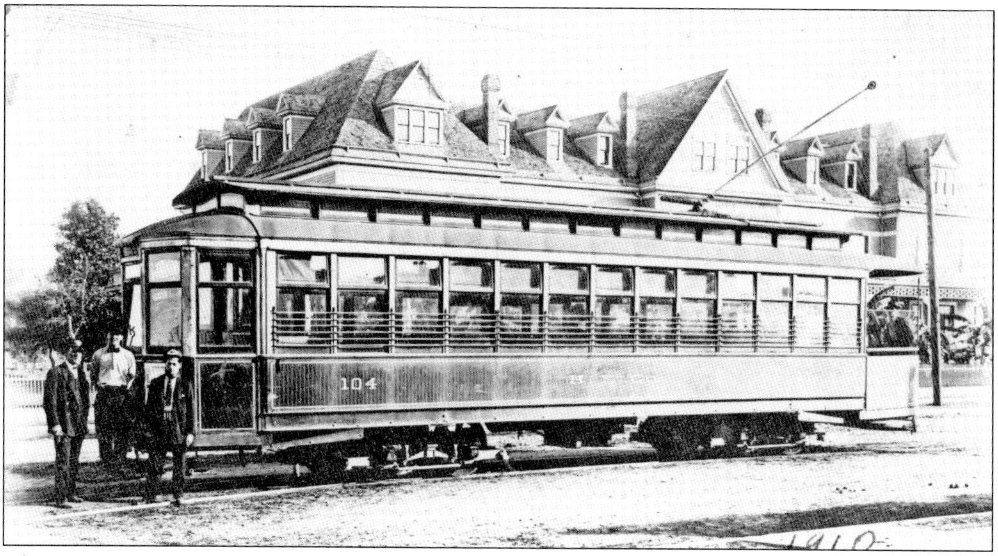

The Houston Electric Company's streetcars operated in corridors where the city's elite often lived. Racial customs prohibited black Houstonians from living in many of these areas, such as Houston Heights, but blacks often found work in these homes as domestics. As few in the black community owned private automobiles, streetcars were often the only means available for many of those domestics to reach these neighborhoods.

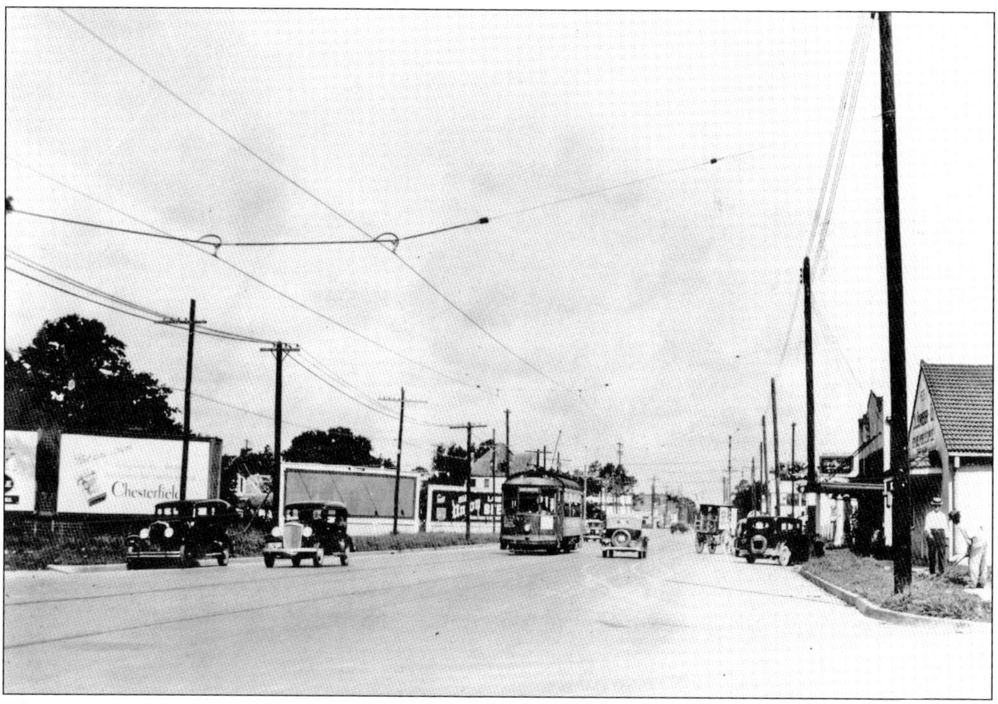

The street scene in a corridor outside of downtown Houston illustrates the use of public spaces by private automobiles and streetcars during the Progressive Era. The city's boosters often cited the ease of access between the downtown and the residential wards as benefits to living in Houston. However, within a few decades, the fluidity of traffic would be replaced by incessant congestion during the building of the interstate highway networks.

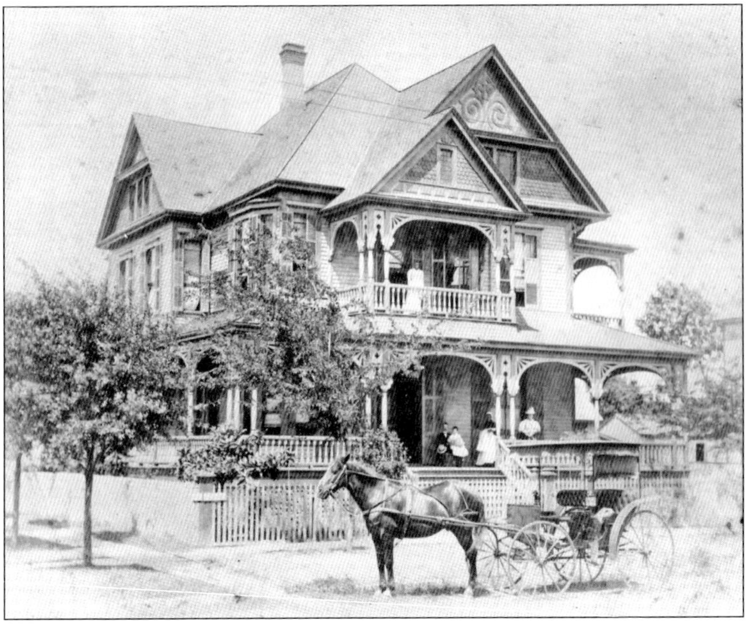

The architecture of many of the homes of the city's aristocracy illustrates their economic power and social influence. Few black Houstonians were counted among the city's aristocracy, but black domestics were commonplace. In this image, the family can be found on the first floor of the home, while a young, black female—most likely a domestic—stands on the second-floor balcony.

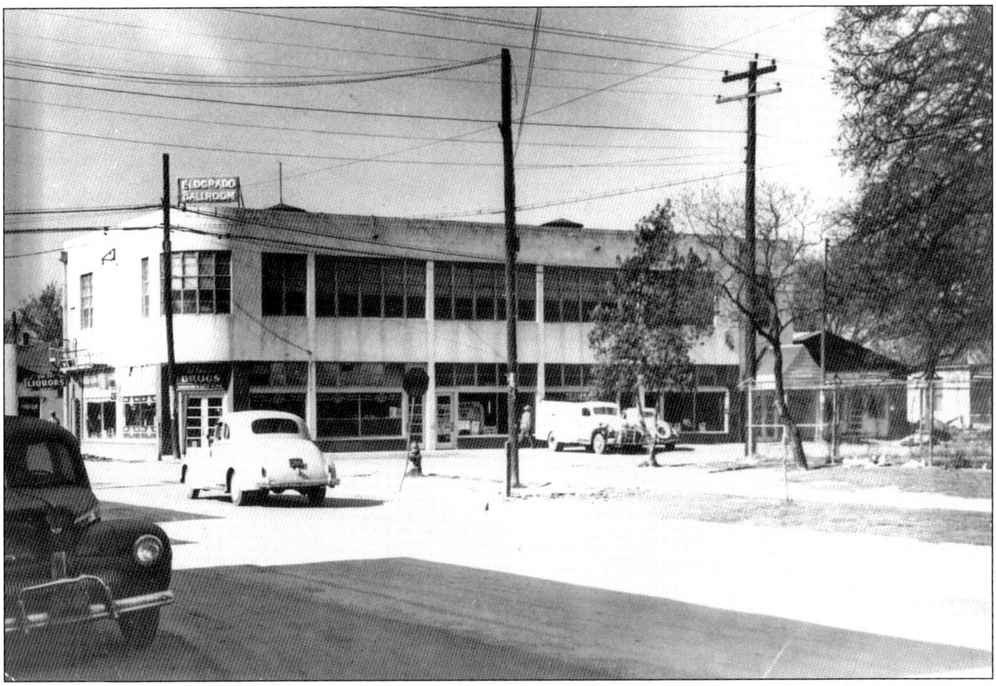

The civil rights movement of the 1950s eradicated many of the Jim Crow laws that prohibited blacks from accessing previously restricted "whites only" facilities. However, black Houstonians gladly held on to many establishments that catered specifically to a black clientele. The El Dorado Ballroom was one of those establishments where the city's black community could enjoy social gatherings outside of white oversight.

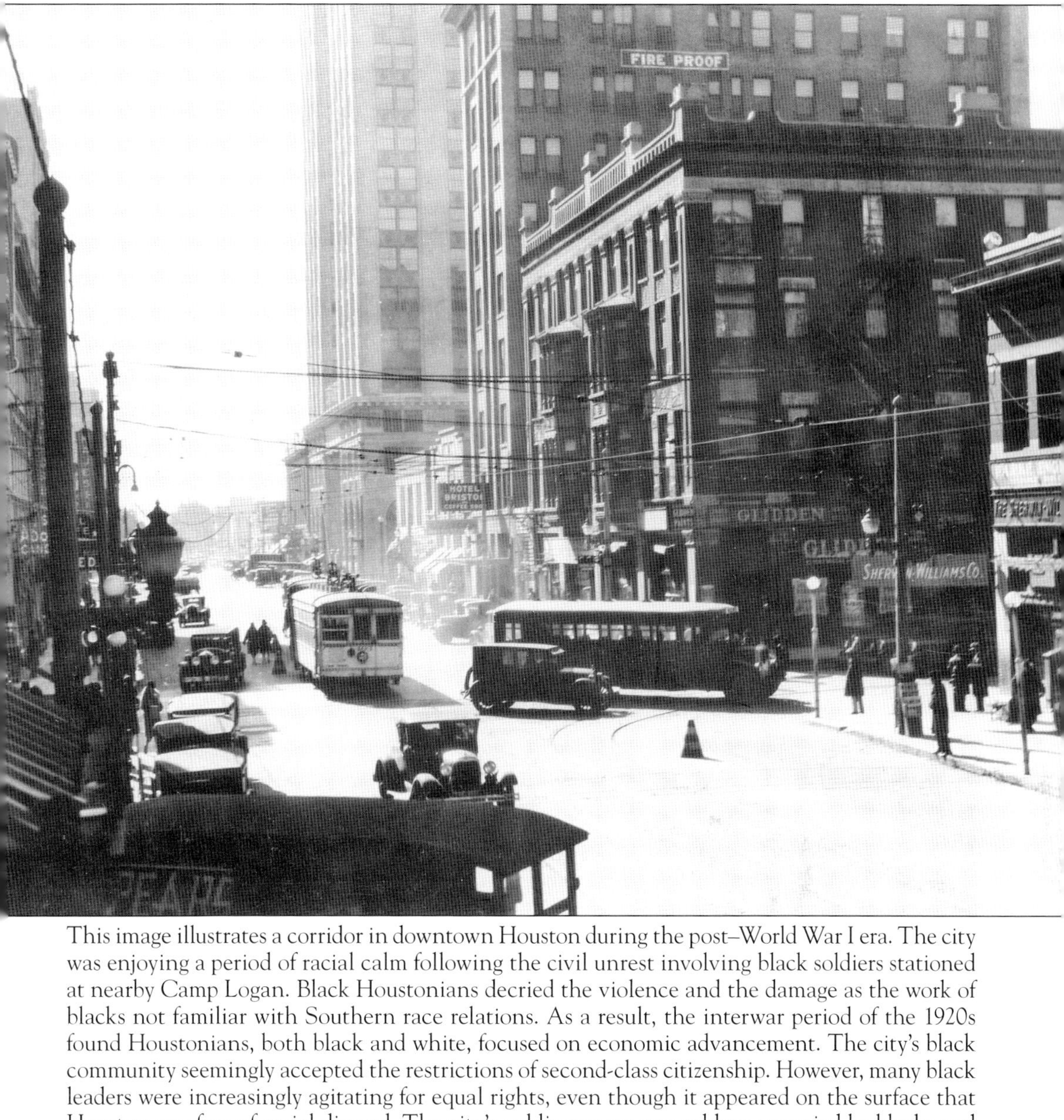

This image illustrates a corridor in downtown Houston during the post–World War I era. The city was enjoying a period of racial calm following the civil unrest involving black soldiers stationed at nearby Camp Logan. Black Houstonians decried the violence and the damage as the work of blacks not familiar with Southern race relations. As a result, the interwar period of the 1920s found Houstonians, both black and white, focused on economic advancement. The city's black community seemingly accepted the restrictions of second-class citizenship. However, many black leaders were increasingly agitating for equal rights, even though it appeared on the surface that Houston was free of racial discord. The city's public spaces were seldom occupied by blacks and whites, as blacks understood the best way to avoid racial conflicts was to not overtly challenge the existing customary racial boundaries.

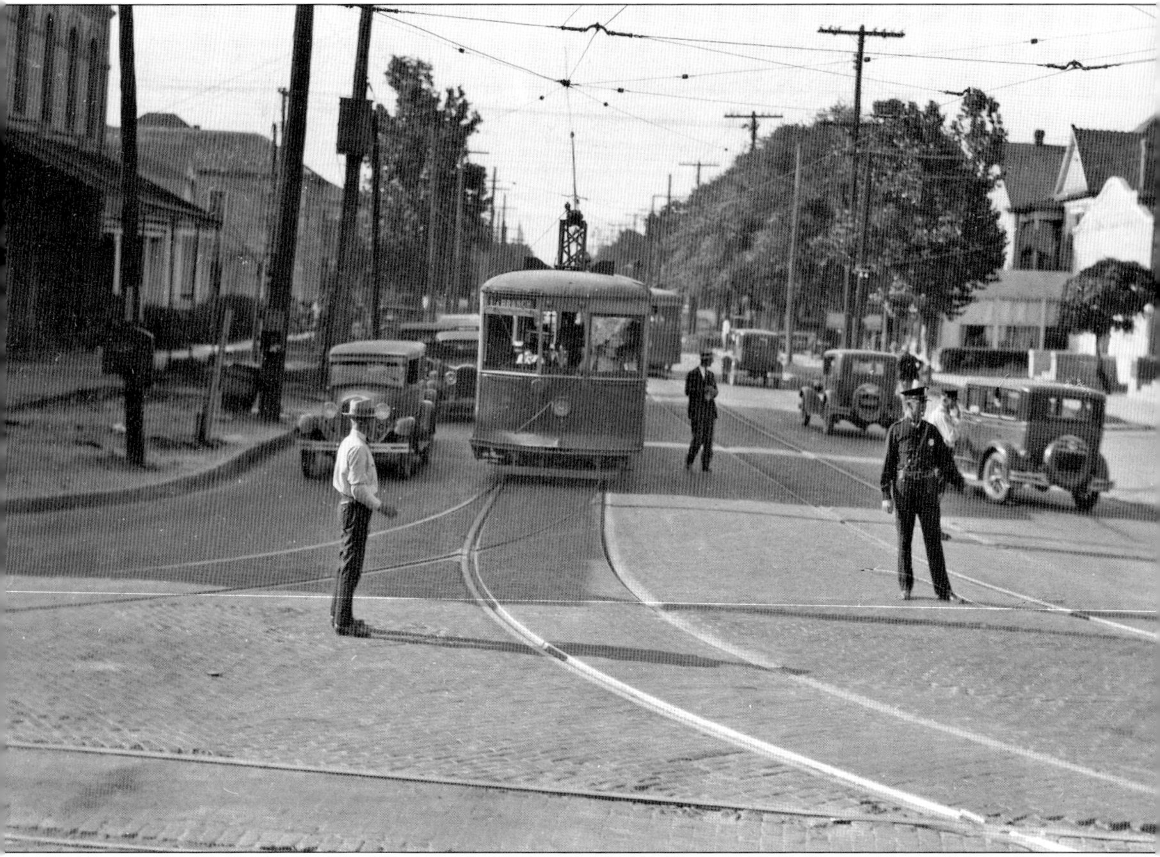

During the interwar period, public spaces were often regulated by Houston's police officers. This image depicts streetcars, private automobiles, and pedestrians outside the downtown area. The tree-lined corridor is indicative of a middle-class neighborhood, where the streets are paved, curbed, and guttered. The public spaces in the city's black community were seldom paved and were infrequently regulated by the police.

Even though Houston is not often thought of as a racially intolerant city, it, like many other Southern cities, held signs that hinted at its (and the state of Texas's) past as a member of the Confederate States of America. "White only" signs were visible throughout the city and in many cases were so common that they did not illicit much attention.

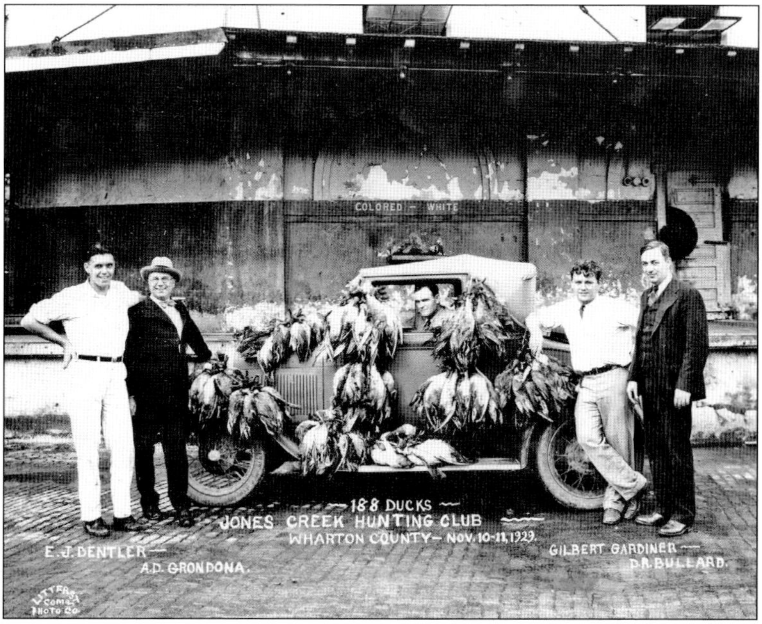

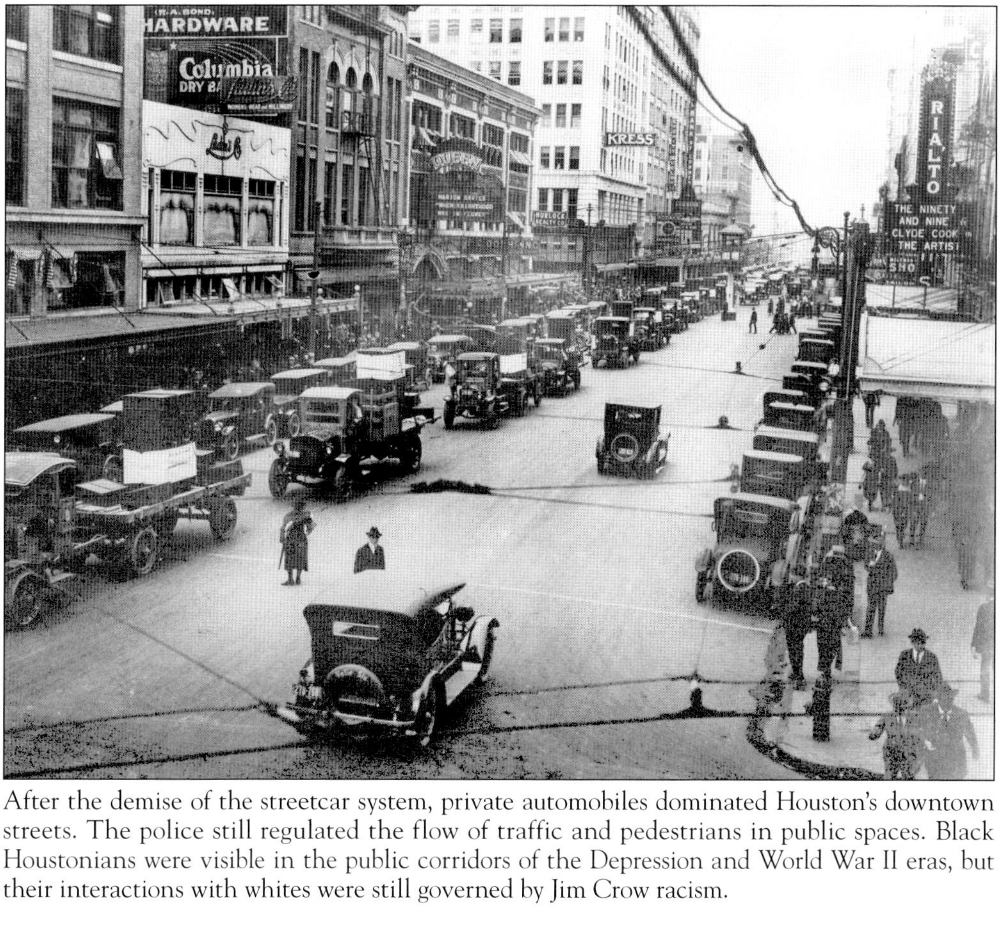

After the demise of the streetcar system, private automobiles dominated Houston's downtown streets. The police still regulated the flow of traffic and pedestrians in public spaces. Black Houstonians were visible in the public corridors of the Depression and World War II eras, but their interactions with whites were still governed by Jim Crow racism.

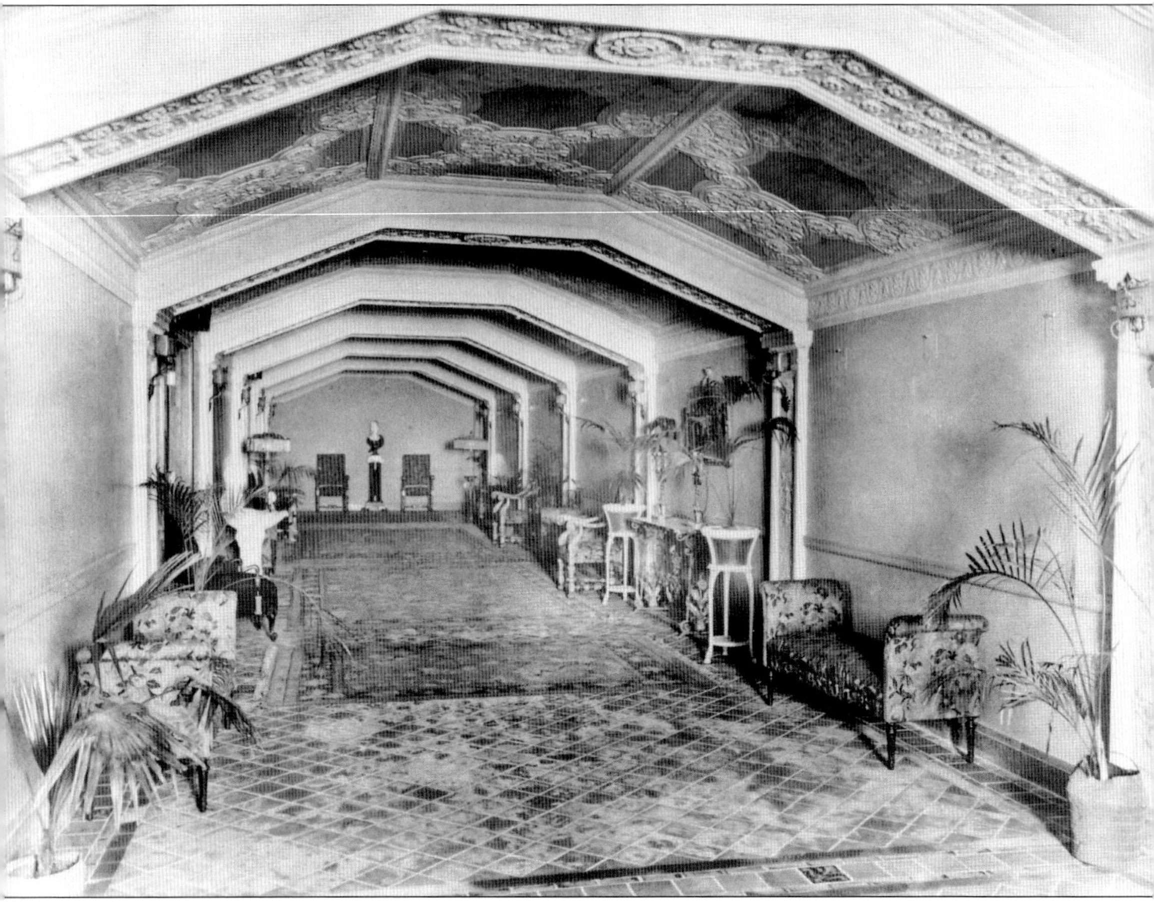

A hallway of the Majestic Theatre exemplifies the architecture and craftsmanship that the city's aristocracy often took for granted. However, the theater was a contradiction of sorts. Its patrons—the city's power brokers and social elites—often did not see the other side of life, where disposable cash was nonexistent and individuals struggled to provide meals for their families. Furthermore, the theater was a reminder to black Houstonians that there was a life of privilege few African Americans would enjoy while it simultaneously reinforced their second-class citizenship. The legacy of slavery was not eradicated by the 13th Amendment, and black Houstonians continued to struggle under economic and social oppression. For all its grandeur, the Majestic Theatre served a specific clientele that had the income to enjoy exclusive entertainment and the force of custom to ensure the only blacks they saw were those in service occupations.

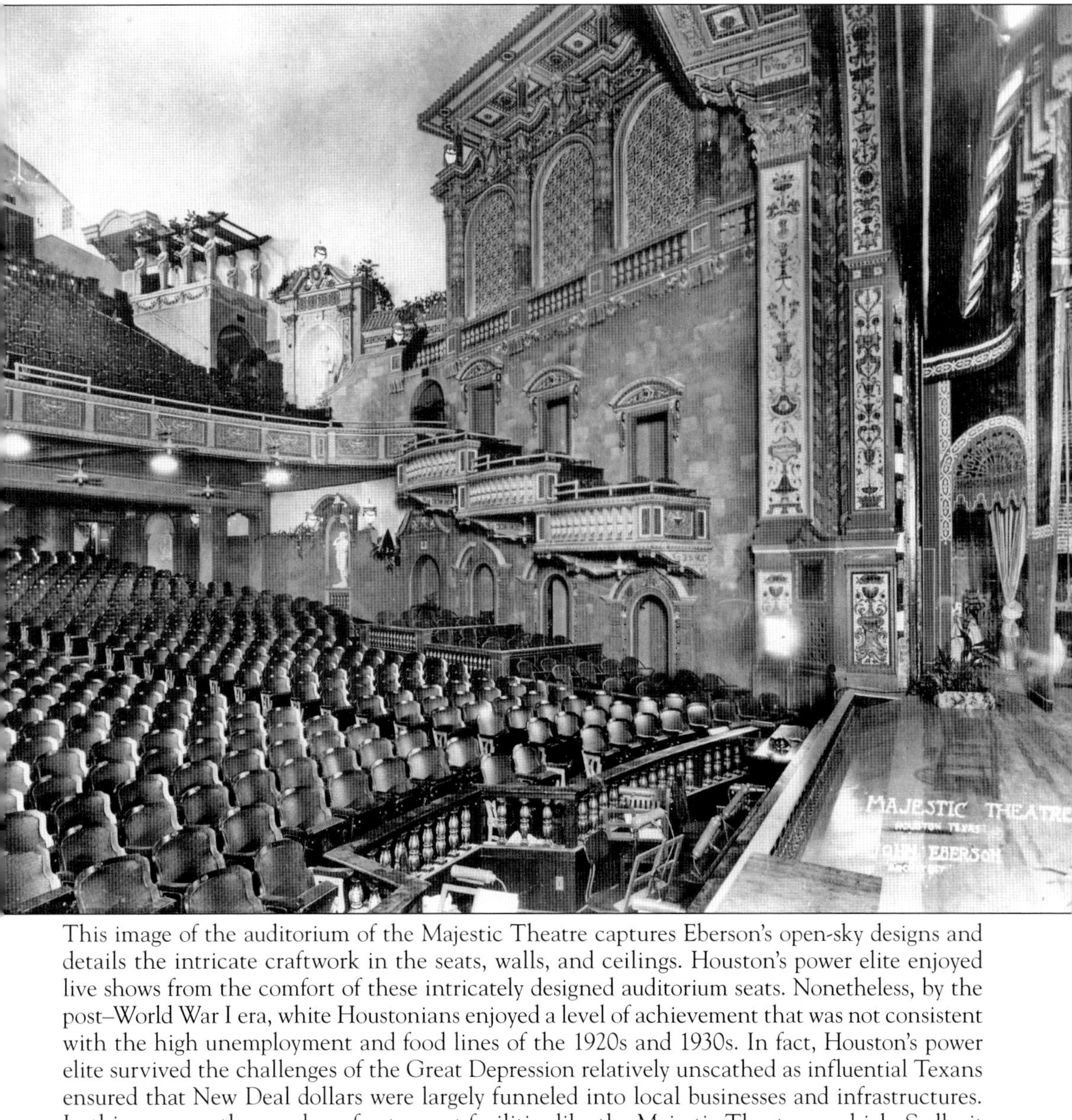

This image of the auditorium of the Majestic Theatre captures Eberson's open-sky designs and details the intricate craftwork in the seats, walls, and ceilings. Houston's power elite enjoyed live shows from the comfort of these intricately designed auditorium seats. Nonetheless, by the post–World War I era, white Houstonians enjoyed a level of achievement that was not consistent with the high unemployment and food lines of the 1920s and 1930s. In fact, Houston's power elite survived the challenges of the Great Depression relatively unscathed as influential Texans ensured that New Deal dollars were largely funneled into local businesses and infrastructures. In this manner, the number of patrons at facilities like the Majestic Theatre was high. Sadly, it included very few African Americans since a majority of Houston's black community remained uneducated and relegated to the periphery of high society.

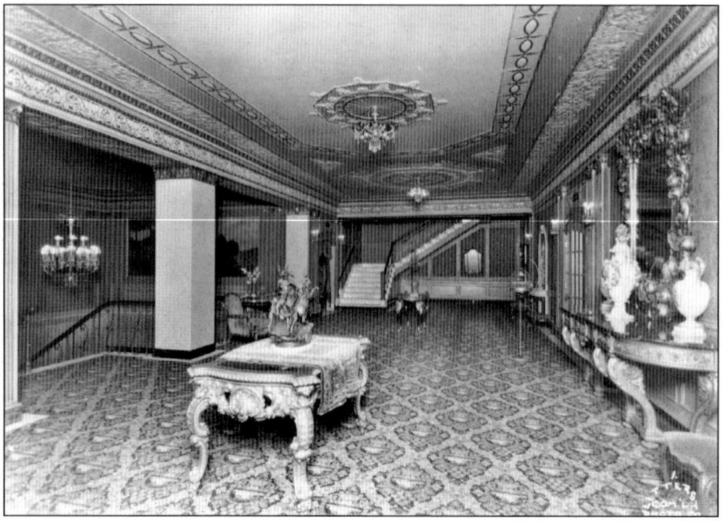

Seen here is a foyer in the Majestic Theatre. The exquisite detail in the furniture, lighting fixtures, floors, and ceilings were all indicative of a society that valued art and culture. However, this is the same society that brutally enslaved a specific population—a population whose physical presence in this country was a source of income and repulsion.

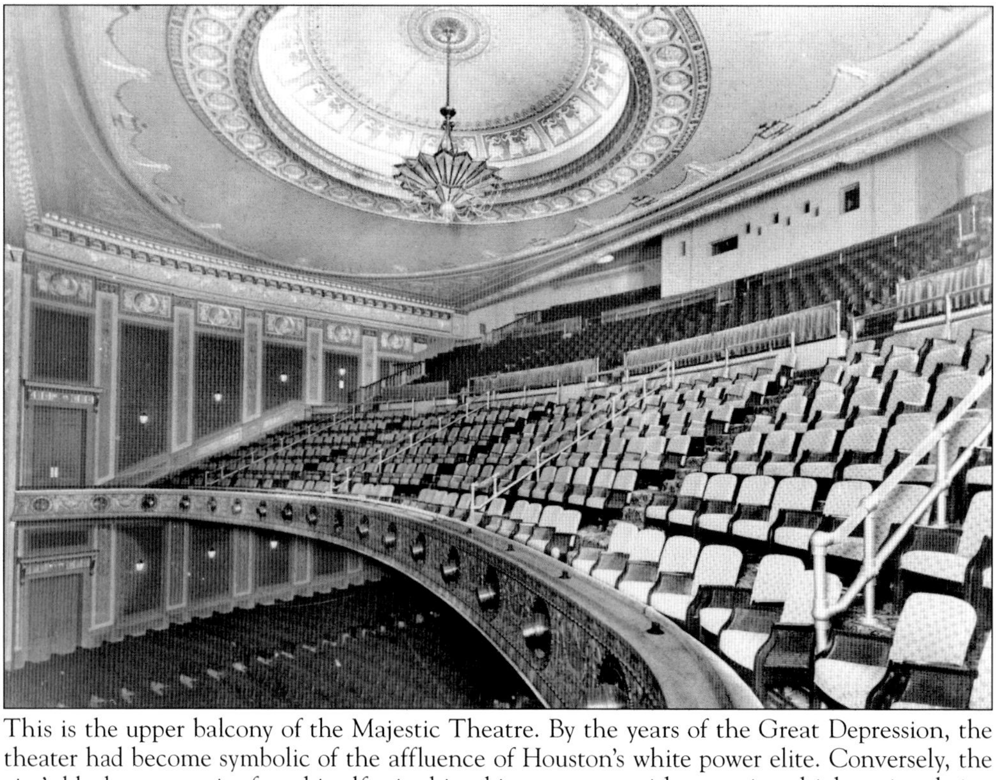

This is the upper balcony of the Majestic Theatre. By the years of the Great Depression, the theater had become symbolic of the affluence of Houston's white power elite. Conversely, the city's black community found itself mired in abject poverty with entry into high society being seldom possible. Nonetheless, the Majestic is revered in Houston's history as a unique structure that symbolized wealth, power, and influence.

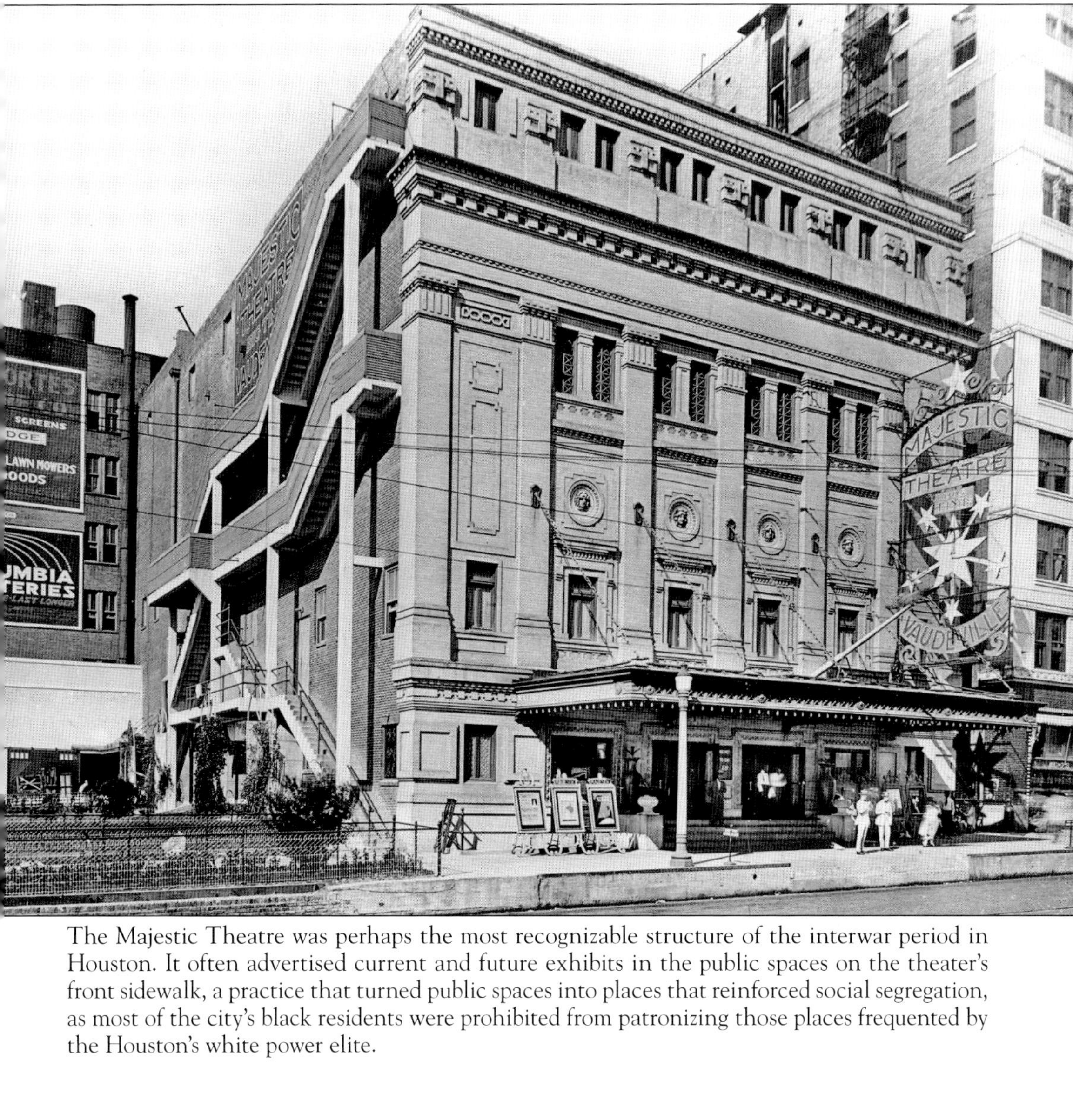

The Majestic Theatre was perhaps the most recognizable structure of the interwar period in Houston. It often advertised current and future exhibits in the public spaces on the theater's front sidewalk, a practice that turned public spaces into places that reinforced social segregation, as most of the city's black residents were prohibited from patronizing those places frequented by the Houston's white power elite.

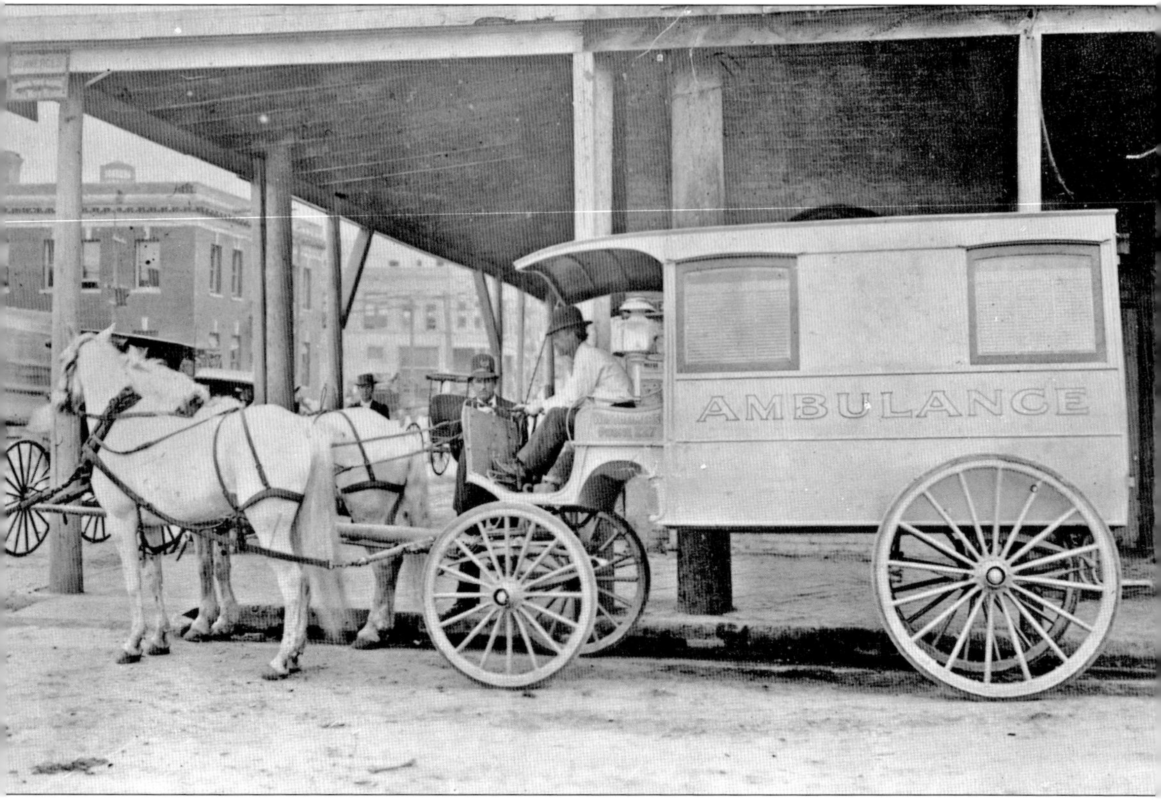

During the Progressive Era, many cities throughout the country saw horse-powered vehicles slowly being replaced by the gasoline-powered, private automobile. This image shows a local horse-drawn ambulance. Unfortunately, this vehicle was only operational when the weather was favorable. Such limitations further led to the demise of the horse as an urban conveyance in favor of private automobiles and paved streets. (Author's collection.)

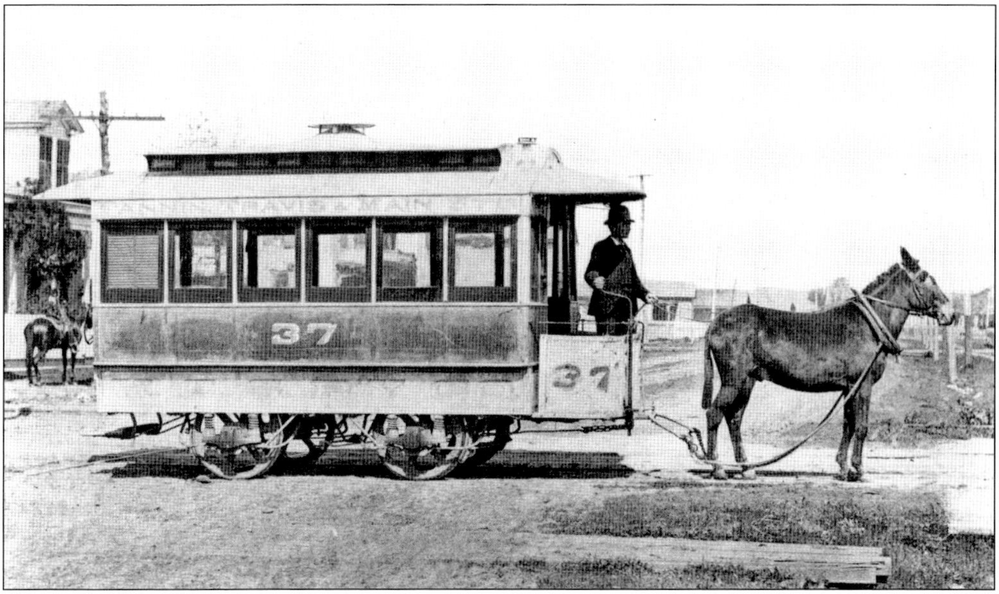

During the last years of the 19th century, streetcars were not electrified but instead animal powered. Houston had not yet begun the process of modernization and economic growth, so animal-powered vehicles remained satisfactory. However, in the years following the hurricane destruction of Galveston, the modernization of Houston began in earnest with the use of pavements and the transformation of public spaces.

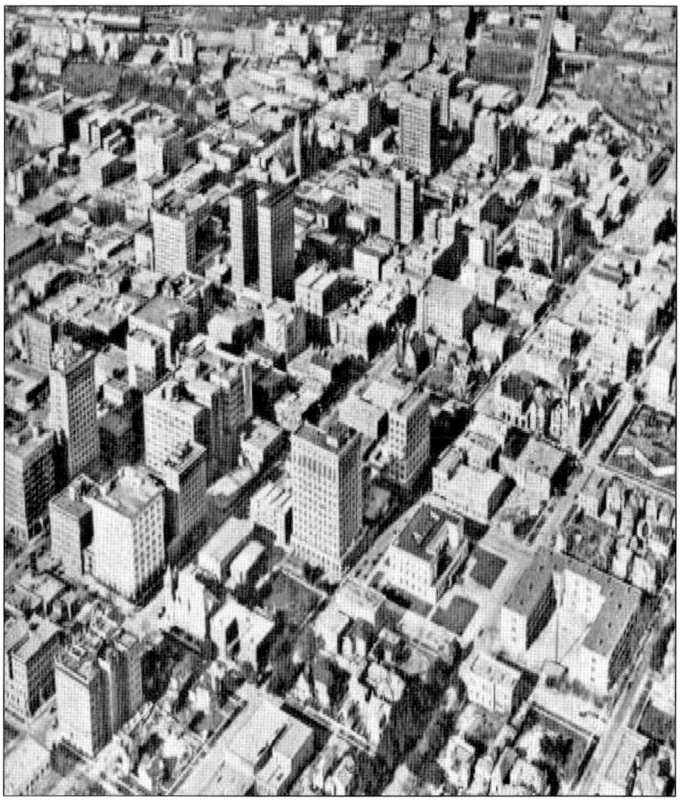

Here is an aerial view of Houston's downtown. The city was becoming a burgeoning metropolis in the years after World War I, but the underside of Houston' growing society hid the segregation of its black populace. Black Houstonians were generally ostracized from participating in the growing economy and were socially restricted from many parts of the city.

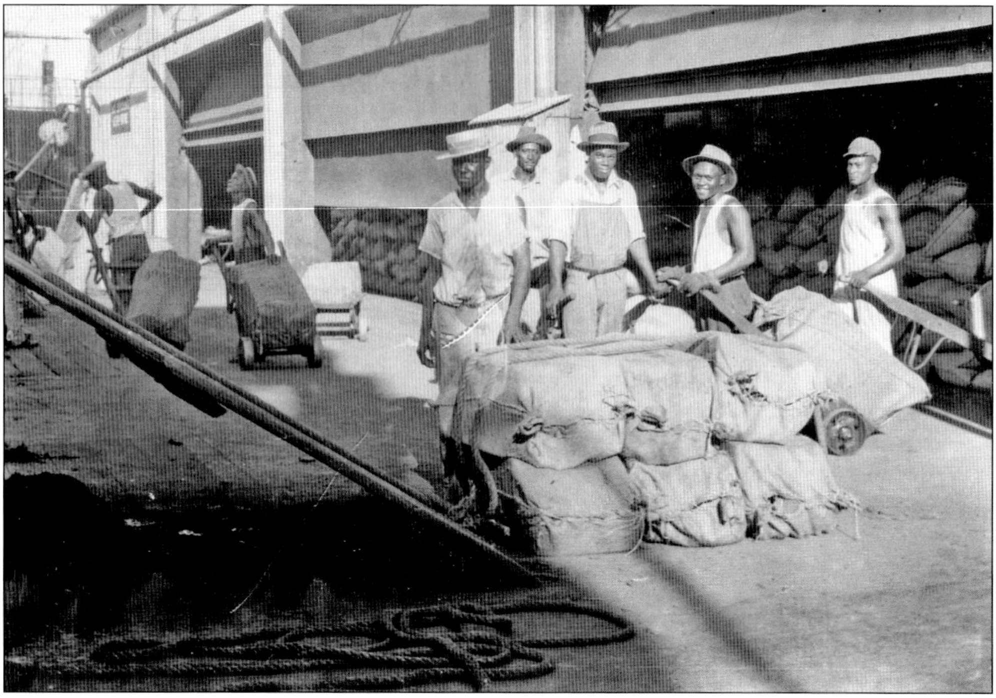

In the first decades of the 20th century, cotton remained a vital exporting crop for Houston's economy. As such, the roles of Houston's black laborers was just as vital.

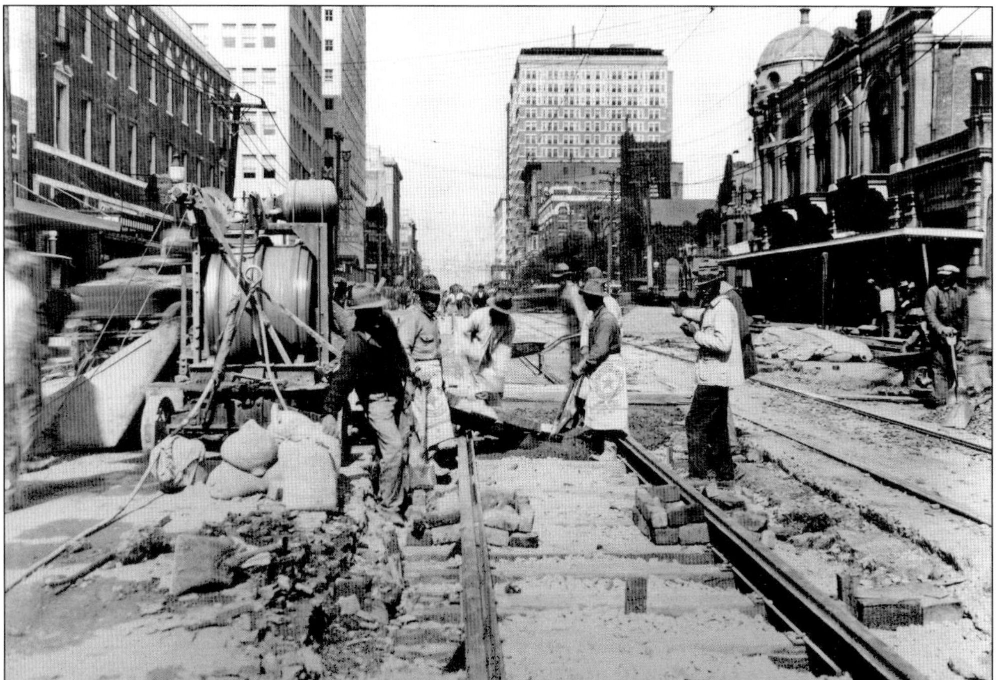

Houston's transportation infrastructure began to take shape during the World War I era. Black labor became crucial to Houston's infrastructure as the city's transportation networks were necessary to support the growing population.

Two

SEGREGATED HOUSTON

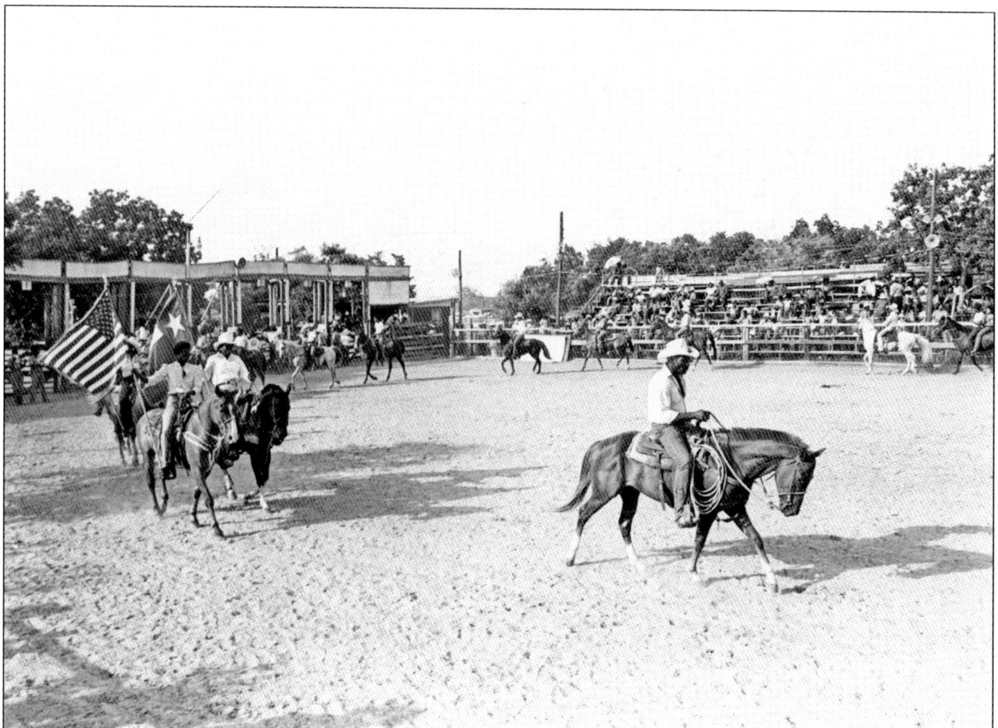

The demise of slavery at the conclusion of the American Civil War did not end the oppression of blacks in this country. In Houston, Jim Crow racism led to the continued separation of the black community that was originally developed during the antebellum South. This image shows the festivities of a black-themed rodeo that celebrated the skills of the Old West's cowboys.

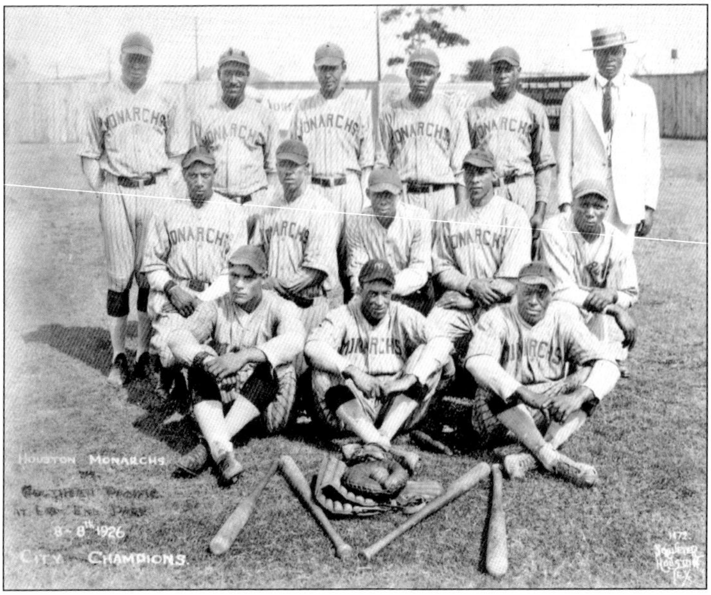

Baseball is known as the American pastime. Sadly, blacks were not afforded access to major-league baseball until the years following World War II. Before that time, however, they participated in segregated "Negro" leagues and developed their own teams and superstars. Unfortunately, Houston's black baseball players played before segregated crowds, and their skills were rarely acknowledged outside the black community.

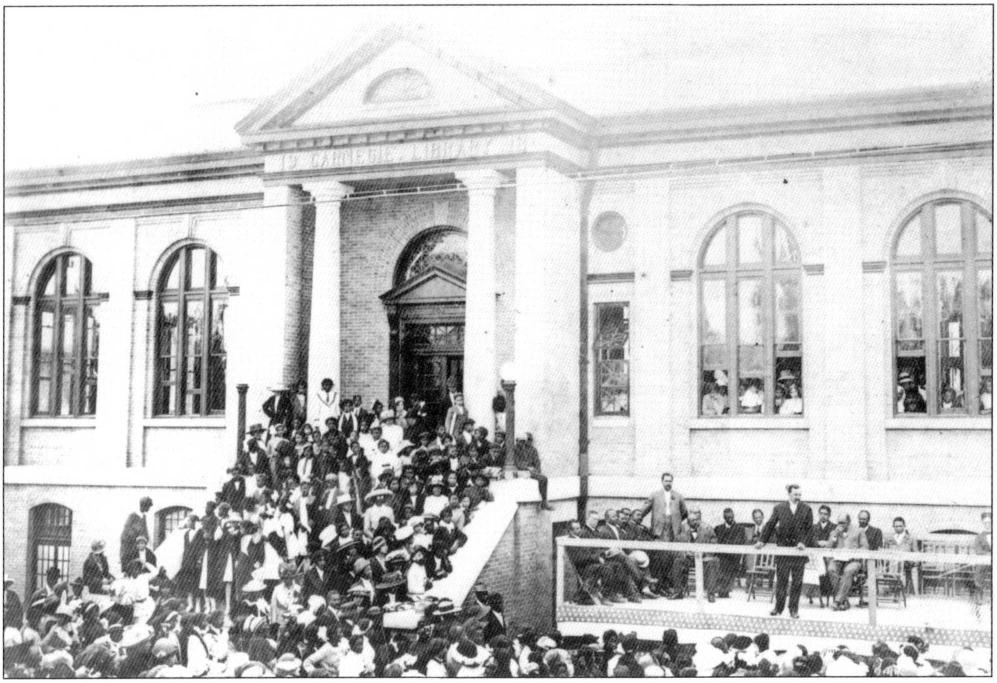

This photograph was taken at the dedication of Houston's Negro Carnegie Library. The city's black community was generally prohibited from accessing many of Houston's public facilities. Funds from philanthropist and steel magnate Andrew Carnegie were used to construct this library for the benefit of the black community.

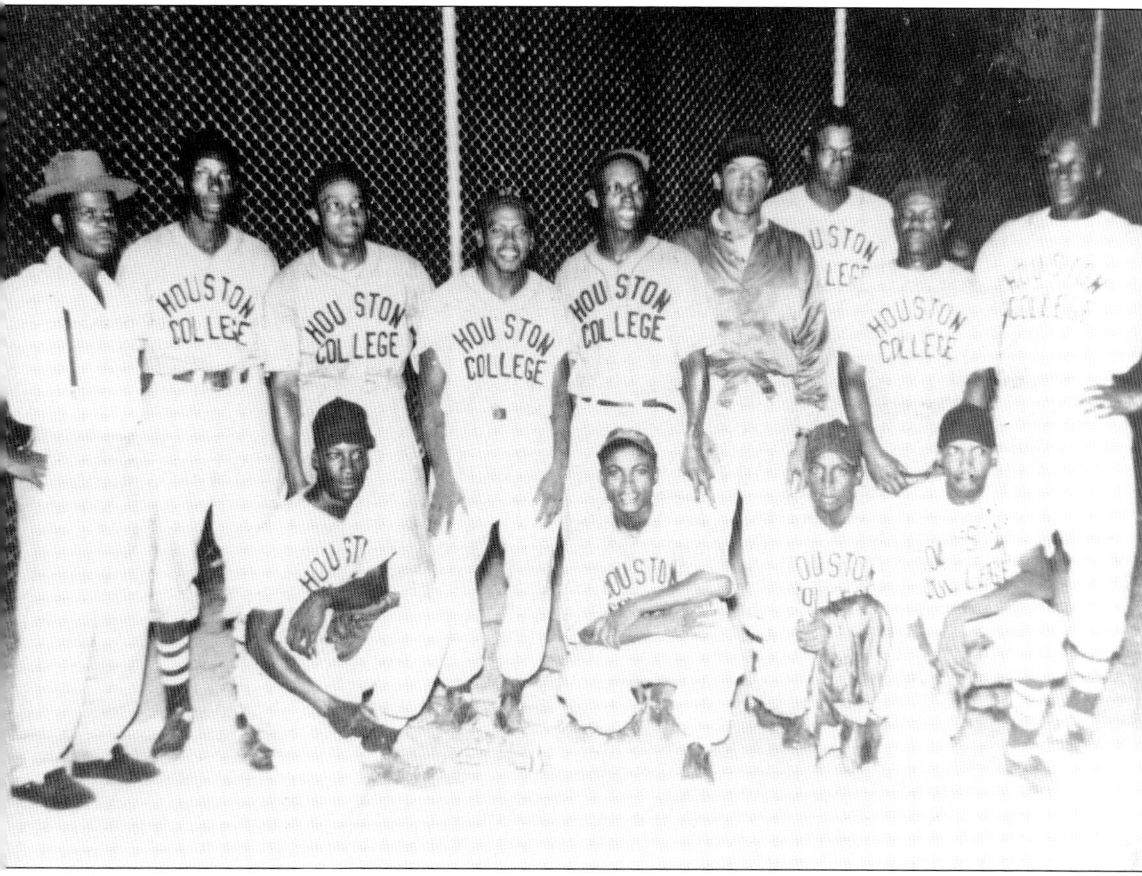

The Houston College for Negroes was the forerunner to Texas Southern University, and the school's baseball team is pictured here. Like their professional counterparts, black and white amateur teams were usually prohibited from competing against each other and were left with no other opportunity to play except in segregated leagues. Black athletes nationwide found their skills marginalized as undisciplined and unable to be coached, and these stigmas were also applied in Houston.

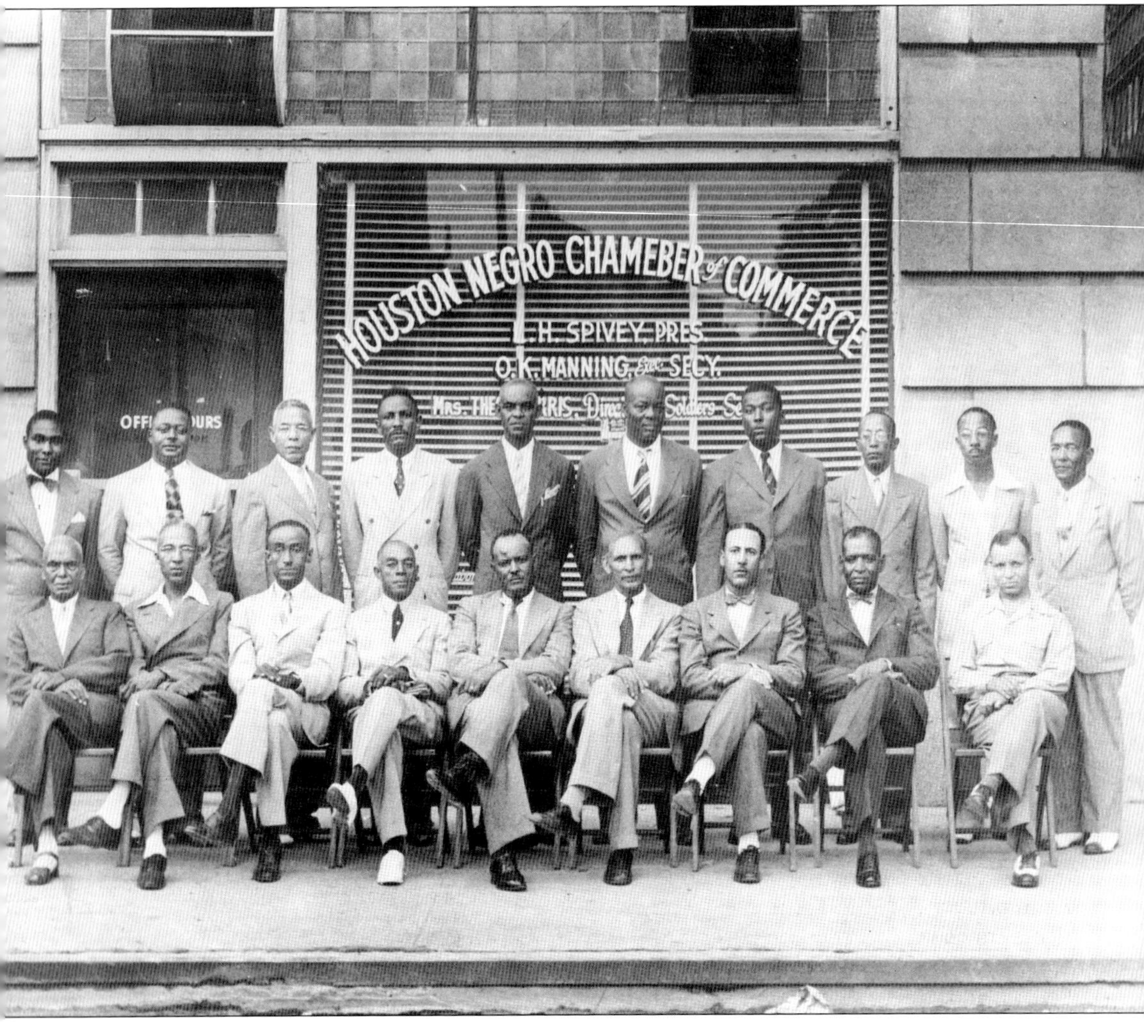

In an effort to mimic their white counterparts, the business leaders of Houston's black community formed the Houston Negro Chamber of Commerce. This organization sought first to encourage the professional development of its members and secondly to encourage the black community to patronize their businesses. During the Jim Crow era, black business thrived in Houston's segregated areas. However, the demise of these enterprises coincided with the demise of Jim Crow. Once white businesses were accessible to black patrons, black business suffered greatly as their typical patrons rushed to support services and products that they believed to be superior.

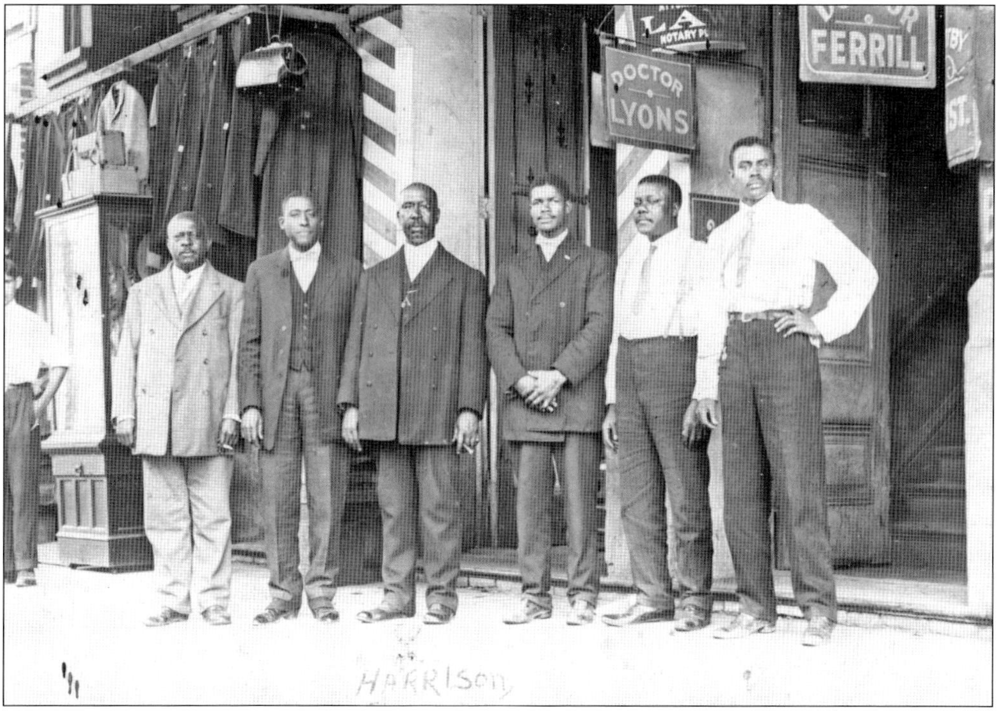

Houston's Fifth Ward is one of the most recognizable black communities in the city. Lyons Avenue was the "Main Street" of the Fifth Ward, and its businessmen operated successfully throughout the era of segregation. As in other communities, the civil rights era had the unintended effect of reducing the influence of black business and black businessmen.

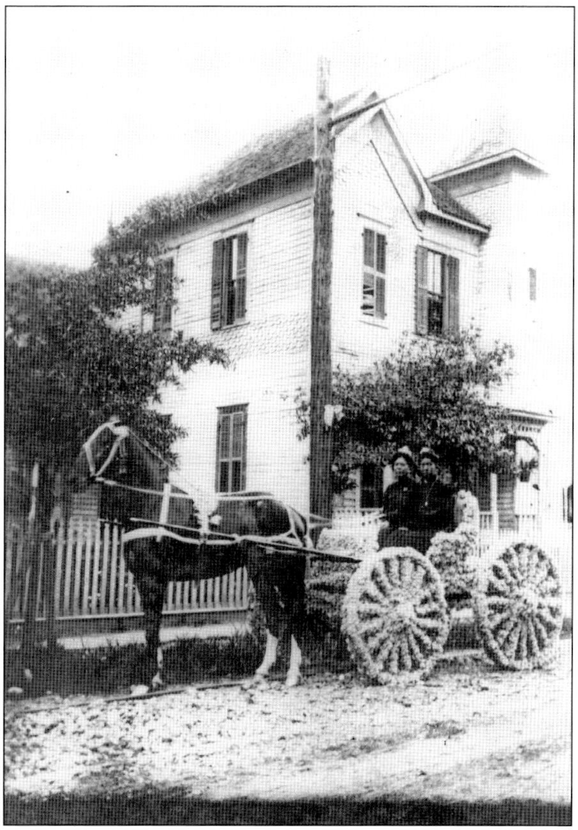

The separation of the blacks and whites in Houston led to separate celebrations and holidays. In Texas, blacks celebrated their emancipation from slavery on the day Union forces arrived in Galveston. Juneteenth is now celebrated in black communities throughout the country, often with the same reverence as the Fourth of July.

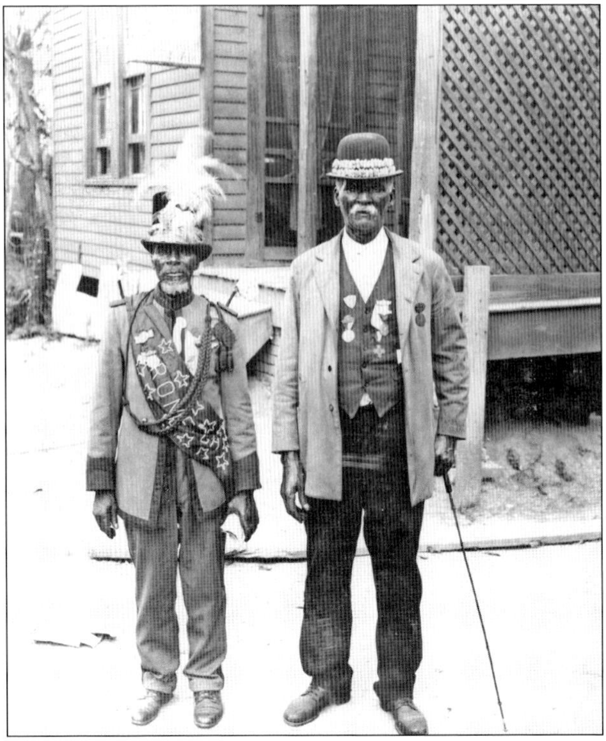

While the state of Texas may be associated with the American Southwest, its history of racism and slavery cannot be eradicated with the passage of time. Texas's participation in the Confederate States of America will forever link the Lone Star State's past with slavery and racial oppression. This image depicts two former slaves participating in a local, segregated parade.

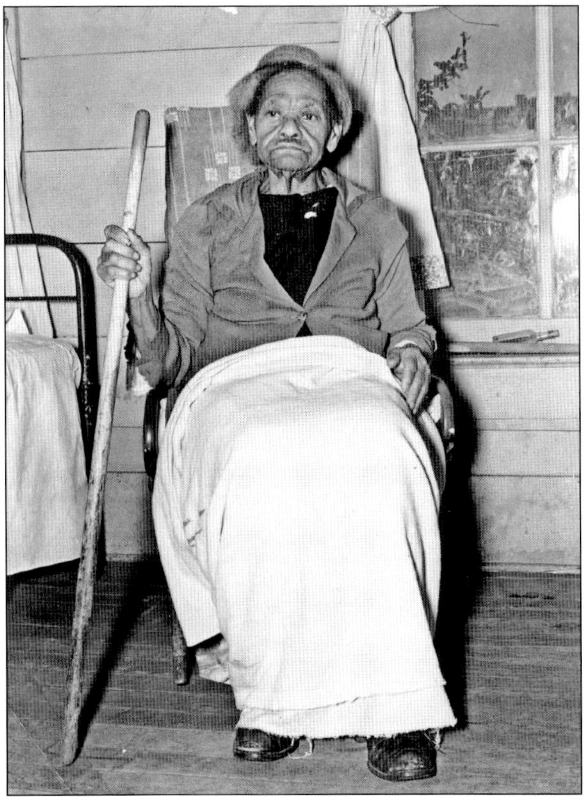

In the 1930s, the federal government's New Deal initiated interviews of former slaves as a means of providing employment for out-of-work white-collar professionals. While many of the New Deal's programs were criticized as frivolous, the narratives of former slaves provided a view of the institution of slavery from the perspective of those enslaved. This is a picture of former slave Mary Armstrong, who was interviewed in Houston in the 1930s.

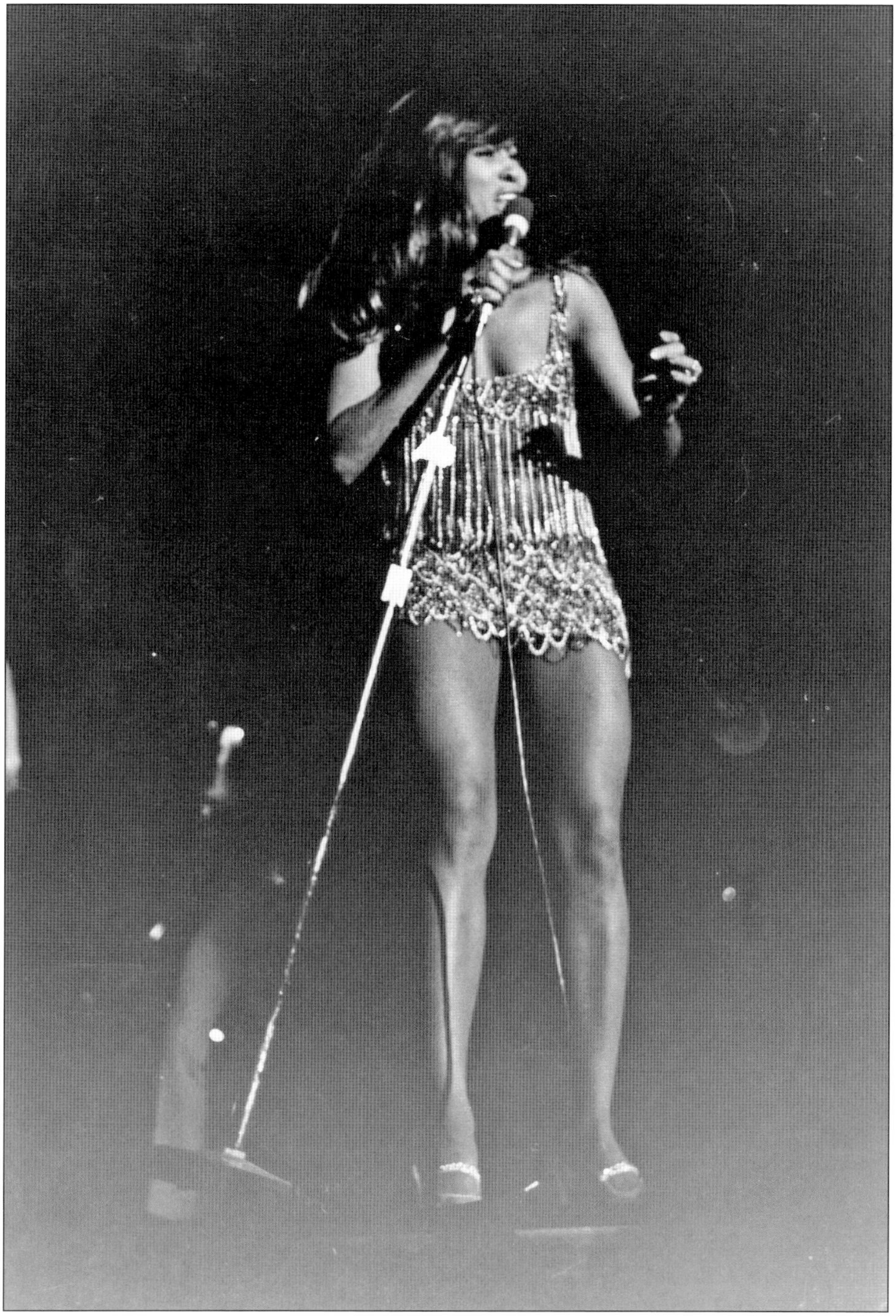

During Jim Crow, many black performers were relegated to performing on the South's Chitlin' Circuit of black clubs and venues. Like B.B. King and Bobby "Blue" Bland, Ike and Tina Turner honed their musical skills before black audiences and later found fame in front of white crowds in the 1960s. Interestingly, their act changed very little after they achieved crossover success, as Tina and the Ikettes exuded a sexuality that would become commonplace in the shows of today's female performers.

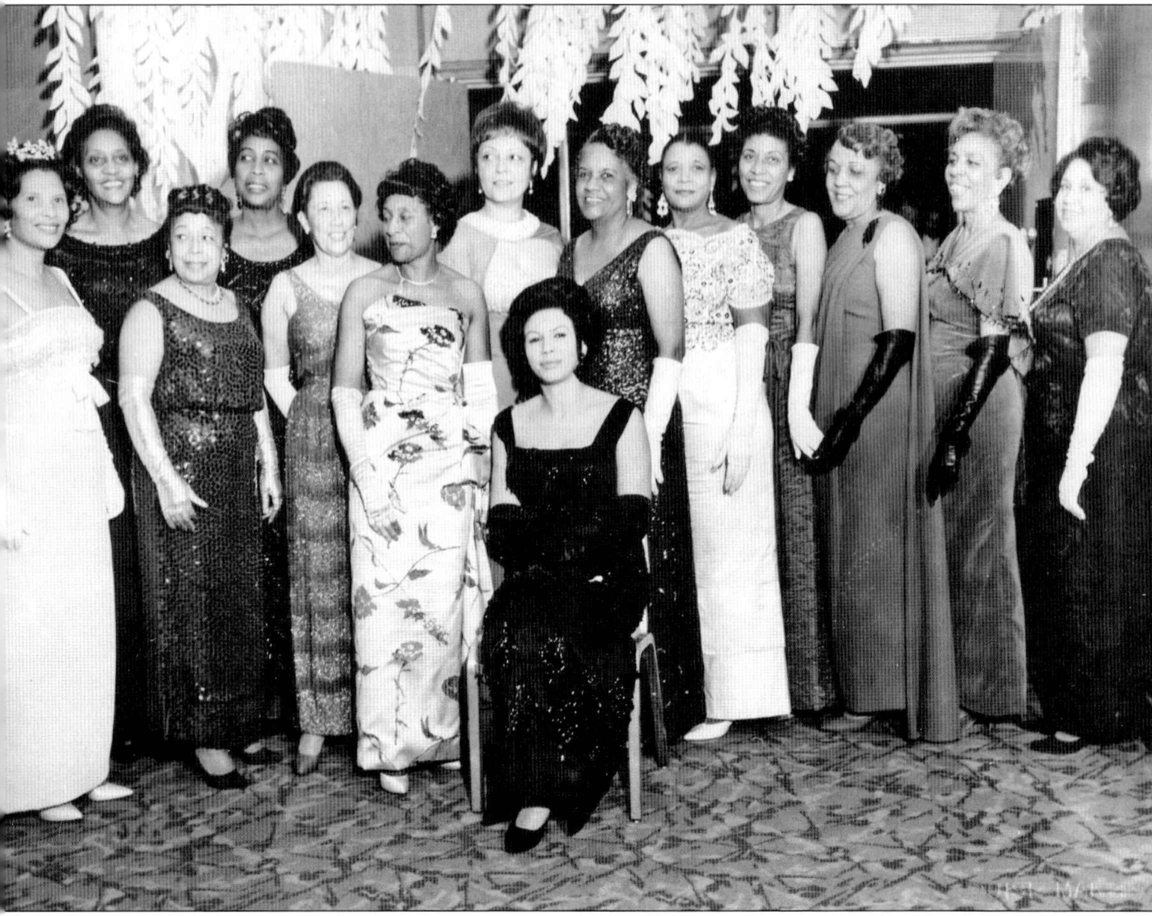

By the 1950s and 1960s, the black community was replicating many of the social norms and customs found in Houston's white society. Debutante balls, formal dances, and social clubs have been key aspects of white society for hundreds of years. In order to mimic the culture of white society, blacks created their own social formalities in order to be more owner than slave.

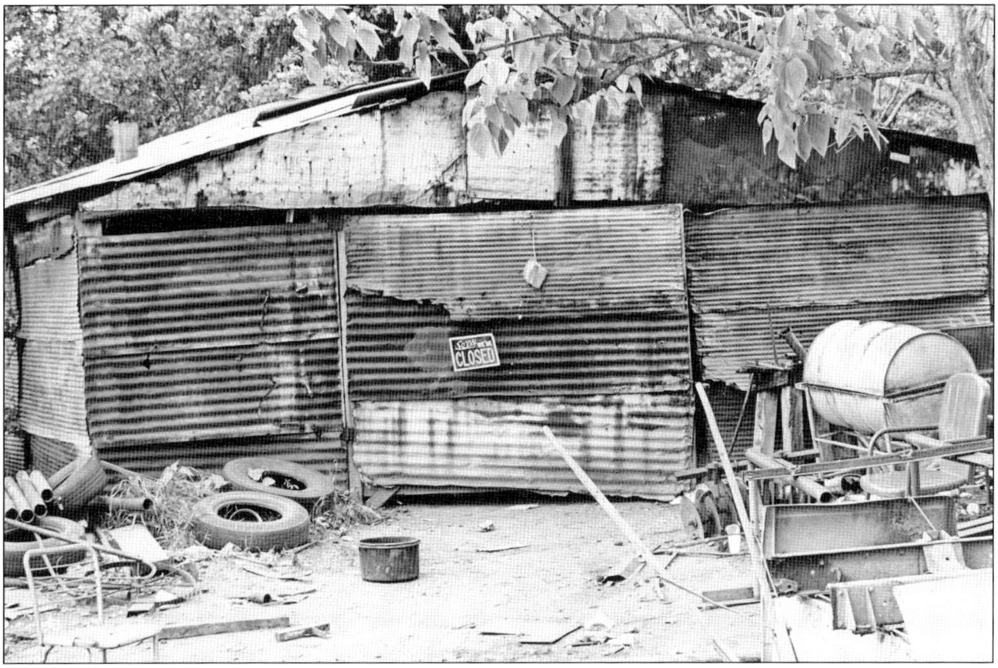

Houston's Third, Fourth and Fifth Wards were the center of Houston's black community. However, the public spaces in these communities seldom had paved streets or curbs, and gutters were often littered with debris. Nonetheless, these public spaces held black culture and were places where blacks interacted with one another out of custom and forced segregation. (Image courtesy of the Hartman collection at Texas Southern University.)

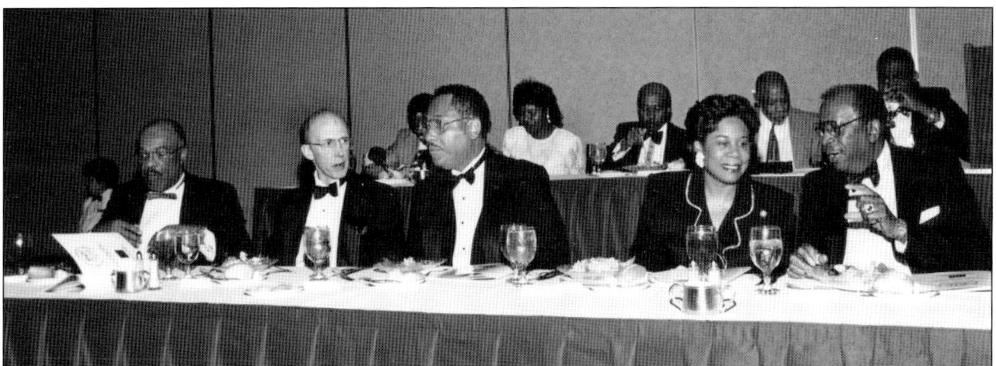

The Houston Citizens Chamber of Commerce routinely honors those in the black community that have made significant contributions to business and politics. The image shown includes Dr. Rod Paige (seated, far left), who lead the Houston Independent School District and served as Pres. George W. Bush's secretary of education; Dr. Lee P. Brown (seated, third from left), who was Houston's first African American chief of police, served as Pres. Bill Clinton's director of Drug Control Policy (drug czar), and in 1998 became the first African American elected mayor of Houston; and the Honorable Sheila Jackson Lee (seated, fourth from left) from Houston's 18th Congressional District, the same district that produced Barbara Jordan and Mickey Leland. Jackson Lee continues the legacy started by Jordan and Leland by tirelessly representing those whose voices have too often been politically marginalized. (Image courtesy of the Houston Citizens Chamber of Commerce.)

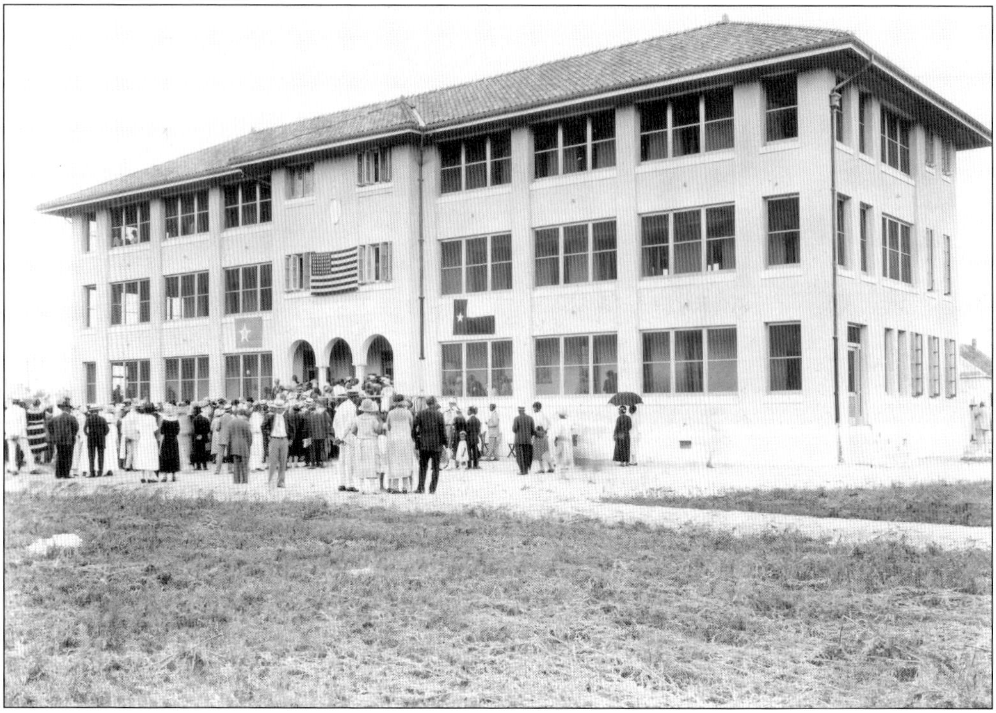

Because of the strict practice of Jim Crow segregation, blacks were not permitted access to "white" facilities throughout the country. In Houston, a hospital was erected specifically for the city's black community following the Supreme Court decision in *Plessy v. Ferguson* that established the concept of "separate but equal." Sadly, such segregated facilities were seldom equal.

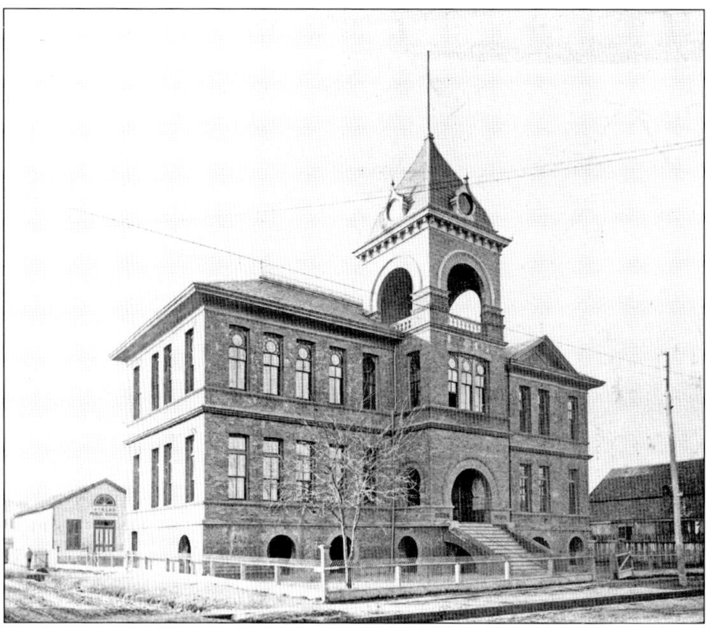

This image shows Houston's "colored" high school in the 1920s. Even though education was seen as the way to a better life, Houston's black community at that time understood the reality that a majority of its members would not achieve a college or liberal arts education. In the years prior to the civil rights movement, blacks were therefore encouraged to obtain skills that would be profitable in such activities as home economics, mechanics, and agriculture.

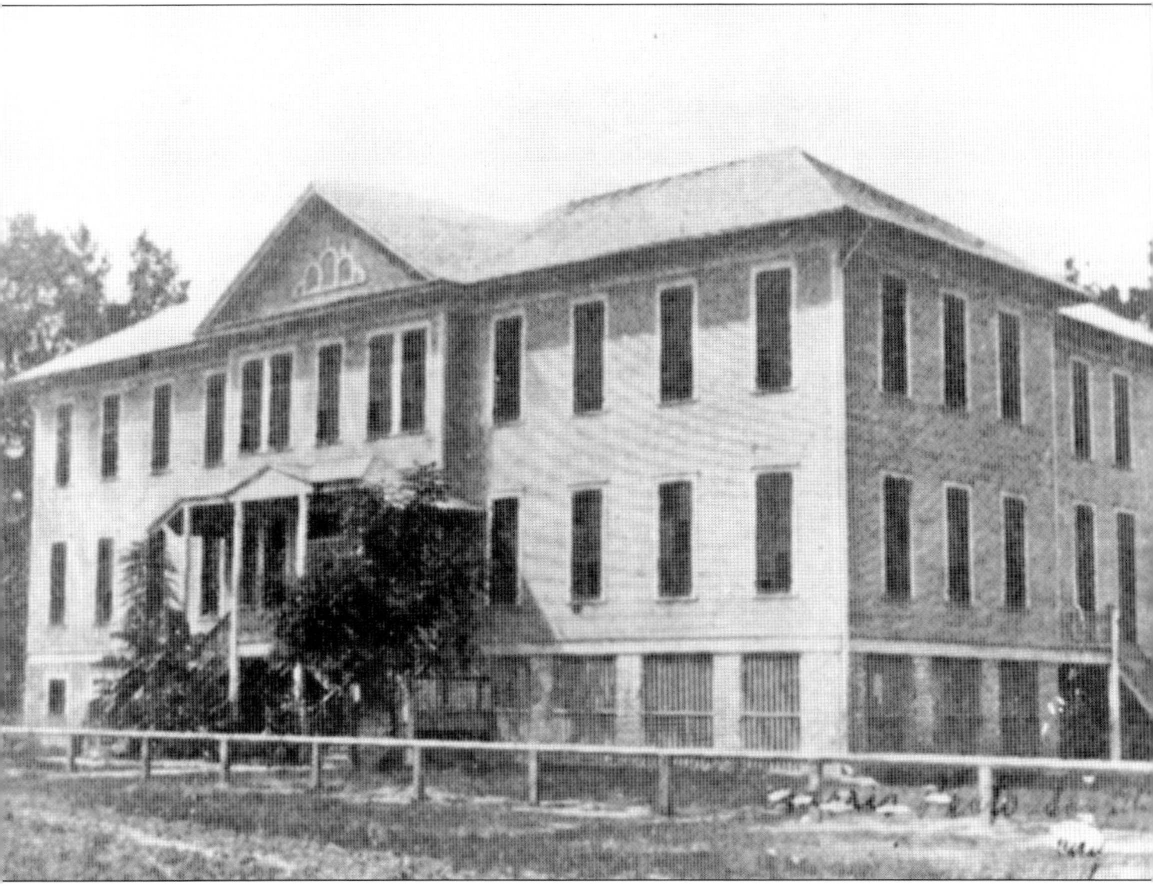

Segregated Douglas Elementary School, located in Houston's Third Ward, was one of the first schools built for Houston's black community. It served not only as a place of education but also as social gathering and meeting place for the community.

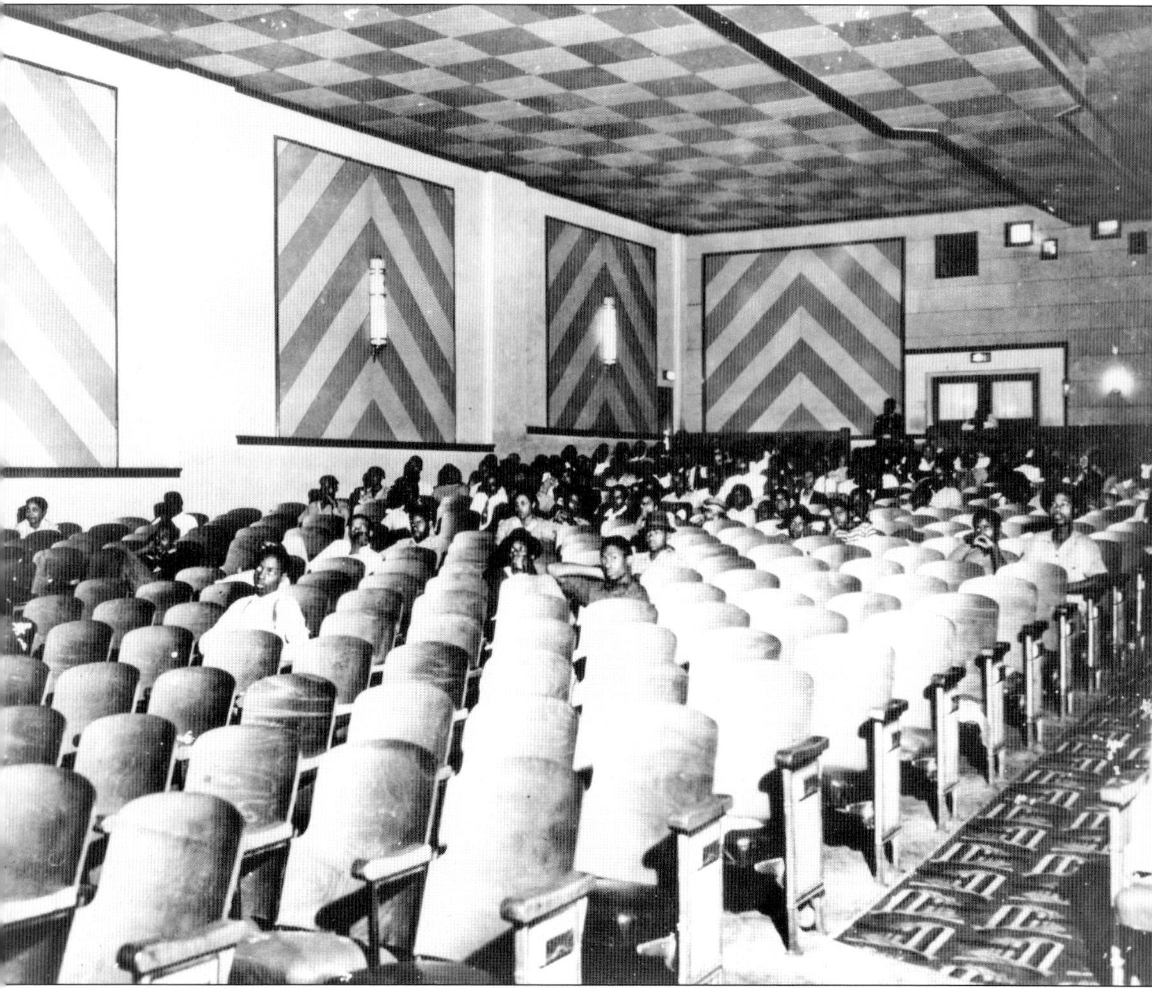

The Dowling Street Theater was one of the segregated facilities accessible to Houston's Third Ward community during the days when blacks were denied access to "white" theaters.

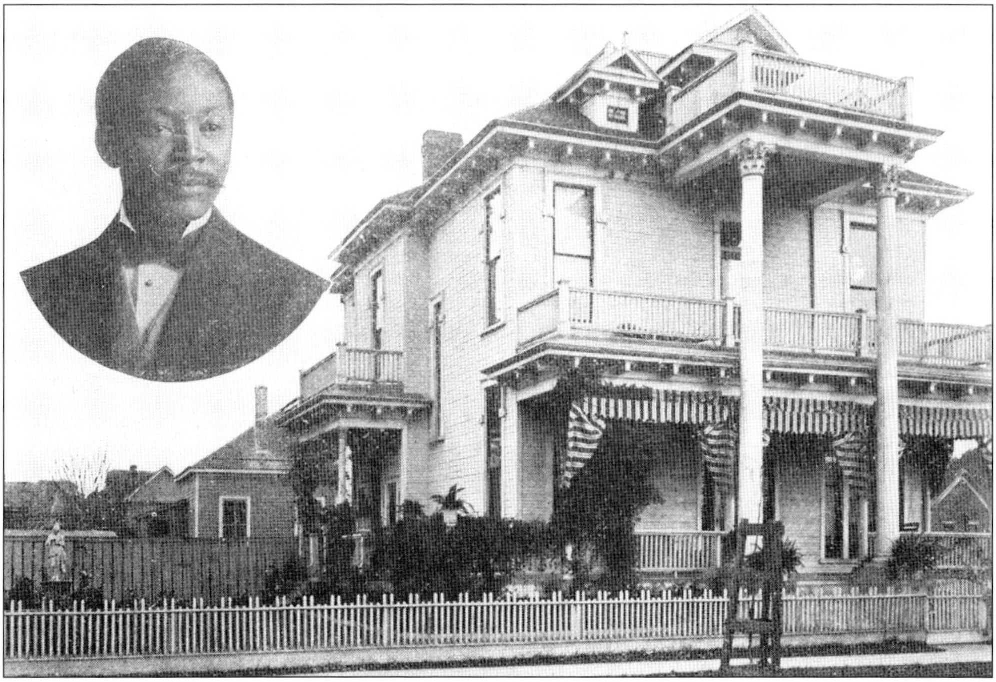

Doctor Covington was the first prominent black physician and faithfully served the city's black community.

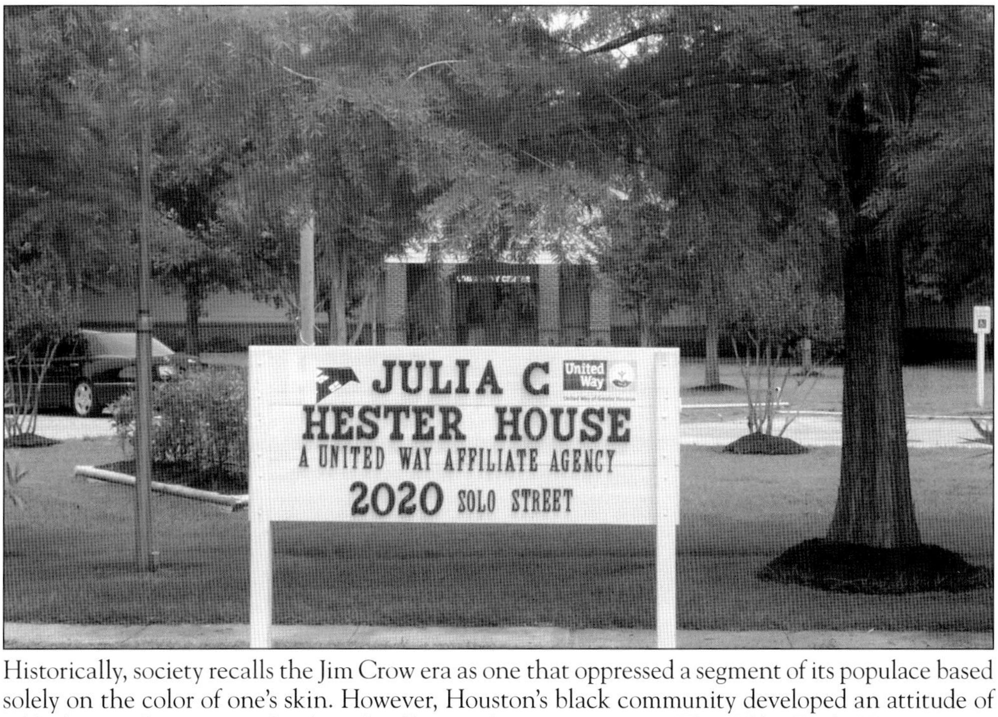

Historically, society recalls the Jim Crow era as one that oppressed a segment of its populace based solely on the color of one's skin. However, Houston's black community developed an attitude of self-reliance, focusing on the shared suffering of generations past. The Fifth Ward's Hester House began in the Jim Crow era and continues providing services to the community more than 50 years later. (Author's collection.)

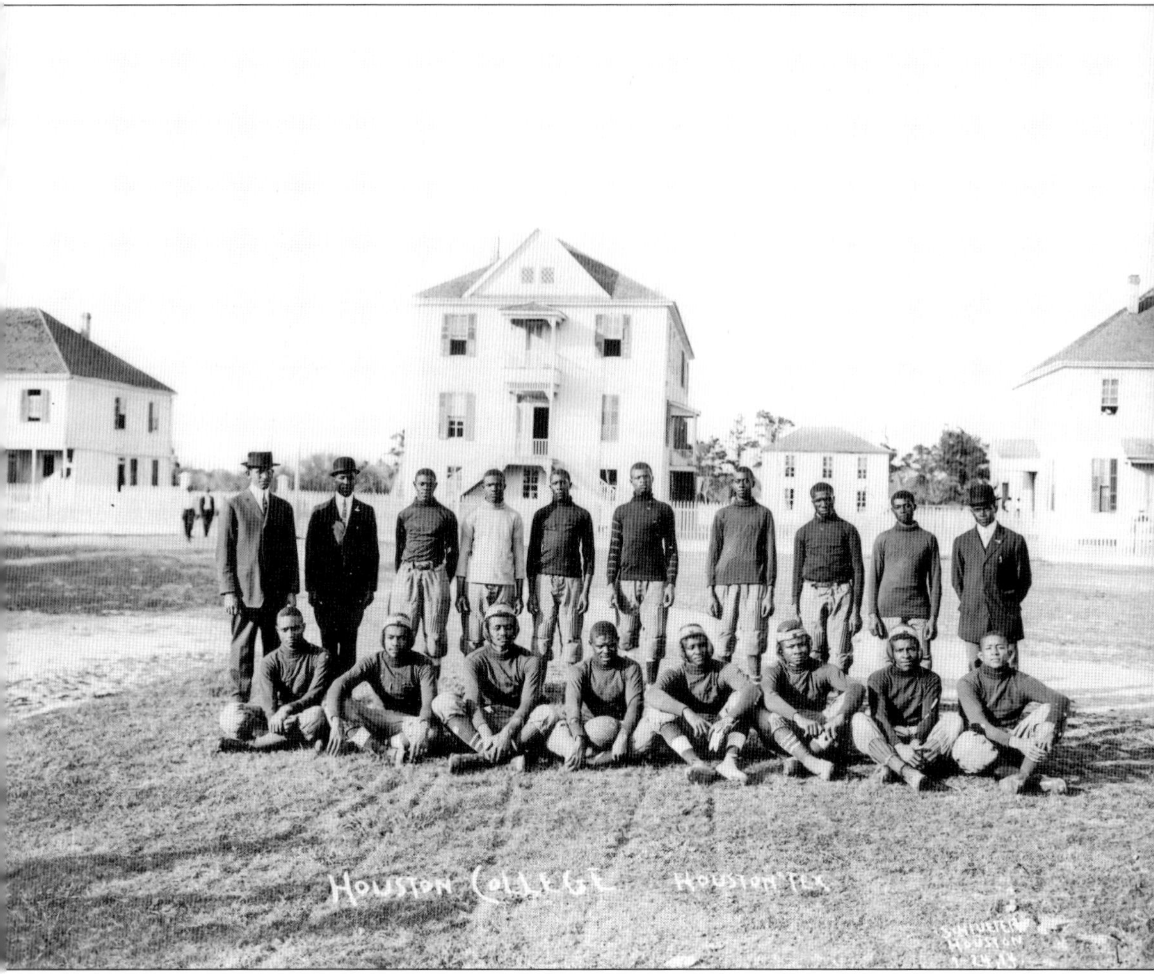

In the most oppressive days of Jim Crow racism, blacks were severely restricted from obtaining any form of education beyond grade school. This image shows the football team for the Houston College for Negroes, the forerunner to Texas Southern University.

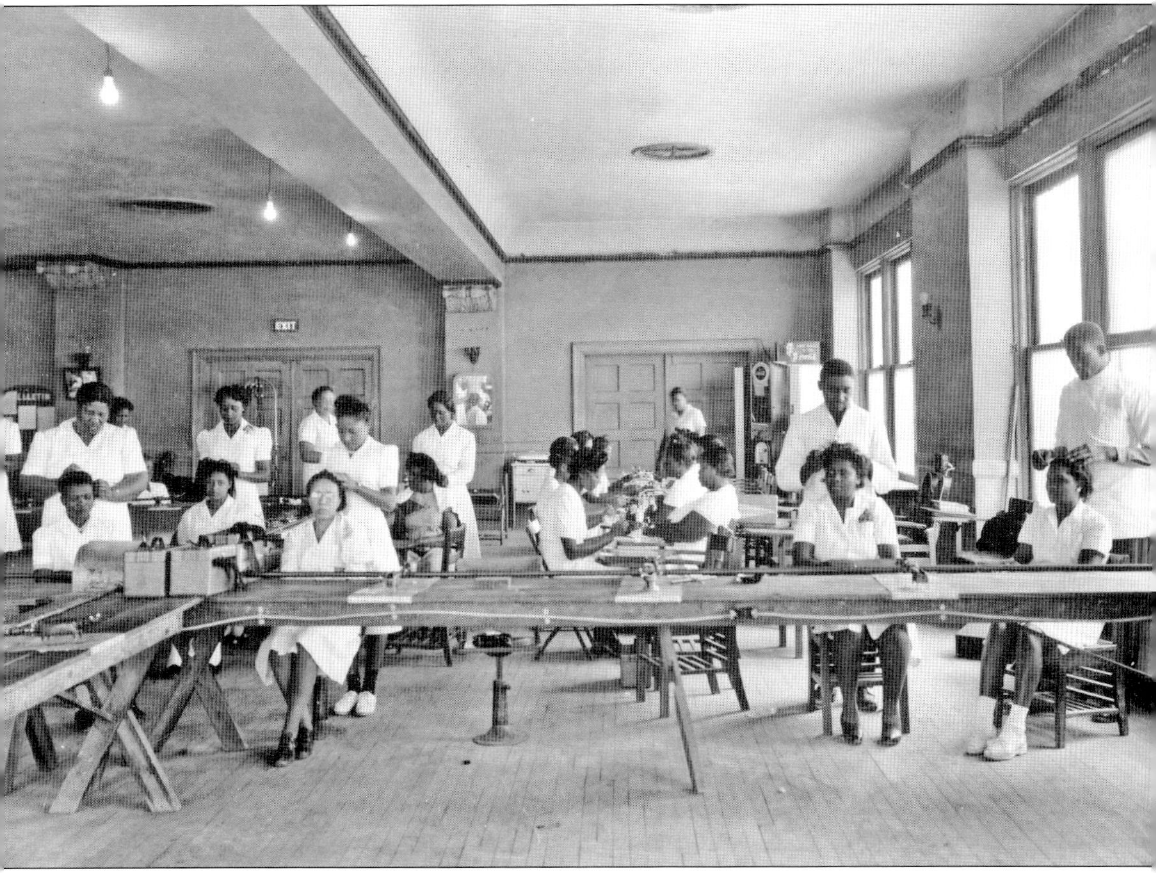

Cosmetology has always been a respected occupation in the black community. In Houston, the Franklin Beauty School trained hundreds to work in the field.

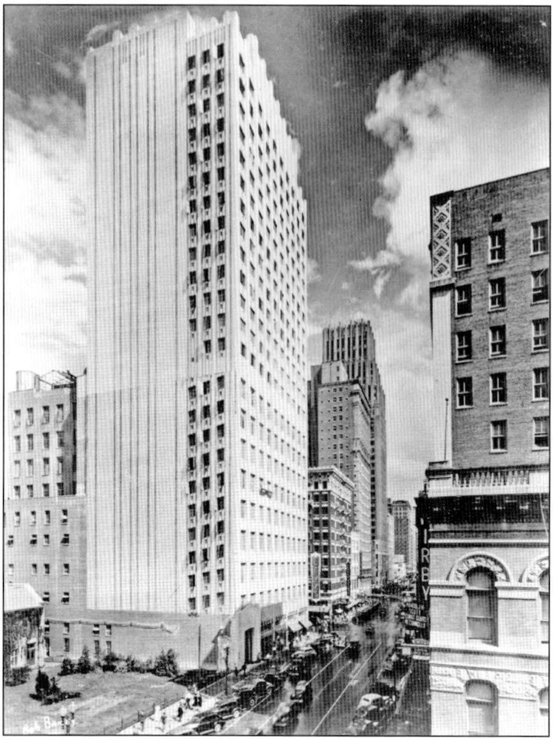

This view of downtown Houston dates to around the 1940s or 1950s. Hidden behind the city's growing skyscrapers were the row houses of city's black community.

One of the public spaces of early-20th-century downtown Houston is pictured here. While these areas of economic activity gave the impression of a modern metropolis, Houston's black community had advanced little beyond the days of slavery and Reconstruction.

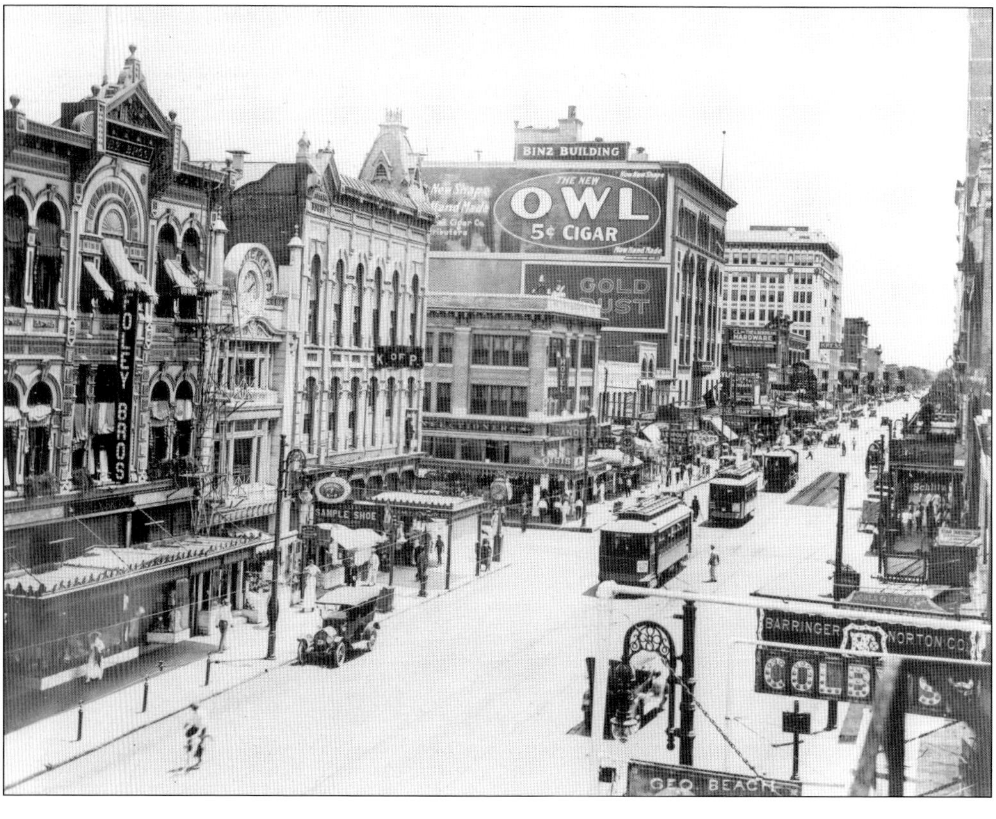

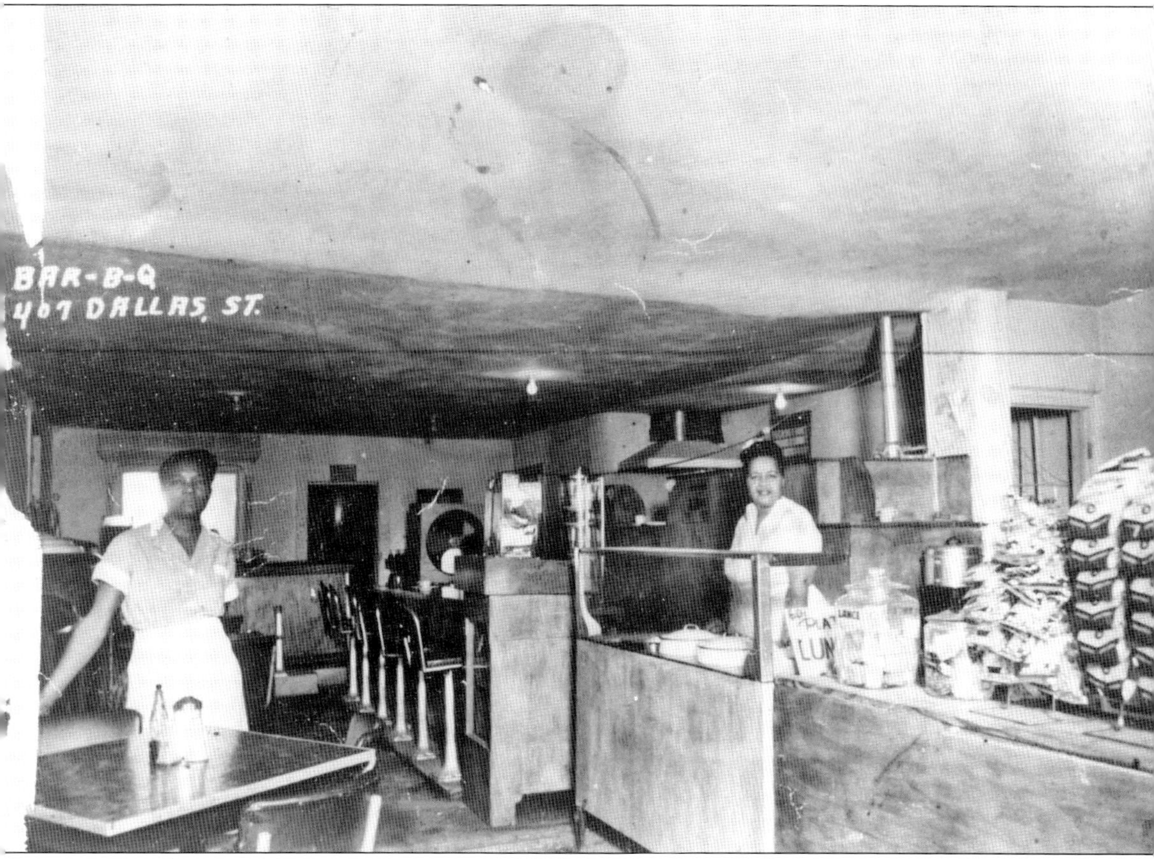

During the years of Jim Crow segregation, black restaurants not only served food and drinks, but also often provided places of social gathering for the community. They had a loyal clientele until demographic changes severely reduced the local population. Sadly, many of these black establishments were unable to survive the black flight into the suburbs during the 1970s and 1980s.

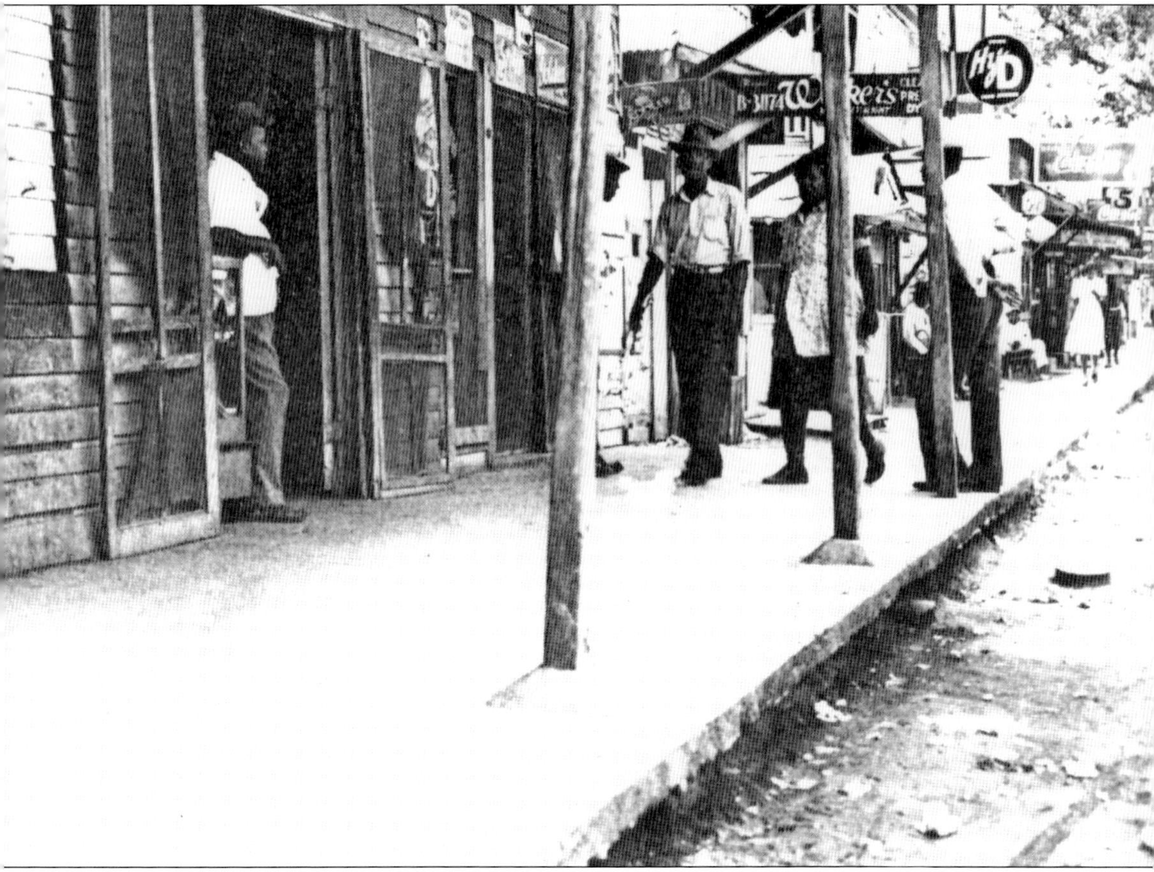

Houston's Fourth Ward was initially settled by former slaves in the late 19th century. Modern historians and community activists have fought mightily to preserve the history of the community in the face of modernization and the land acquisition efforts of real estate developers.

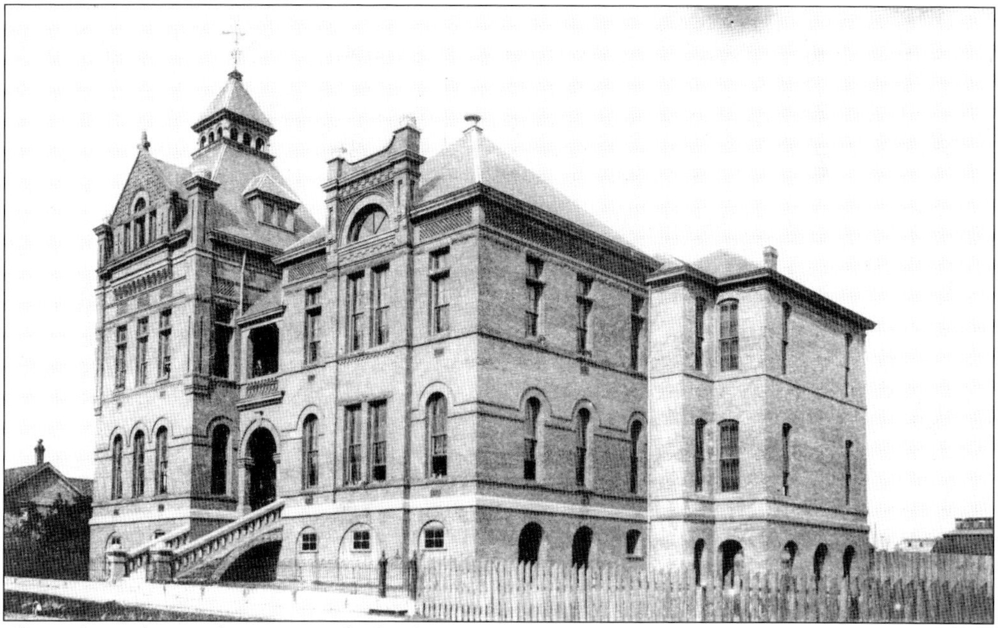

Throughout the South, segregated schools were the only places that educated the children of black communities. That education often went beyond that found in textbooks, also incorporating lessons in pride and self-respect that would be necessary for survival in a racist, segregated society.

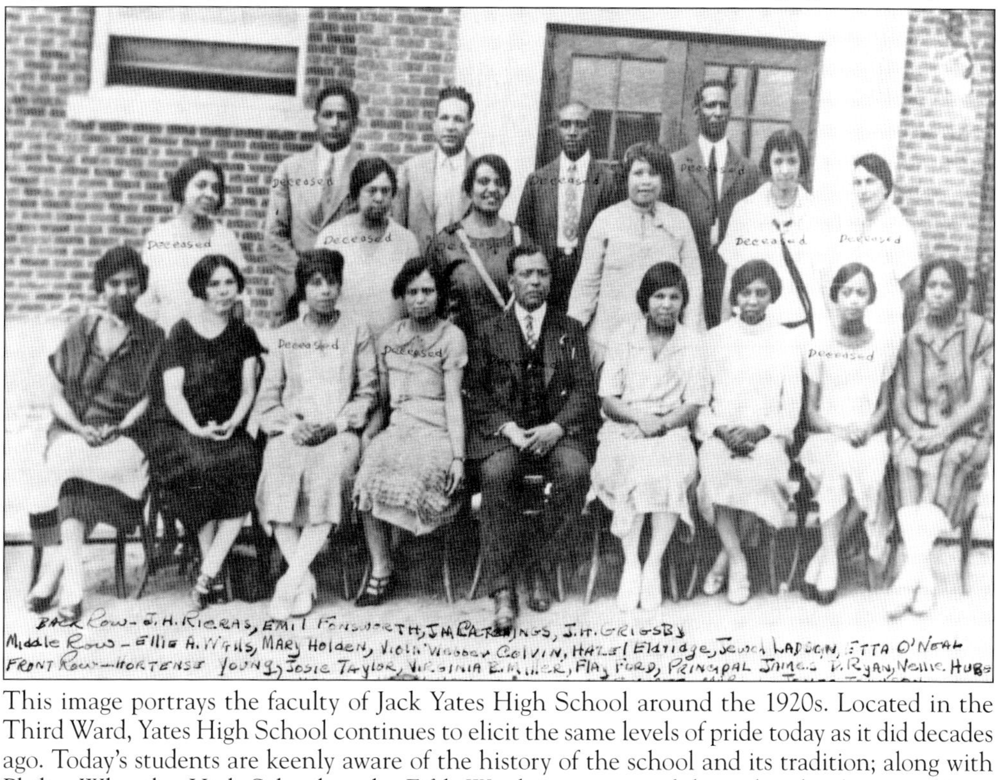

This image portrays the faculty of Jack Yates High School around the 1920s. Located in the Third Ward, Yates High School continues to elicit the same levels of pride today as it did decades ago. Today's students are keenly aware of the history of the school and its tradition; along with Philiss Wheatley High School in the Fifth Ward, it was one of the only schools accessible to black Houstonians for multiple generations.

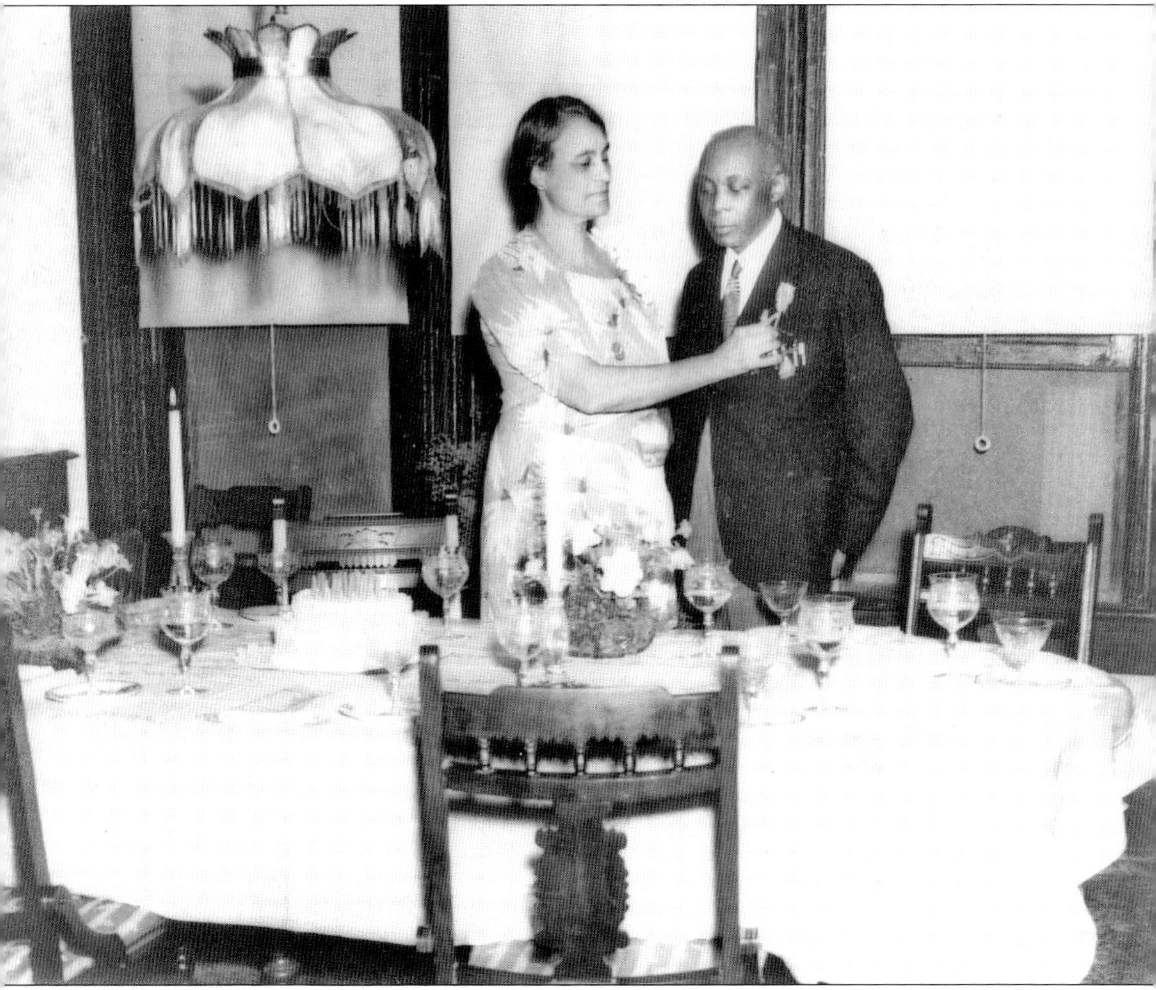

Black physicians were rare in the decades before the eradication of the Jim Crow. Dr. Covington was one of those rare individuals and is said to have served the black community with professionalism, grace, and class.

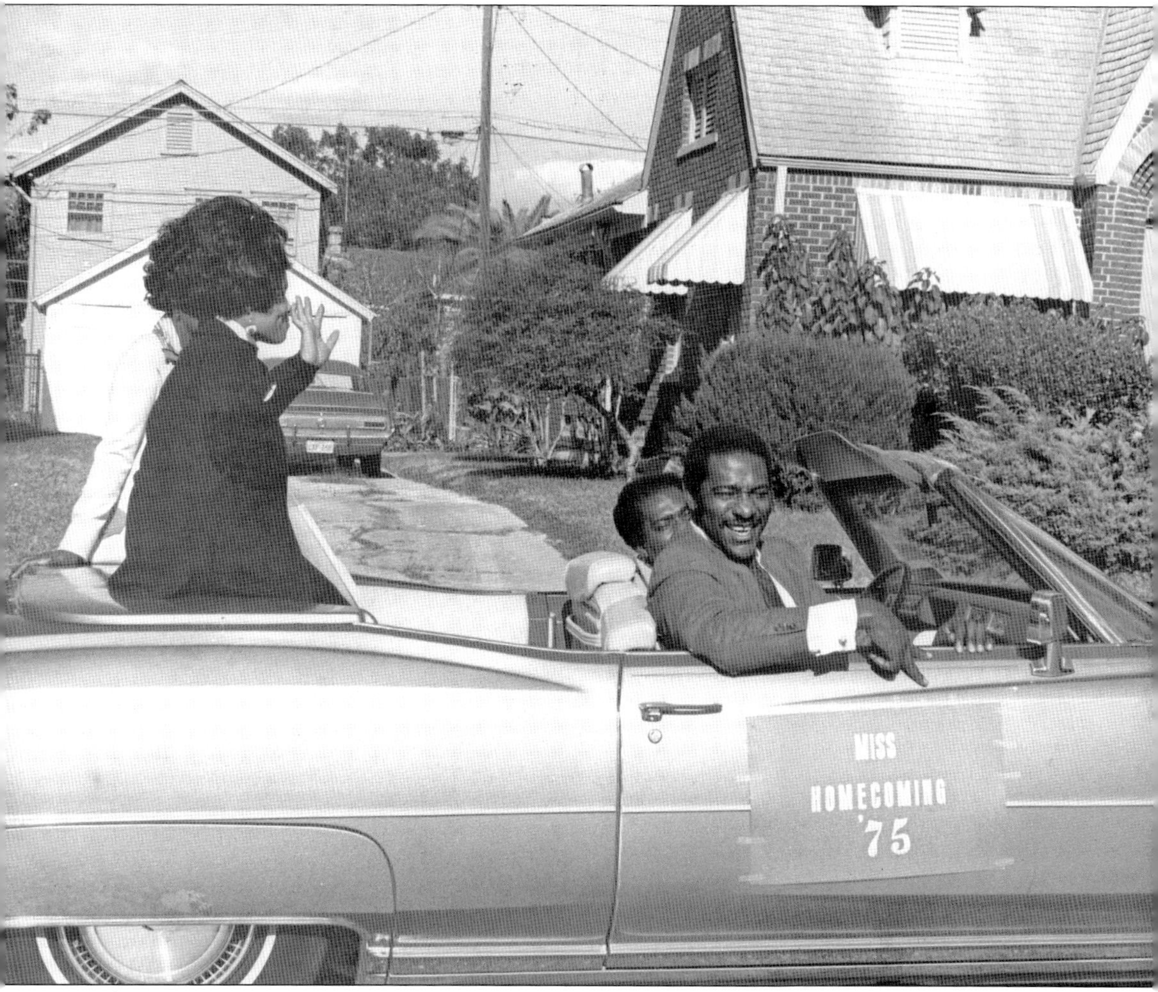

By the 1970s, most remnants of Jim Crow were fading under the rapid modernization of Houston. Still, the black community sought to preserve some of the customs that had originated under Jim Crow as a way to honor those who had sacrificed to create a community where opportunities were available to all. Texas Southern University's homecoming activities encouraged not only its alumni, but also those of the black community fortunate enough to have escaped the limitations of the inner city for the newly built suburbs that sprouted up around Houston's outer regions to return home. (Image courtesy of the Heartman Collections at Texas Southern University.)

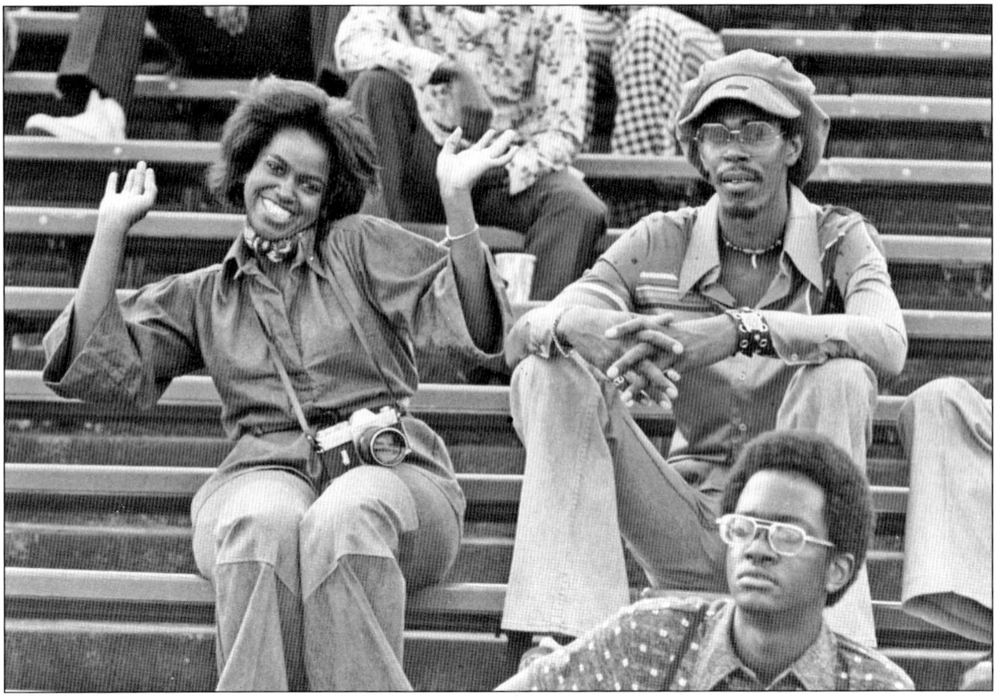

Athletic events were always a source of pride in the black community during Jim Crow. It was often rumored that the segregated black teams would be able to successfully compete against their white counterparts if ever given the opportunity. In the post–Jim Crow era, the black community no longer questioned whether their teams could compete but came out to support them nonetheless. The end of segregation meant the best black athletes were free to go to previously "white" institutions and generate millions for their coffers while seldom successfully matriculating their classrooms. (Image courtesy of the Heartman Collections at Texas Southern University.)

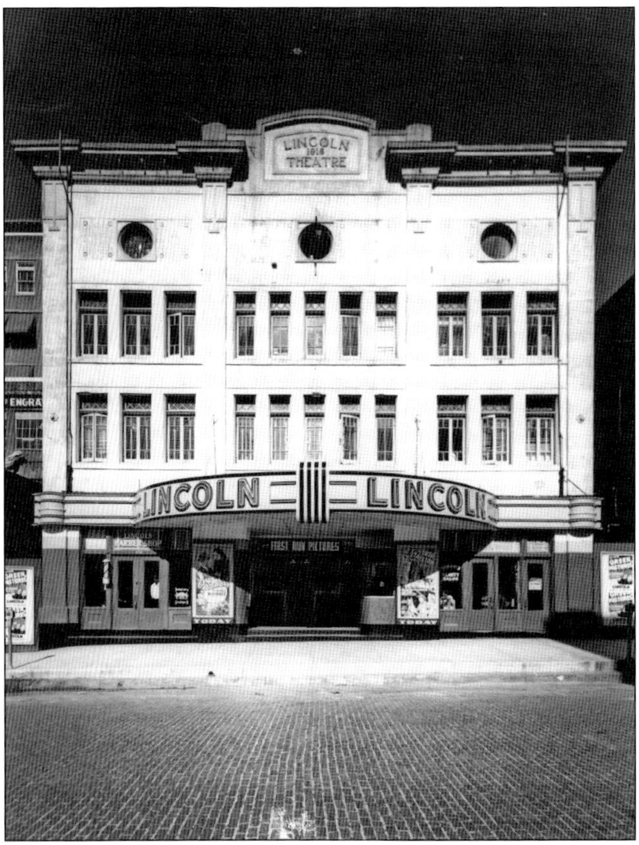

The Lincoln Theater was one of the most celebrated institutions in Houston.

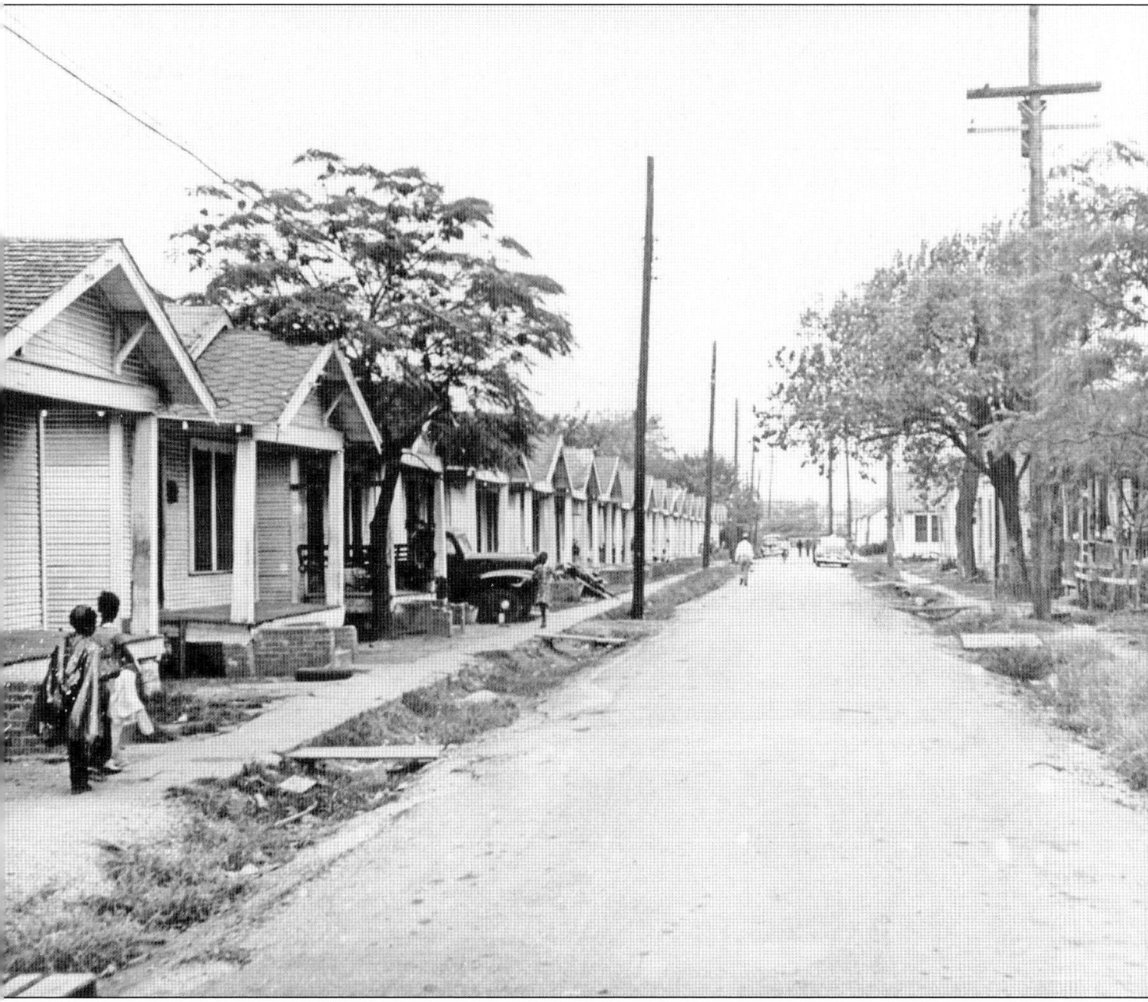

Shotgun row houses were a common sight in Houston's black community. This simplistic architectural style encouraged dense communities, which in turn fostered the sense of communal kinship. However, the end of Jim Crow led to a slow destruction of that sense of a close-knit community.

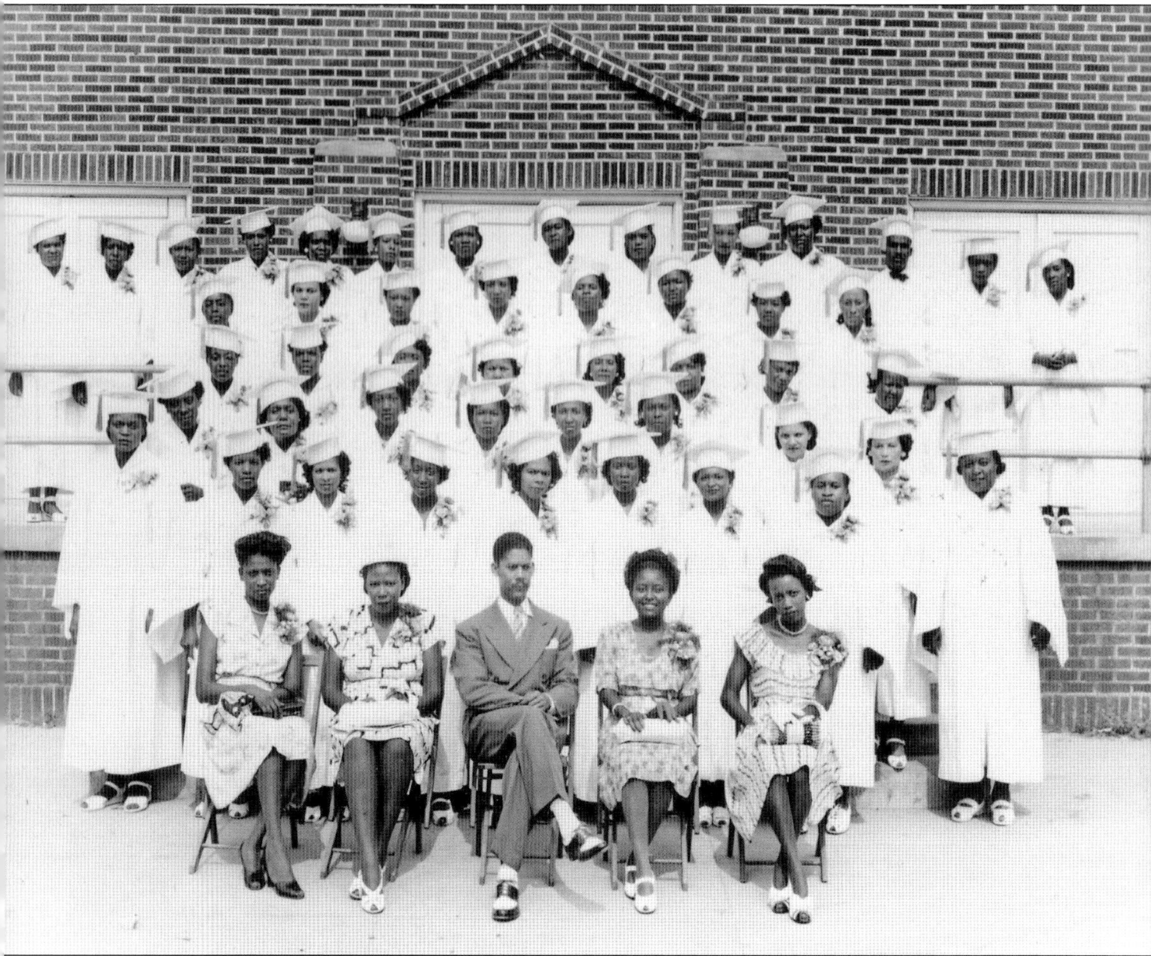

Houston's black community had few opportunities to pursue educational training. This image shows the graduating class of the Franklin Beauty School.

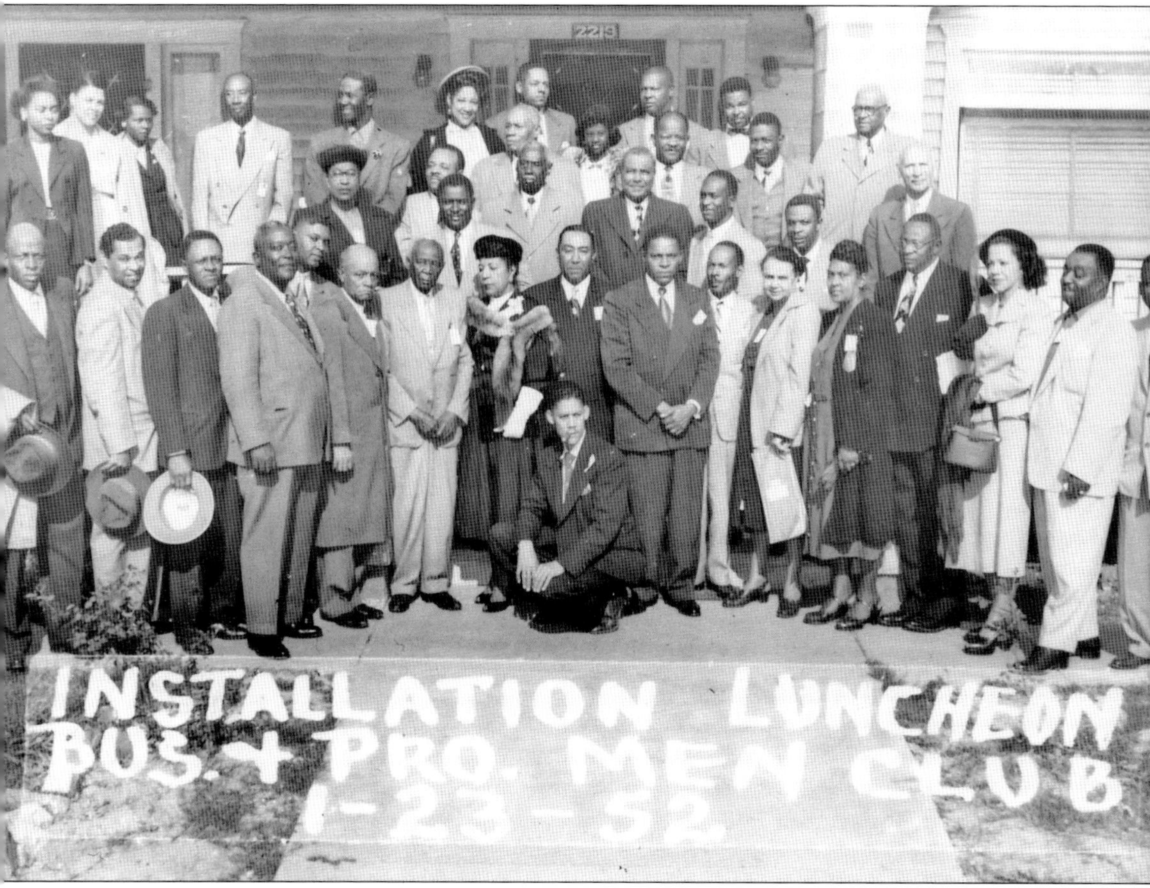

Meetings of black business and professional associations often mimicked those of the white business establishment.

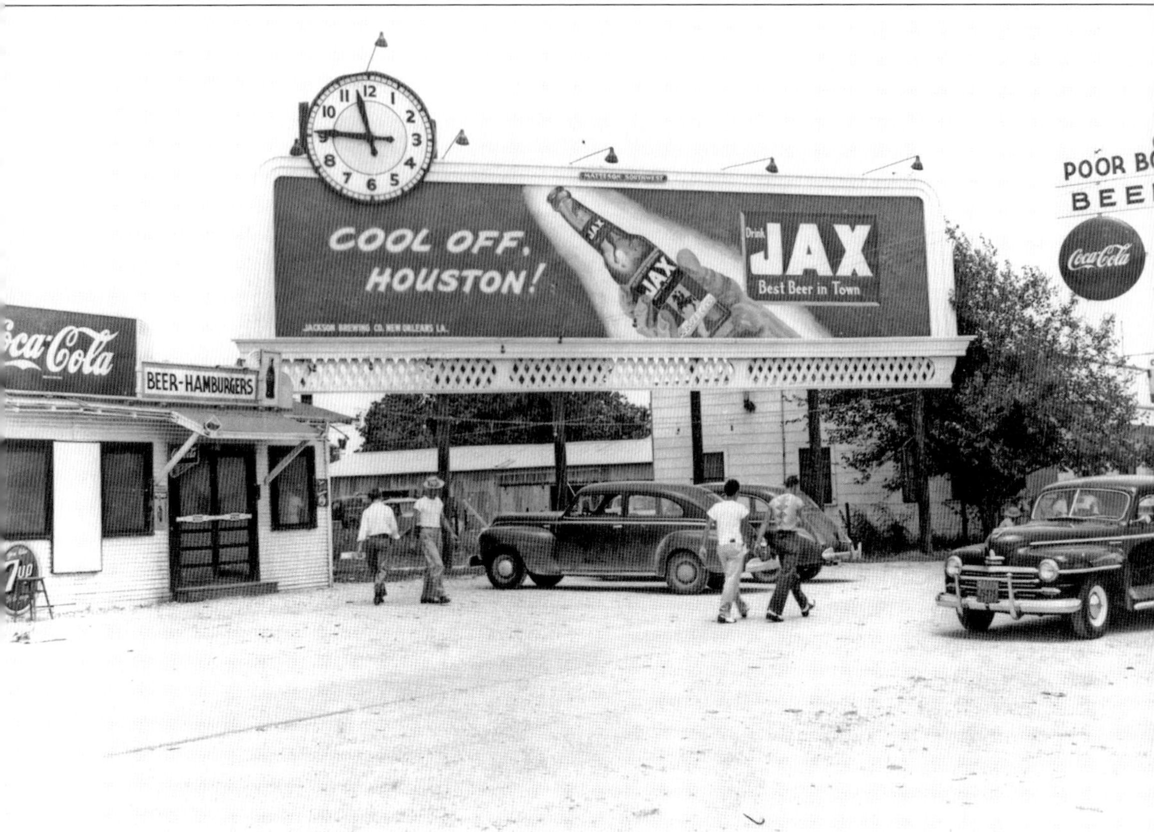

This is a c. 1940s image of a public space in one of Houston's black communities. Municipal services and financing for Houston's black communities often lagged far behind those of the white community. While Jim Crow was often seen as a means of socially separating the races, it also had a tangible impact in the ways that funds were administered throughout the city. Many areas in the black community did not have paved streets or curbs and gutters until the 1970s.

Three

PROTEST

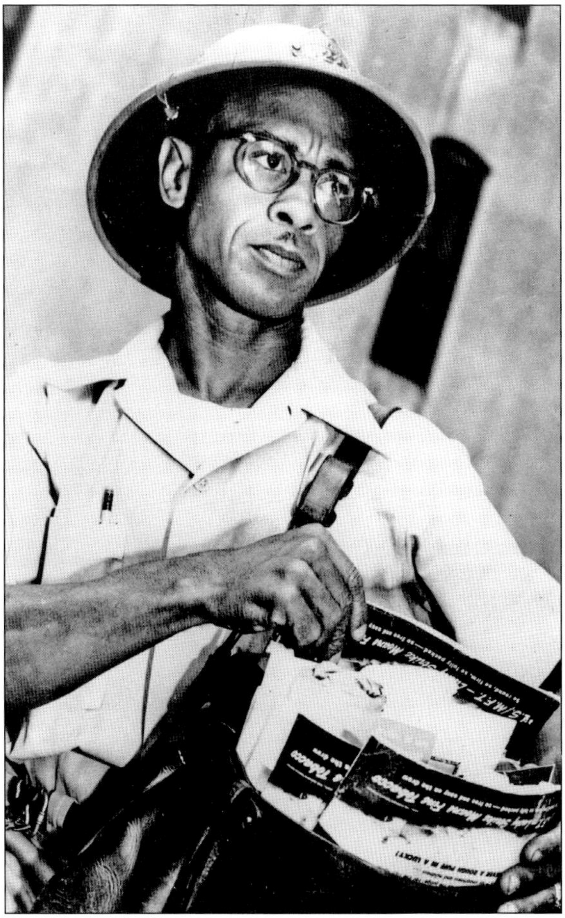

In 1946, supported by Thurgood Marshall and the NAACP, Houston mail carrier Heman Sweatt applied for admission to the University of Texas School of Law and was summarily denied admission based on his race. In order to comply with the Supreme Court's previous ruling in *Plesssy v. Ferguson*, the regents of the University of Texas hurriedly assembled a law school for blacks. Opening in 1947 as the Texas State University for Negroes (later renamed Texas Southern University), the regents sought to maintain the "whites only" student body of its flagship institution. However, the Supreme Court ruled in 1950 in *Sweatt v. Painter* that the newly assembled law school did not meet the intent of separate but equal, and Heman Sweatt was granted admission to the University of Texas School of Law. This case was one of the stepping stones to the NAACP's successful litigation efforts in *Brown v. Board of Education*, which led to the reversal of the cherished Jim Crow policy of separate but equal. This image is of the plaintiff in that case, Heman Sweatt. (Image courtesy of the Heartman Collection, Texas Southern University.)

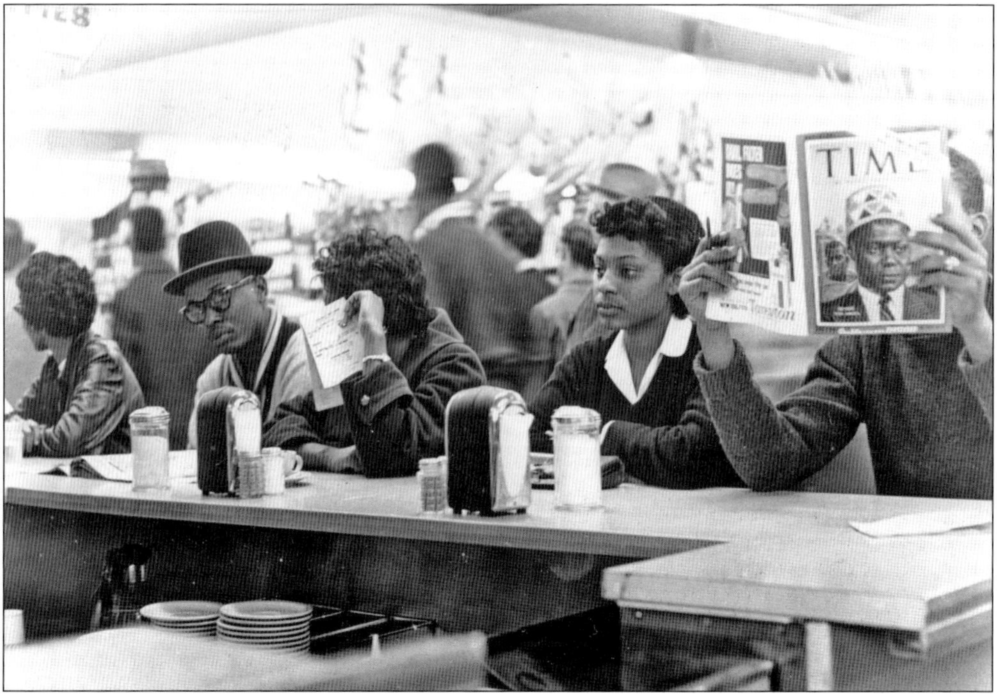

By the 1960s, black students were protesting their inability to access public facilities across the South. In Houston, students from Texas Southern University protested unequal facilities throughout the city.

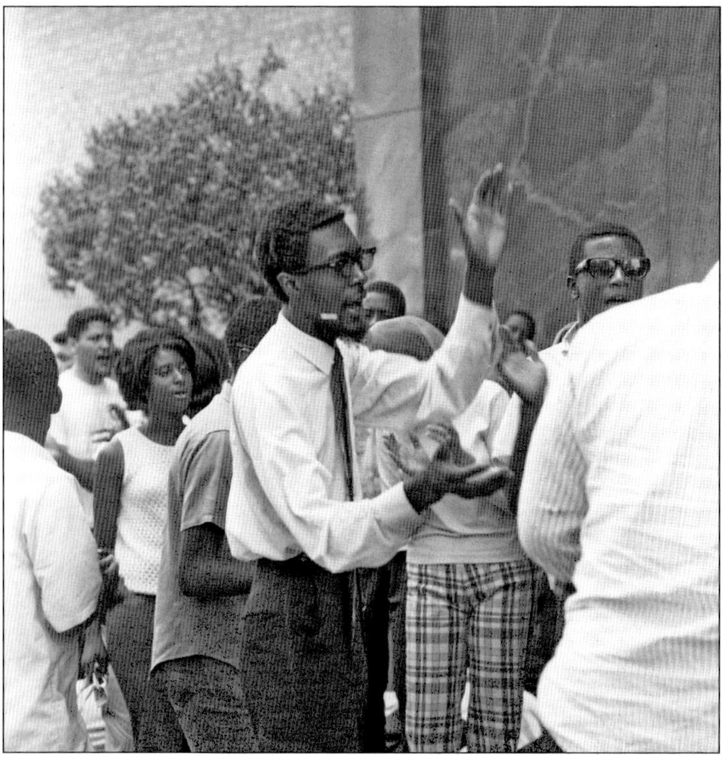

These students protest in downtown Houston in a manner reminiscent of the youth protests of the 1960s. The civil rights movement of the 1960s was motivated by the energies of young black and white college students. Even though Houston did not generally experience the same degree of violence as other urban areas, Houston's black community still successfully agitated for an end to Jim Crow policies and equal rights under the law.

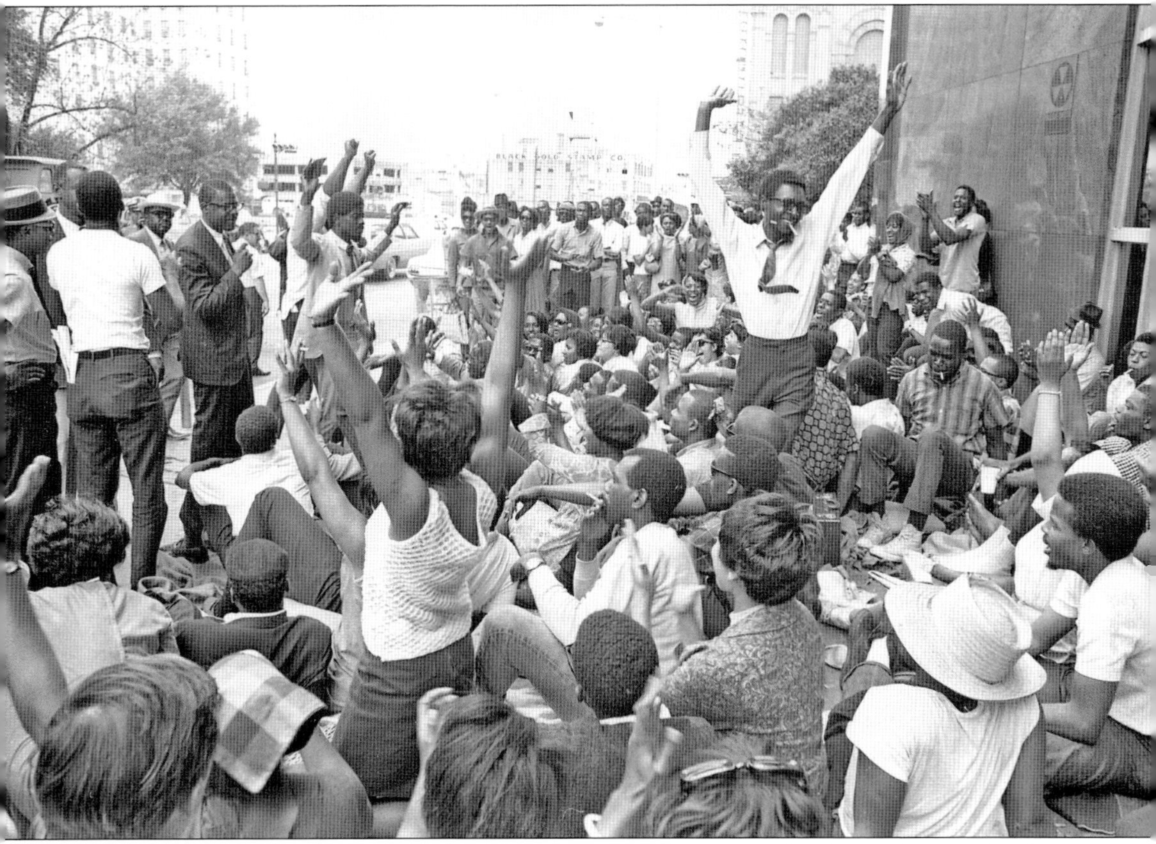

Most historians credit the Montgomery bus boycott as the impetus for the modern civil rights movement. However, the sit-in movement initiated by college students brought attention to the inequities of segregation in public facilities. In the early 1960s, Houston's black student movement often met at the YMCA in the Third Ward to plan strategies for integrating the city's public spaces.

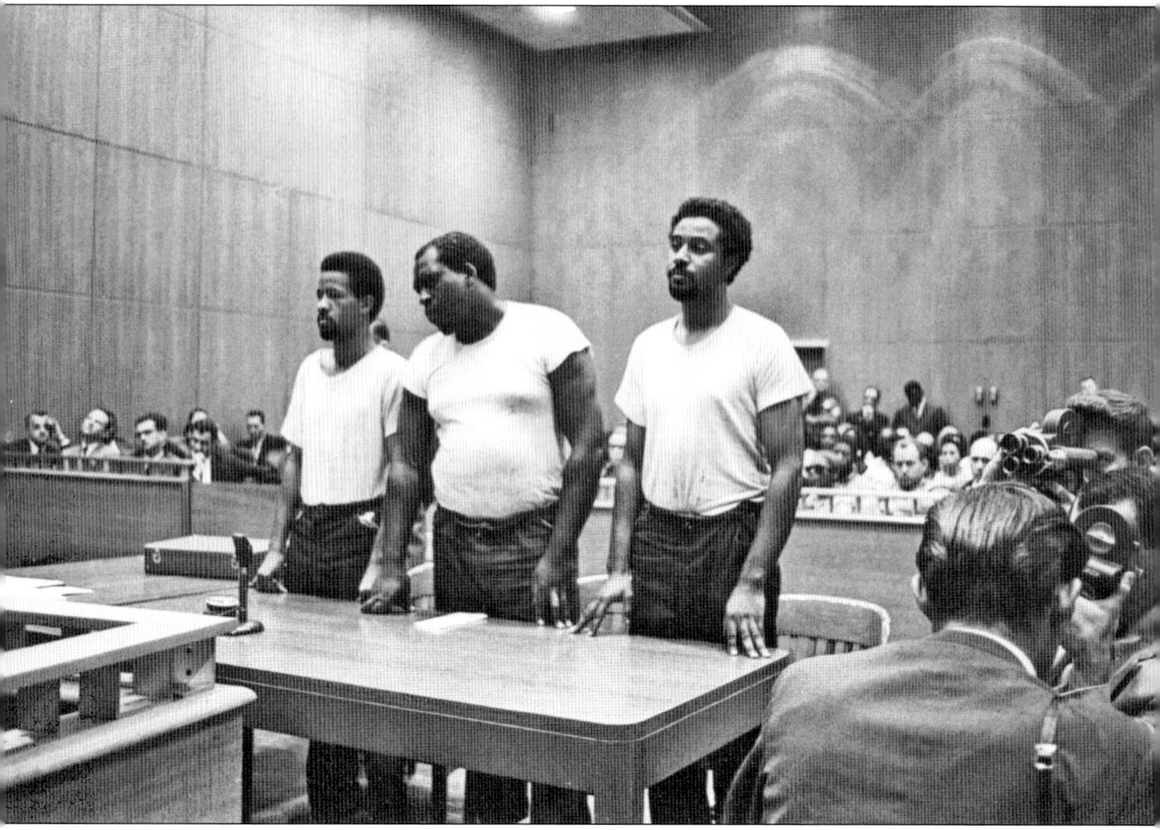

These black defendants are in custody after the shooting of a white police officer during a violent conflict between police and students on the campus of Texas Southern University. Evidence later indicated that the killing bullet was from a fellow officer's gun. After the incident, both sides worked quickly to repair the splintered relationship between city officials and the TSU community.

During the conflict between Houston police officers and TSU students, numerous students were arrested, and evidence suggests they were mistreated and physically threatened upon arrival at police headquarters. (Image courtesy of the Heartman Collections at Texas Southern University.)

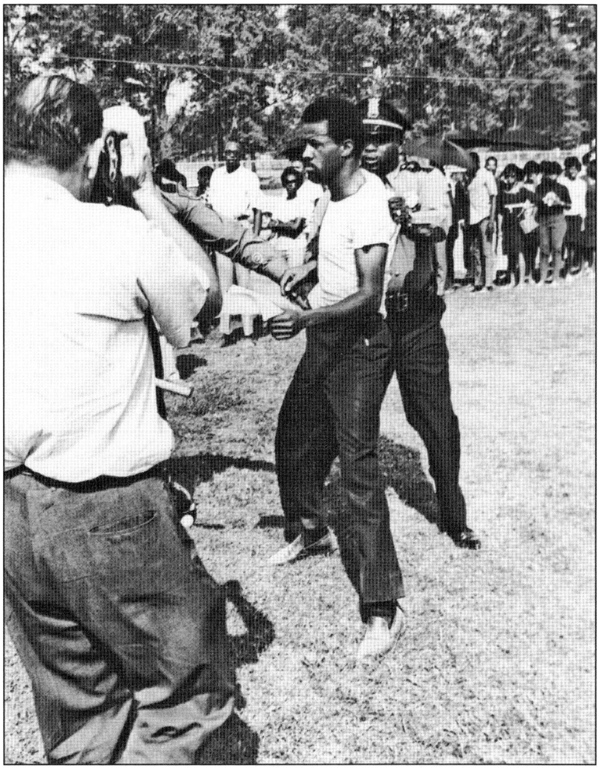

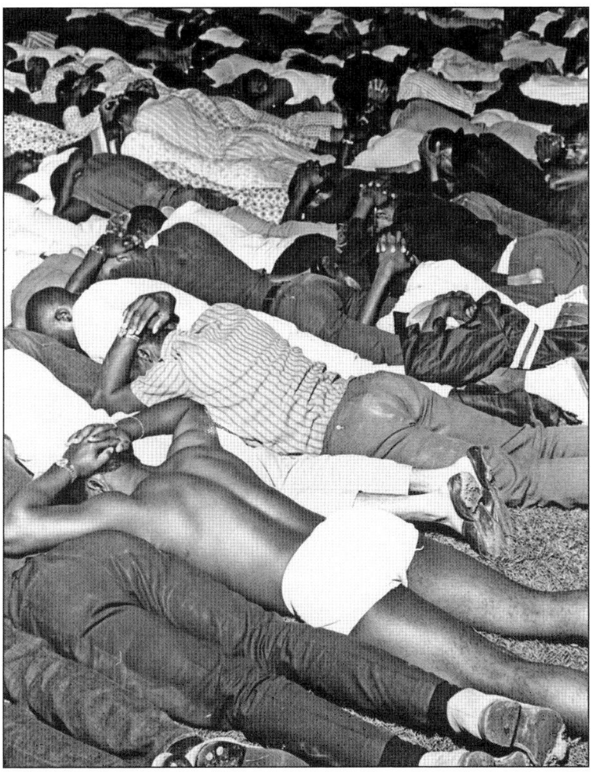

These students are pictured outside their dorms after the TSU riots. In the aftermath of the conflict, police officials ransacked dormitories in search of the gun believed to have been used in the killing of an officer. No gun was found, but the treatment of students was reminiscent of images from places like Montgomery and Selma. (Image courtesy of the Heartman Collections at Texas Southern University.)

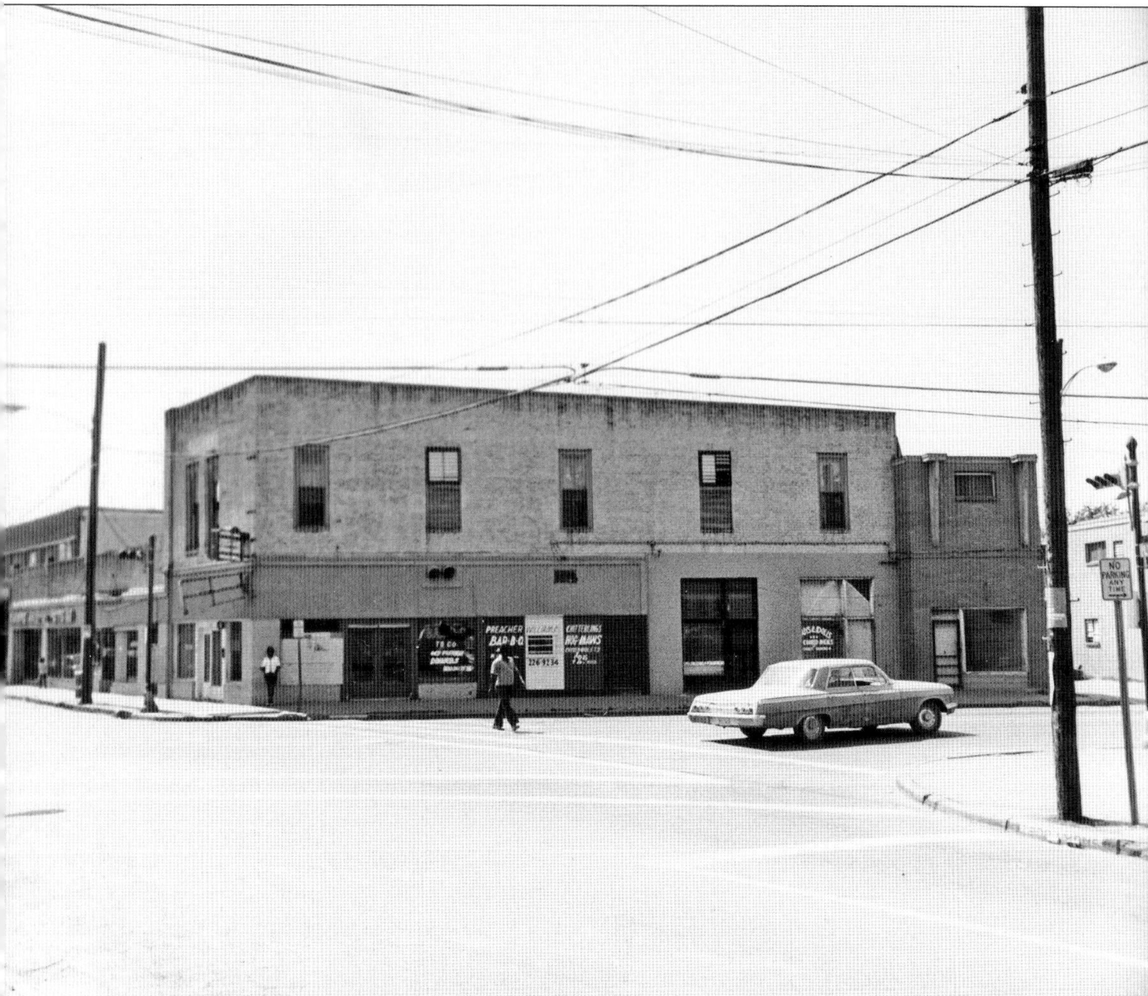

Storefront businesses were common in Houston's Third Ward, as many black communities were self-contained during the Jim Crow era. The black community took pride in the way in which they operated outside the control and oversight of whites. The end of Jim Crow meant the end of these self-contained communities as blacks followed their white counterparts to the suburbs.

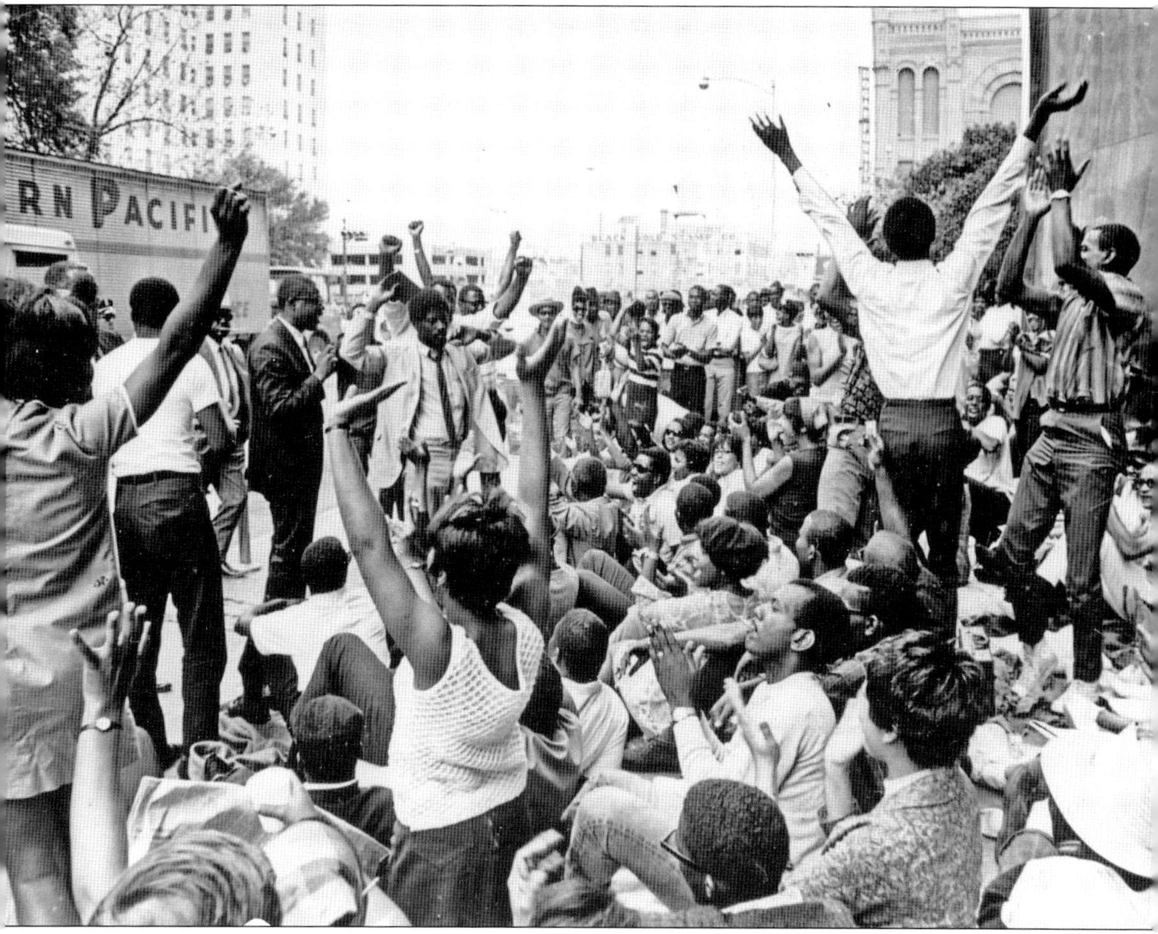

Students in Houston's black community were politically active in the early 1960s. However, black students were not involved in the process that led to the integration of Houston's lunch counters, facilitated by city leaders and the president of TSU, and negated some of their initiatives. Nonetheless, young people in the black community continued to protest when they felt their rights were being infringed upon.

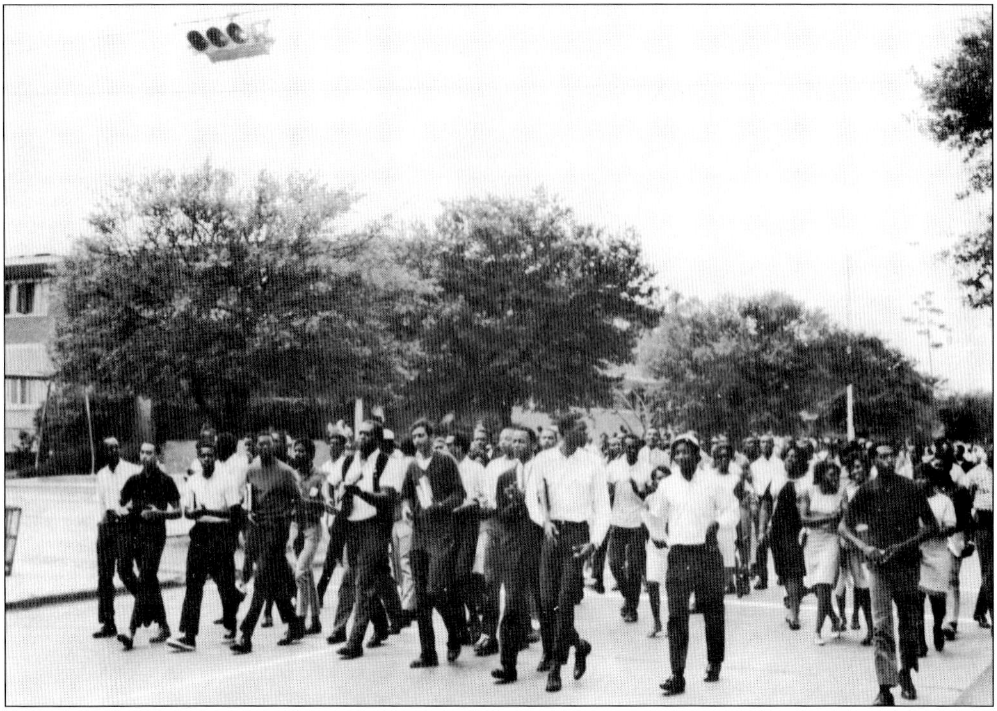

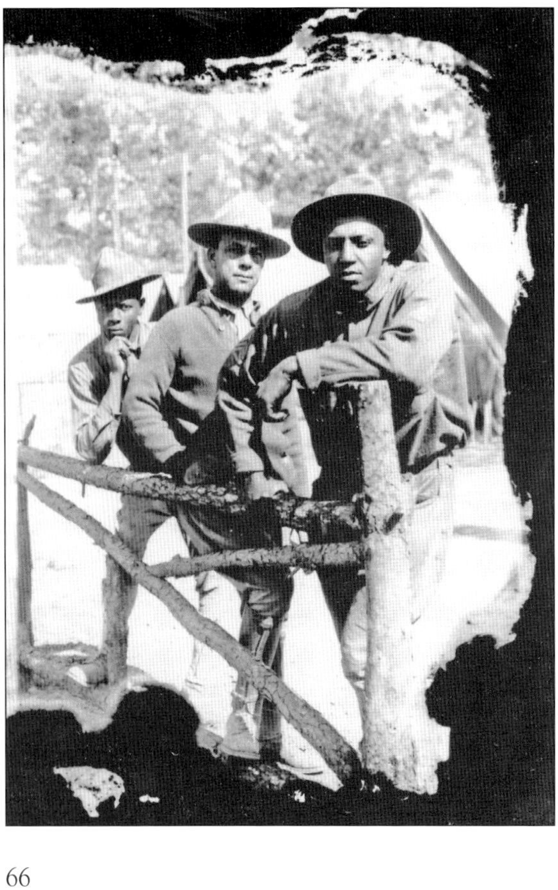

Black college students across the South began protesting for equal access to public facilities in the 1960s. A lot of these demonstrations led to confrontations with authorities, many of whom wanted to maintain the status quo of Jim Crow segregation. In Houston, city officials manipulated the press to prevent the integration of a downtown restaurant from being publicized. As a result, Houston integrated without fanfare, violence, or negative publicity.

Buffalo Soldiers were black soldiers serving in the US military during the years and decades following the Civil War and Reconstruction. In the 20th century, the US Army maintained segregated units through World War II. Camp Logan was a segregated military facility located just outside Houston's city limits during World War I.

Four

African American Houston

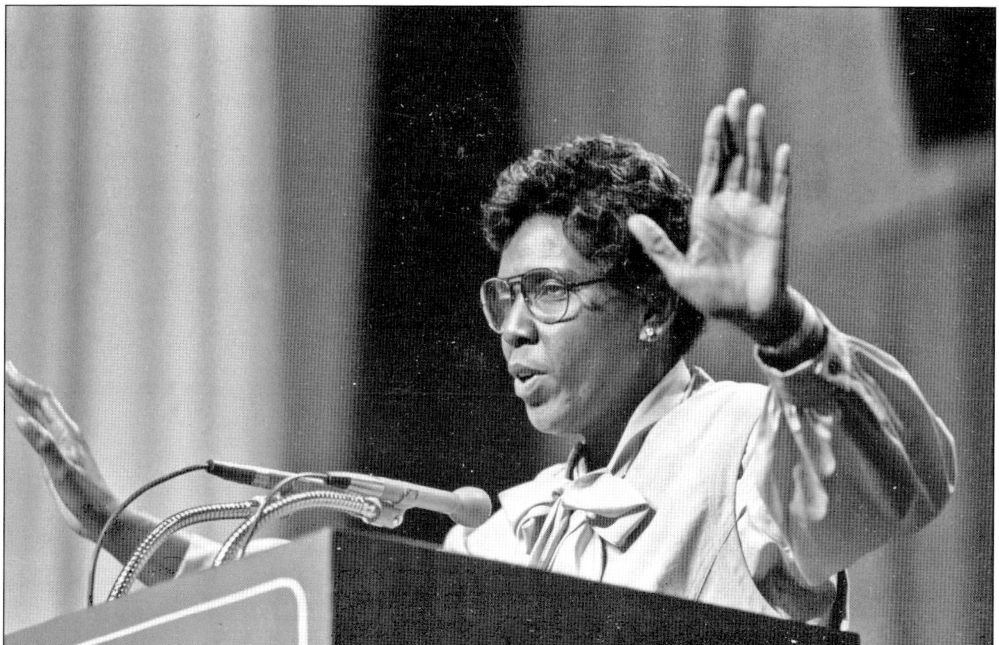

US congresswoman Barbara Jordan electrified audiences with her distinct oratory style, a style she admitted was learned during her years on the Texas Southern University debate team under the leadership of Dr. Thomas Freeman.

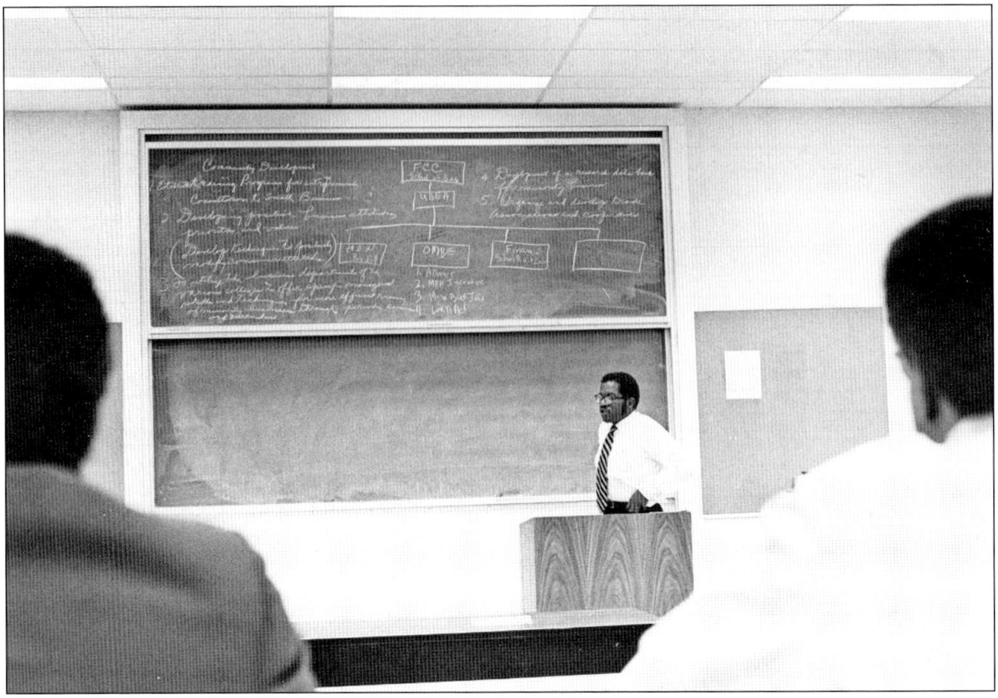

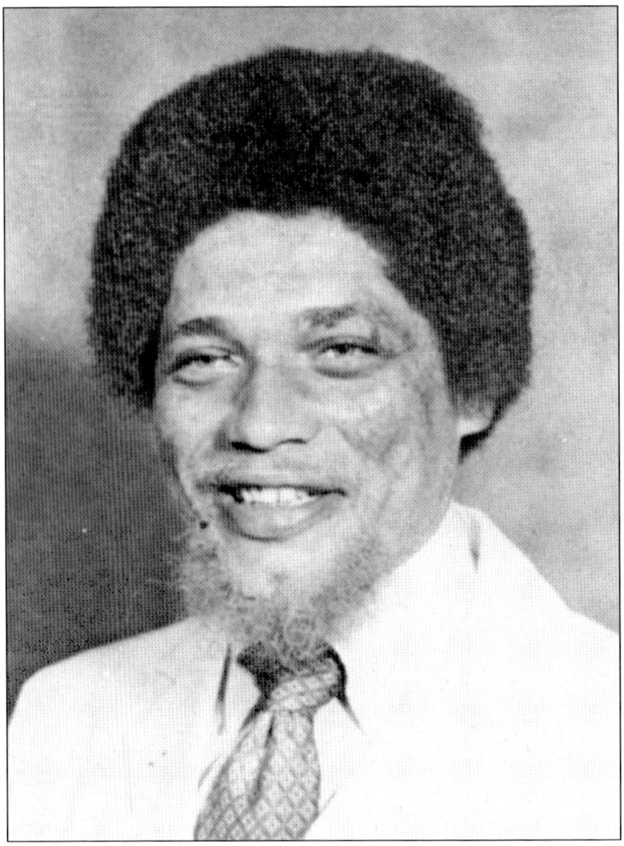

The civil rights era opened many educational doors for the black community, and a number of African Americans pursued graduate degrees and found faculty positions at TSU and Prairie View A&M University. Many students in the post–Jim Crow era often commented that the learning experiences were heightened because their professors could relate to them on a social level. (Image courtesy of the Heartman Collections at Texas Southern University.)

US congressman Mickey Leland was one of the area's most influential congressmen during an all-too-brief political career. Leland perished during a humanitarian trip to Africa. His legacy of activism still reverberates throughout the community, especially at the Texas Southern University School of Public Affairs, which shares his name.

The Fifth Ward's Julia Hester left a legacy of service to the community, particularly those who have difficulties serving themselves.

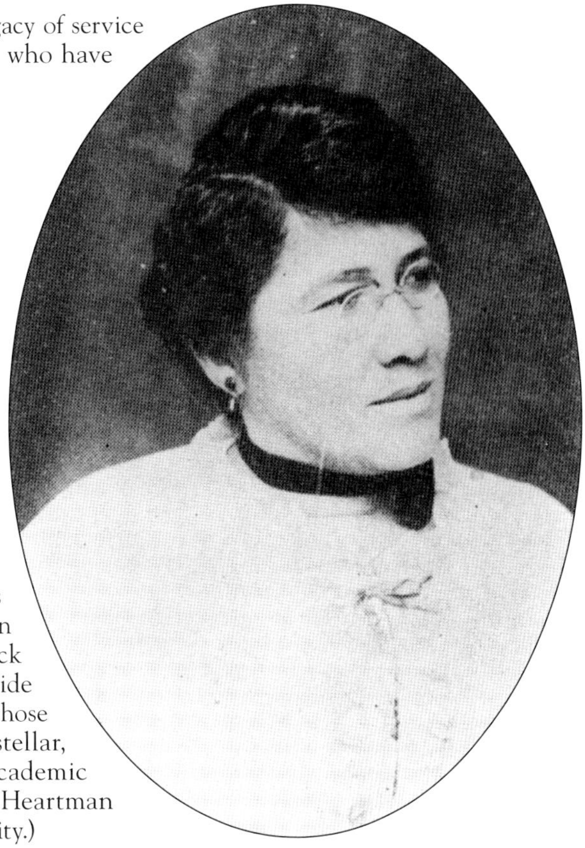

This image shows two children participating in homecoming activities in the 1970s. Homecoming was more than a university function; it generally involved the entire community. This was indicative of the role Texas Southern University played in Houston's black community. TSU continues to provide educational opportunities not only for those whose academic record may not be stellar, but also to students of exemplary academic achievement. (Image courtesy of the Heartman Collections at Texas Southern University.)

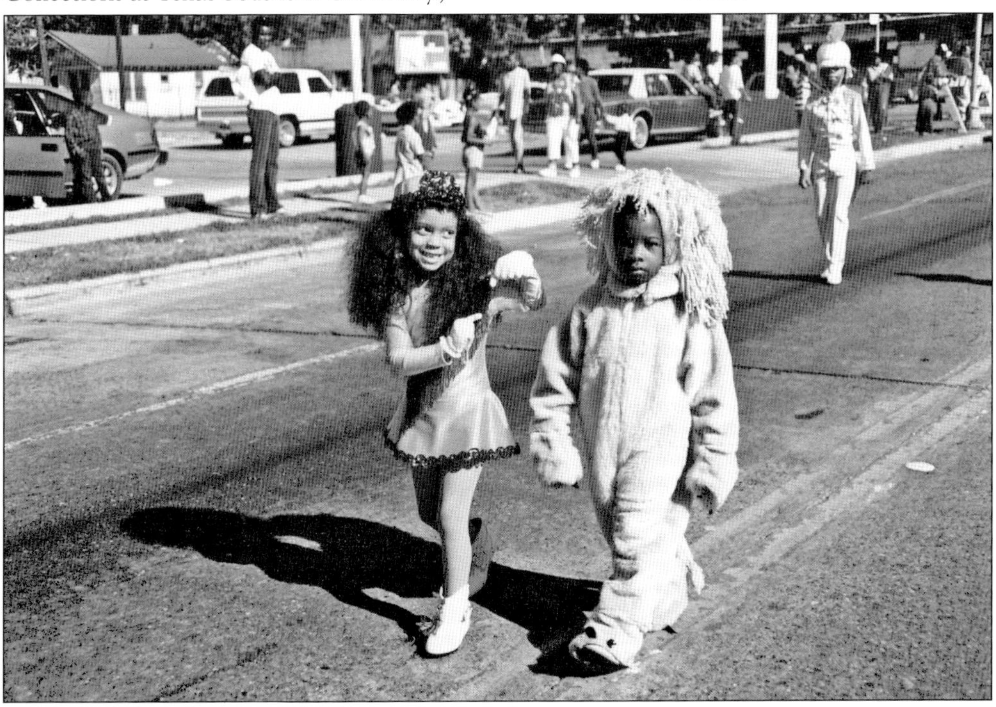

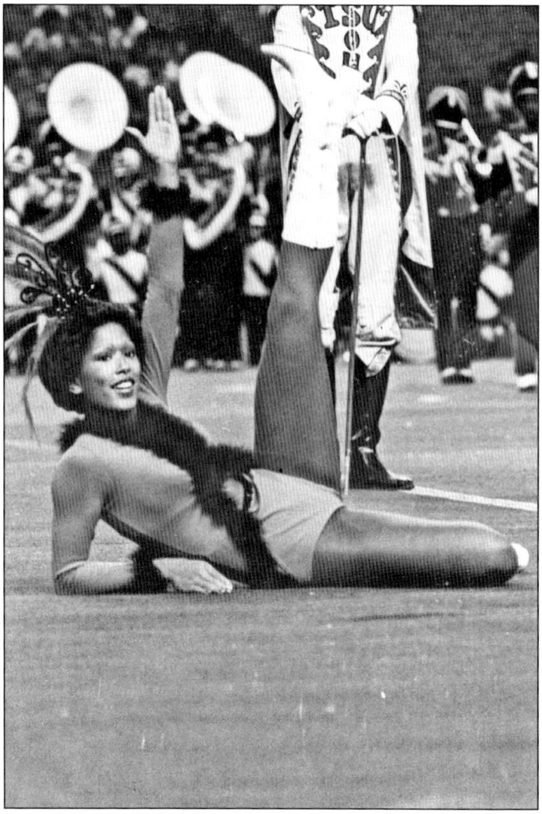

Throughout the South, football fans who supported the teams of historically black colleges and universities (HBCUs) knew to get their refreshments during the second quarter of the game in order to be back in their seats when the halftime performances began. It did not matter if it was Grambling, Southern, Prairie View, or Mississippi Valley, the halftime shows never disappointed and left the entire stadium breathless. (Image courtesy of the Heartman Collections at Texas Southern University.)

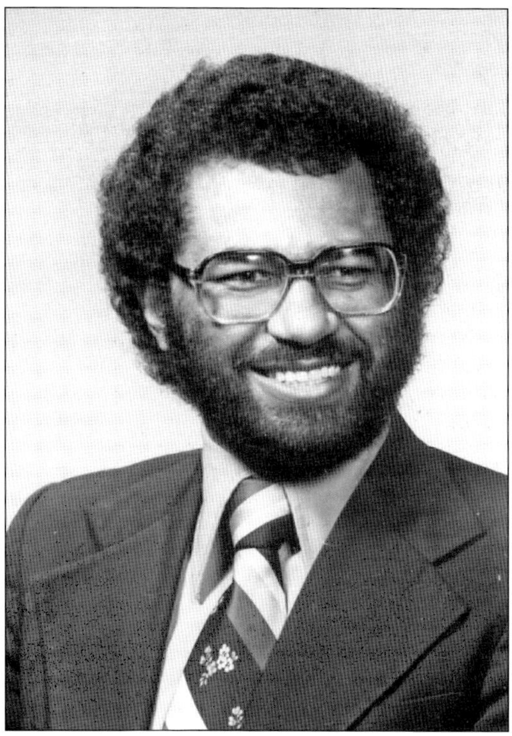

US congressman Al Green has served the Houston community as a defender of personal liberties. He served as Precinct 7 Harris County justice of the peace for 26 years beginning in 1978. In 2005, Green became the US congressman from Texas's 9th district, a position he currently holds. (Image courtesy of the Greater Houston Black Chamber of Commerce.)

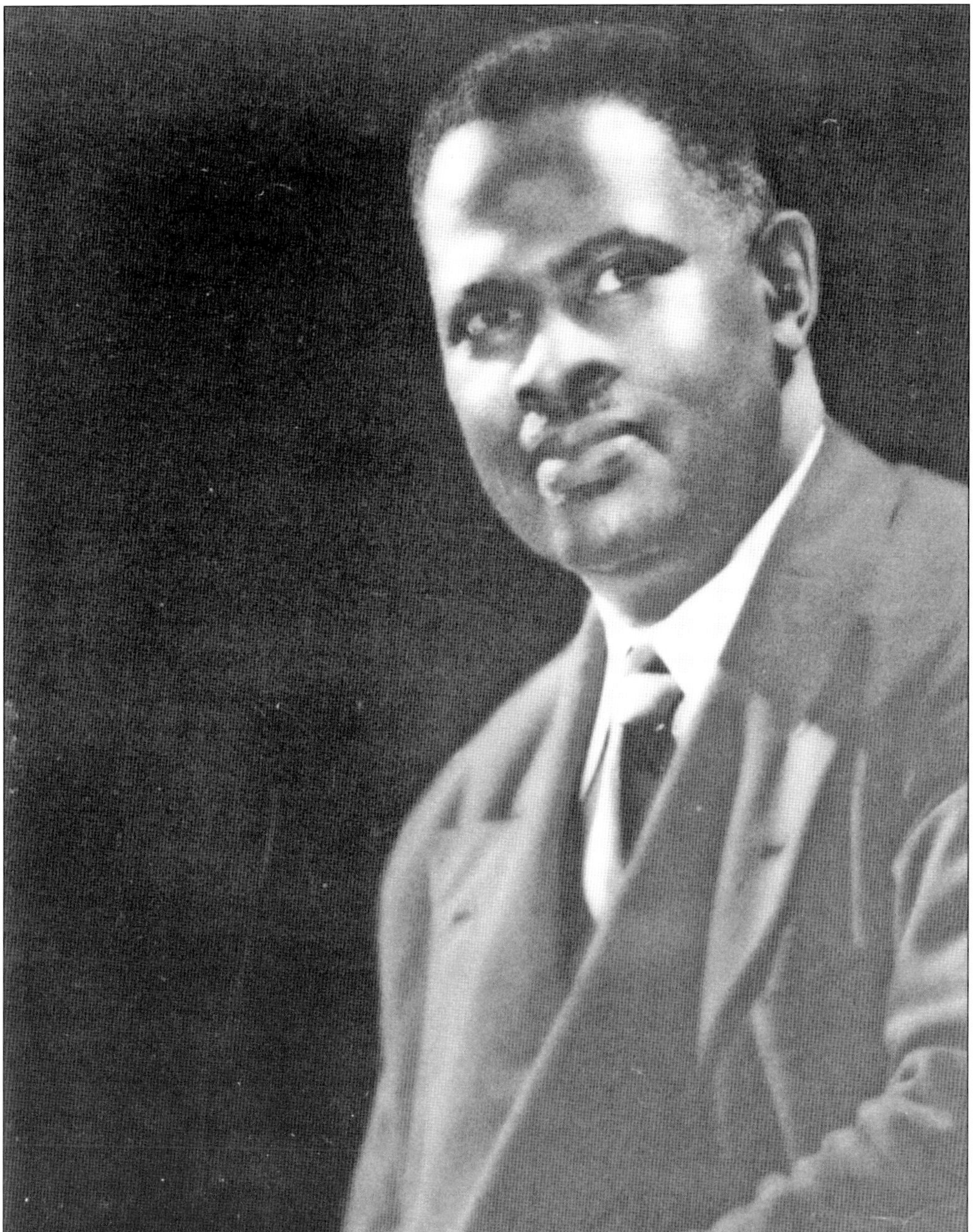

Texas Southern University's first president, Dr. Raphael O'Hara Lanier, was given the charge of establishing the new institution with a few buildings and a limited budget. While no one was sure how this experiment in educating primarily black Houstonians would turn out, Lanier provided the confidence and leadership that was most needed during those volatile early years. (Image courtesy of the Heartman Collections at Texas Southern University.)

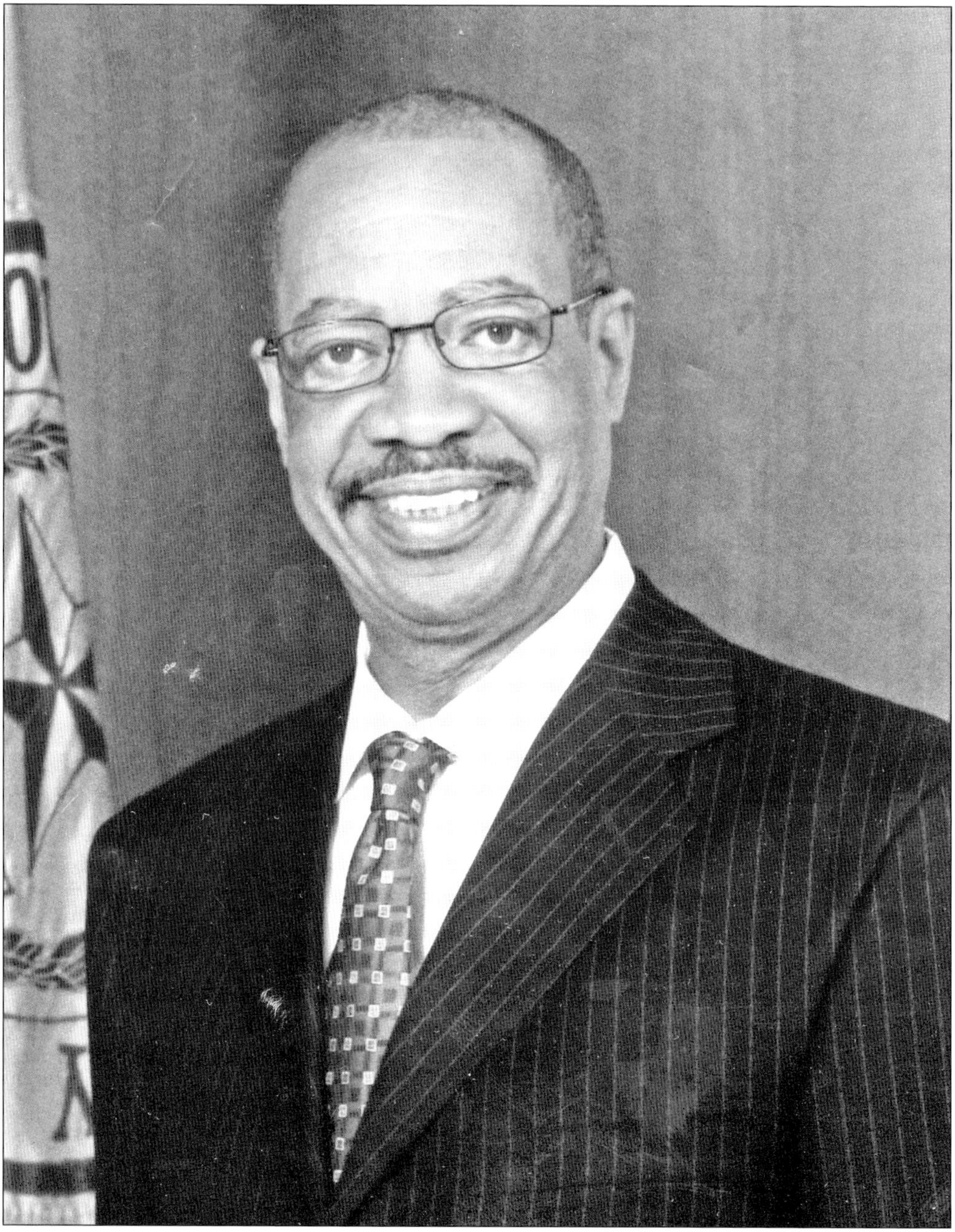

Texas Southern University's 10th president, John Rudley, assumed the helm during a tumultuous period in the history of the university. Nonetheless, he is poised for a long tenure that will ultimately see TSU transform from a place that originally offered an education to those locked out of other institutions to a 21st-century institution second to none in the country. (Image courtesy of the Heartman Collections at Texas Southern University.)

Local commissioner El Franco Lee has been a positive presence in local politics in the most influential political body in county government. His support of affirmative action and the activities of the black community has ensured that he will remain an influential political figure for the foreseeable future.

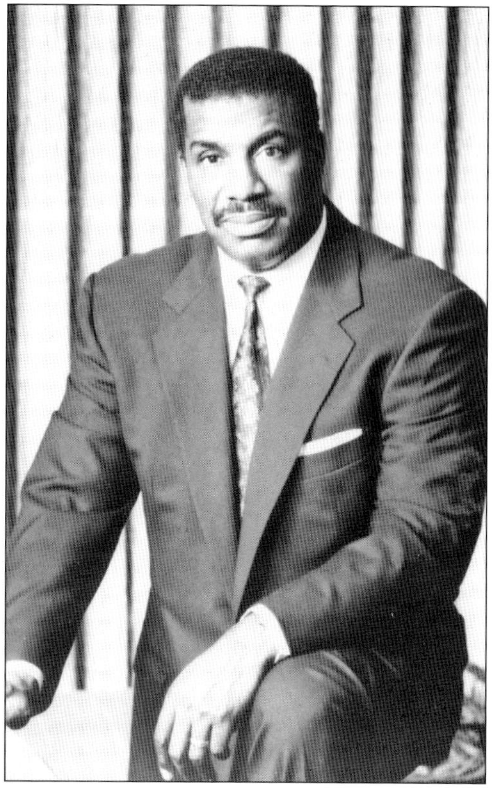

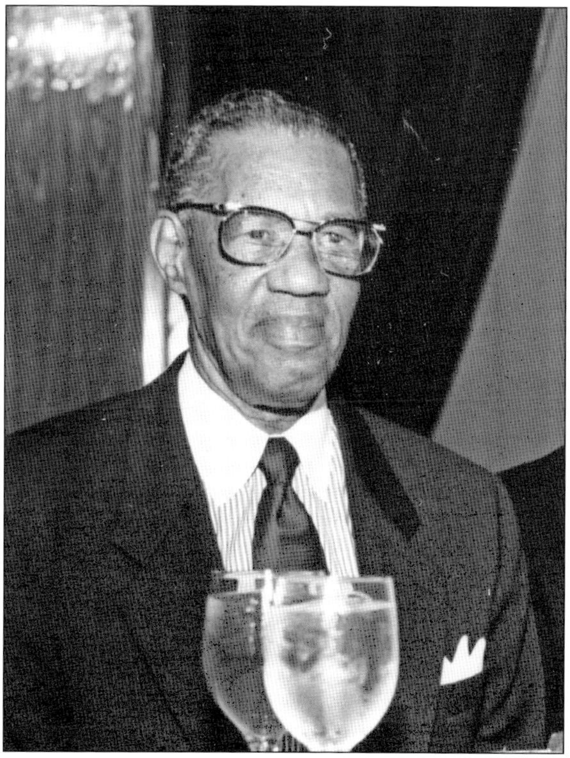

William Lawson, pastor emeritus of the Wheeler Avenue Baptist Church, was one of the most influential persons during the quiet and seamless integration of Houston's public facilities. While other Southern cities often erupted in violence during the integration process, Lawson was one of the mediators ensuring Houston did not suffer the same fate during this pivotal period in the country's history. (Image courtesy of the Heartman Collections at Texas Southern University.)

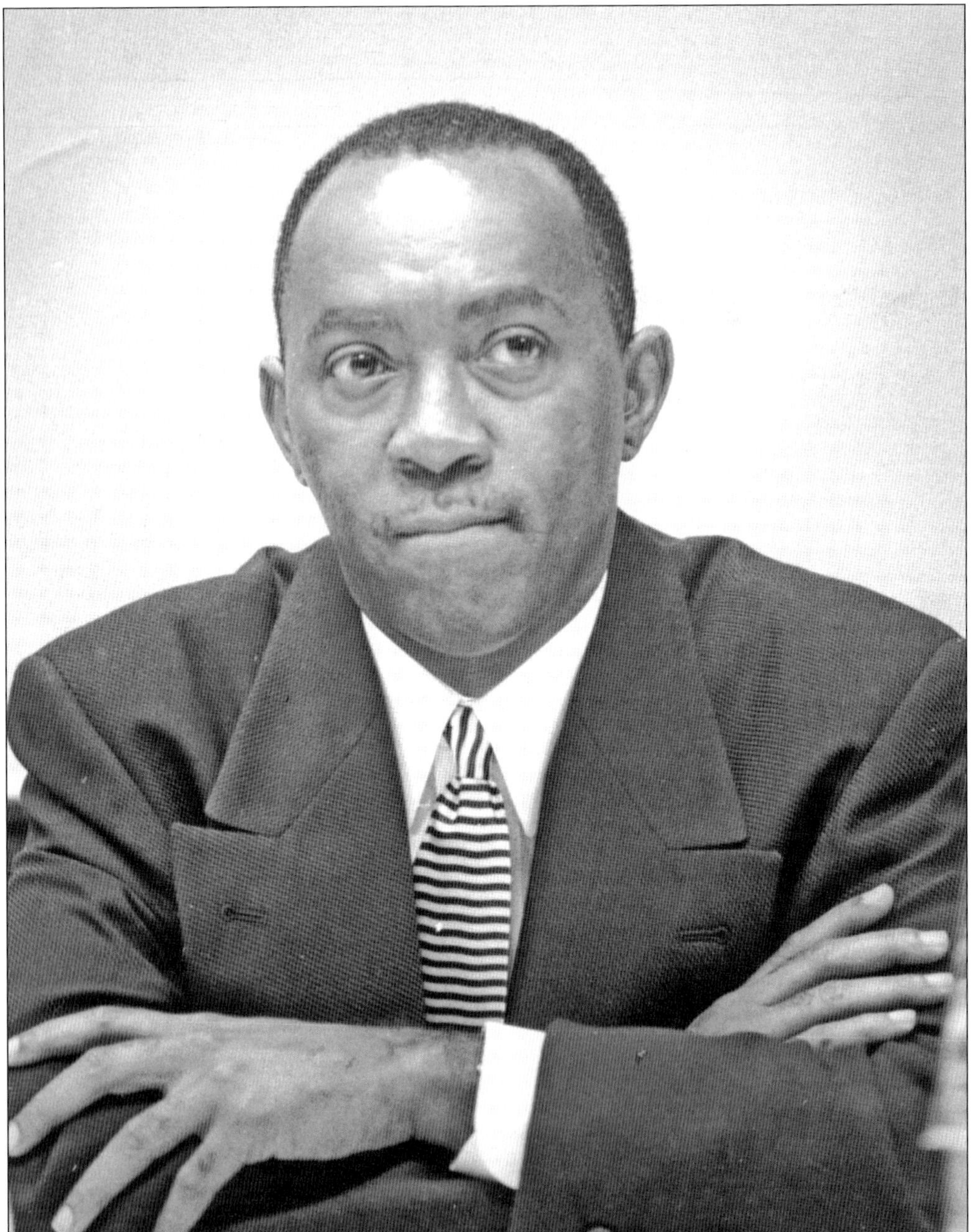

Rep. Sylvester Turner has served his Houston district with distinction and pride. A one-time candidate for Houston's mayor, Turner has consistently been an example of unapologetic political skill and dignity for the next generation of black politicians.

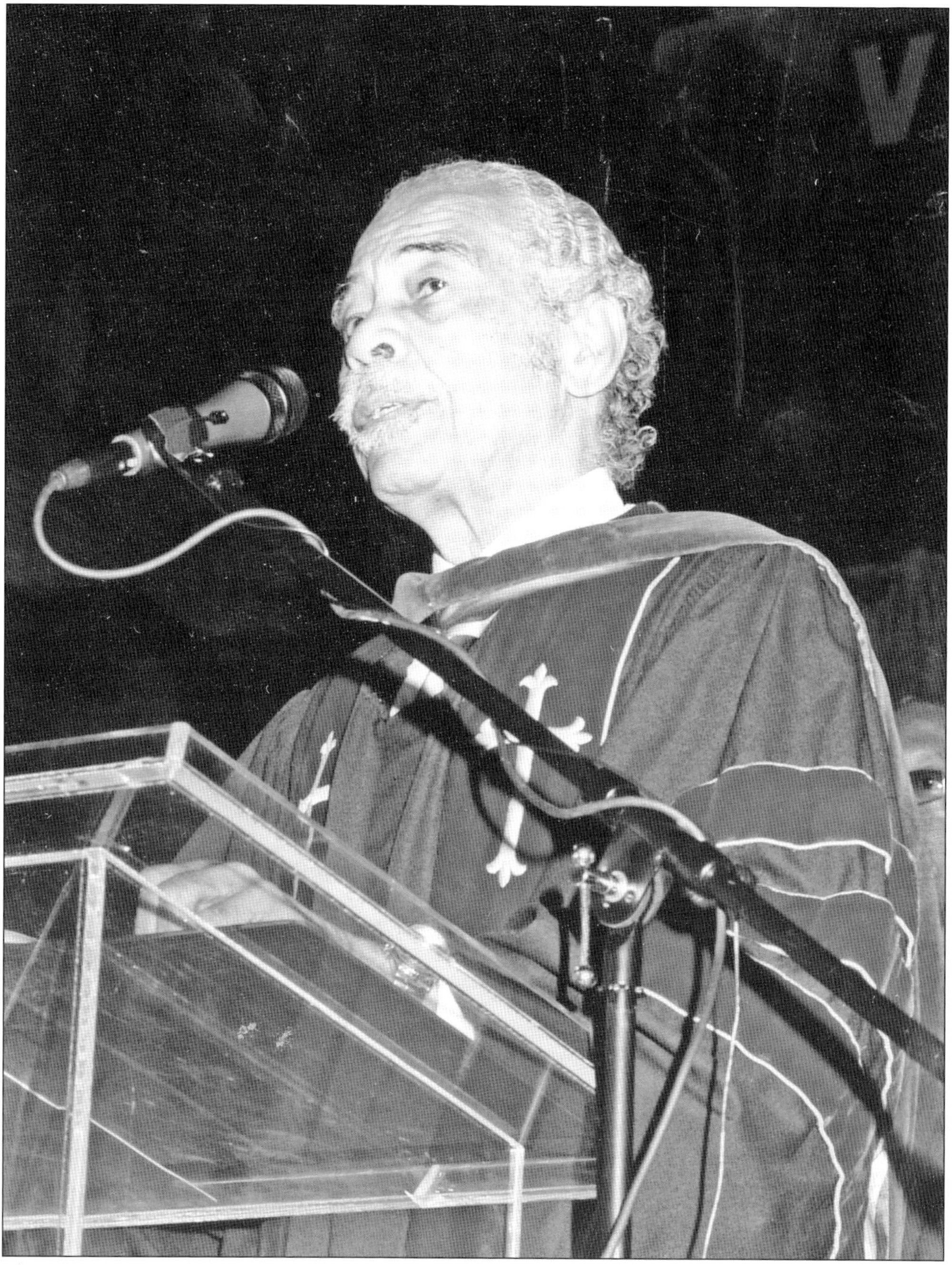

Thomas Freeman, Texas Southern University's famed debate coach, is pictured here. Freeman served as mentor to a young Barbara Jordan during her undergraduate studies at the university. Jordan often commented that it was Freeman's diction and vocal cadence that positively influenced her well-known speaking style. (Image courtesy of the Heartman Collections at Texas Southern University.)

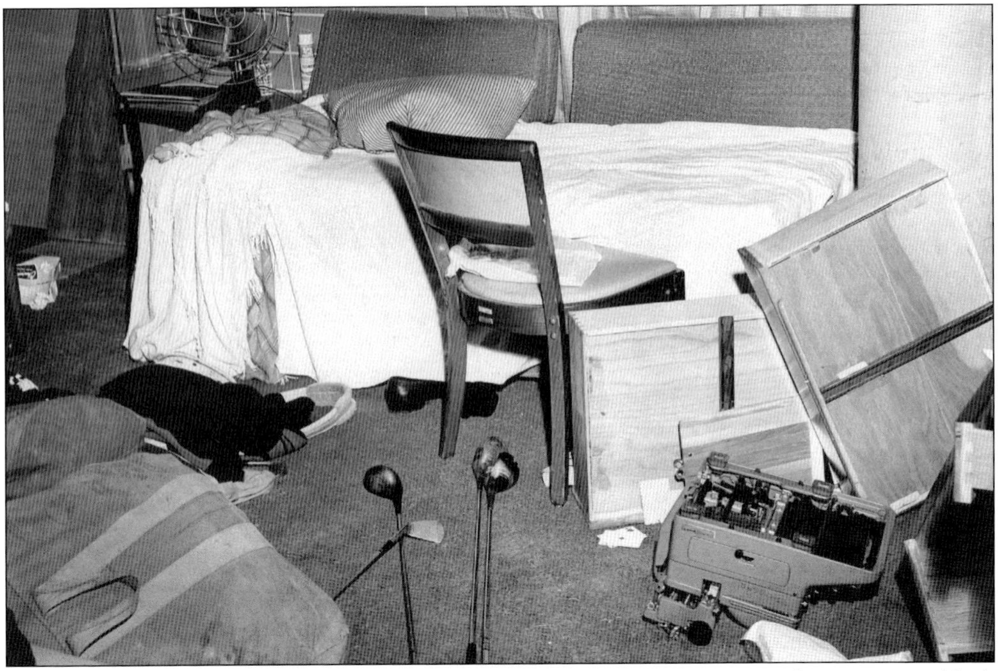

Americans fondly remember the 1960s as the decade that placed a man on the moon. For black Houston, it will be remembered as a time when city leaders and the police were fearful that the black community would erupt violently like other black communities had across the South. Texas Southern University was believed to be the potential flash point for racial violence which ultimately became a self-fulfilling prophecy. Did the police overreact? Some community leaders believed so. Regardless of the rumors of hidden guns and dangerous revolutionaries, an institution of learning was unapologetically turned upside down in an effort to suppress any potential acts of political dissent. (Image courtesy of the Heartman Collection, Texas Southern University.)

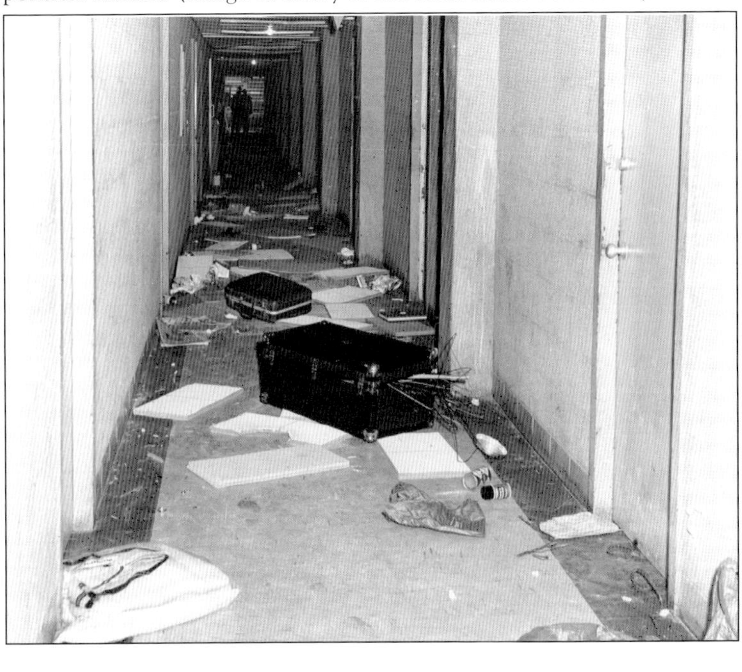

These are the hallways of a dormitory on the TSU campus after Houston's police ransacked the rooms in search of a gun supposedly used to kill an officer. Evidence eventually found that the death was a result of a random shot fired from the gun of a fellow officer. (Image courtesy of the Heartman Collections at Texas Southern University.)

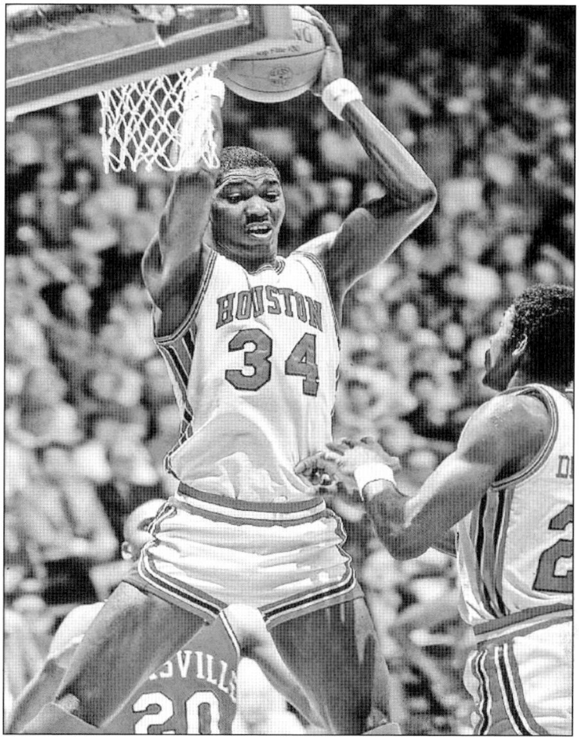

Former University of Houston and NBA star Hakeem Olajuwon was a Phi Slamma Jamma teammate of Clyde Drexler's. Admittedly, his basketball skills were raw when he began studying under perhaps the game's best "big man," Moses Malone. (Both, image courtesy of the Special Collections at the University of Houston.)

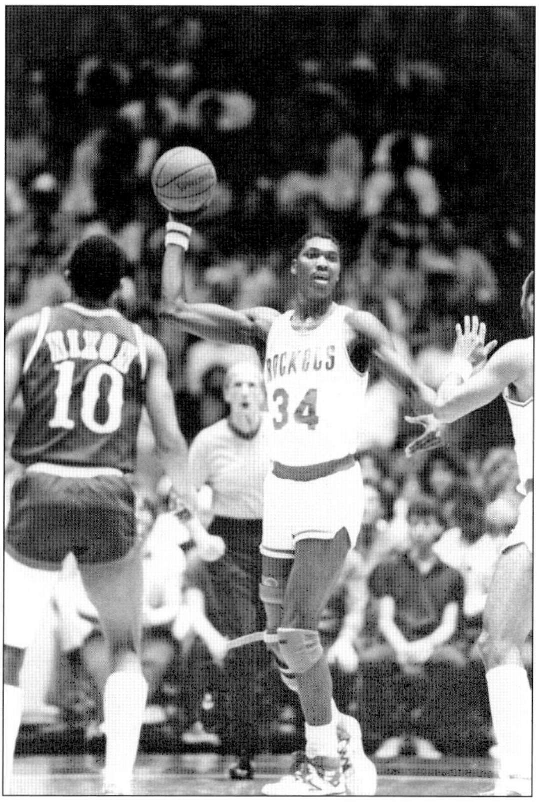

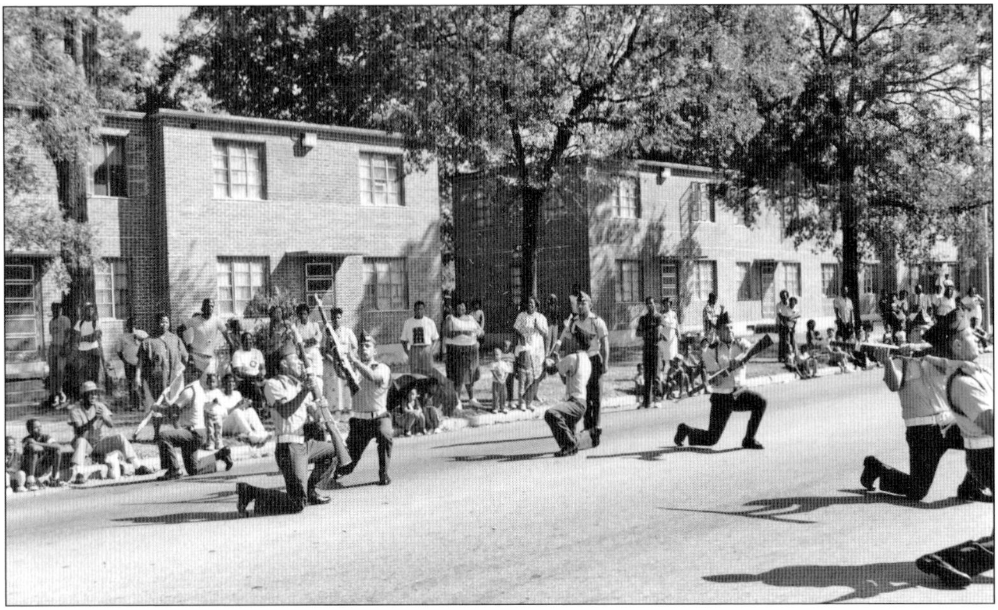

During Jim Crow, many black citizens coveted a high school education as a remarkable achievement. In later years, education beyond high school became possible for many in the black community. Still, the role of the high school in the black community changed little, and support for high school athletes and students remains a priority. This image depicts a local Junior ROTC unit participating in a parade in the city's Third Ward. (Image courtesy of the Heartman Collections at Texas Southern University.)

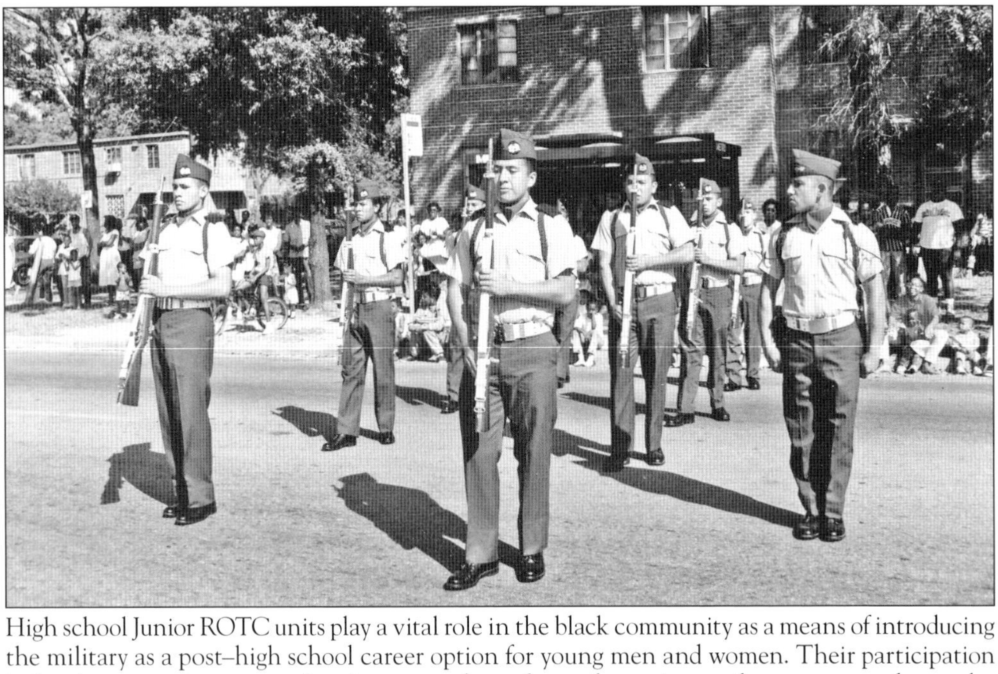

High school Junior ROTC units play a vital role in the black community as a means of introducing the military as a post–high school career option for young men and women. Their participation in local community events oftentimes served as a form of recruitment for younger students who become drawn to the uniforms, the precise drill movements, and the obvious camaraderie among the units. (Image courtesy of the Heartman Collections at Texas Southern University.)

Heisman Trophy winner Andre Ware revolutionized college football in the late 1980s at the University of Houston with the then unorthodox run-and-shoot style of offense. Passing for 400 yards a game may seem commonplace in the 21st century, but football in the 1980s was generally characterized by fleet-footed runners. But in his senior year, Ware's mind-boggling numbers led to his being recognized as college football's most outstanding player. (Image courtesy of the Special Collections at the University of Houston.)

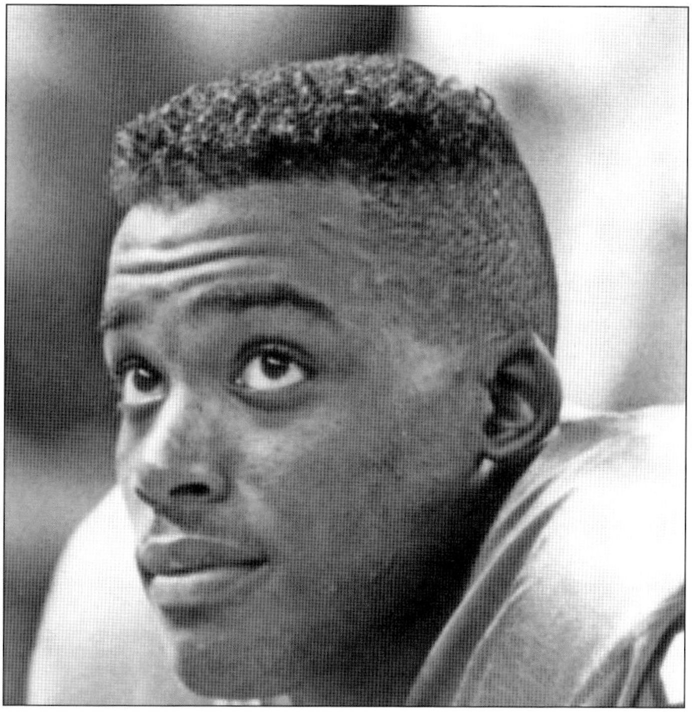

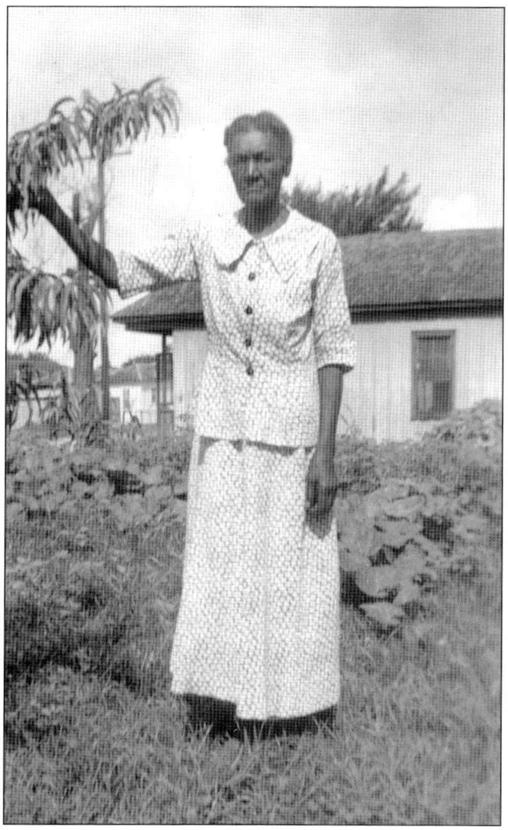

This image is of Sarah Ford, and it was taken during the interviews for the New Deal's Slave Narratives project. Unemployed writers throughout the country were tasked with interviewing surviving slaves to gather their recollections of slavery. Ford was interviewed in Houston but was a slave on a plantation in West Columbia, Texas, minutes south of Houston. Of her memories of slavery, Ford shared that field hands were not allowed to marry on that particular plantation. However, she said, "dey jus' puts a man and breedin' woman together like mules. Iffen the woman don't like the man it don't make no diff'rence, she better go or dey gives her a hidin'."

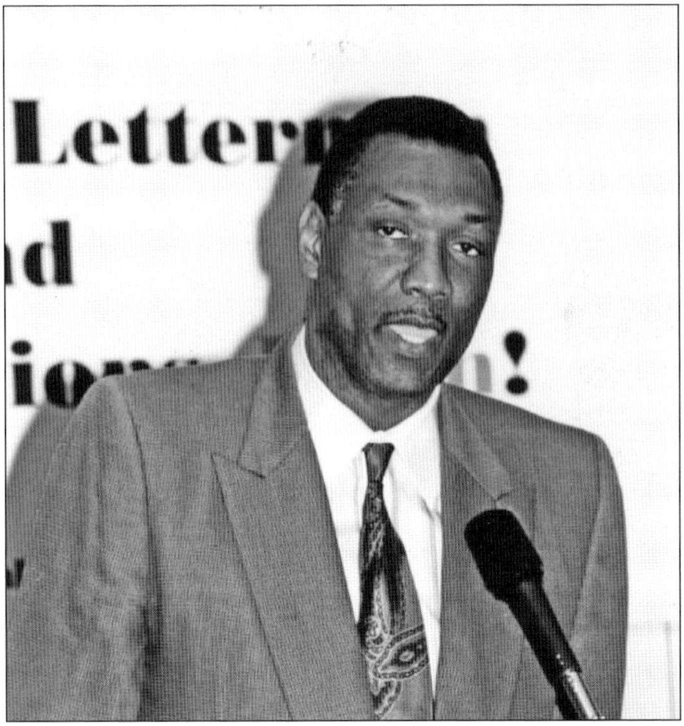

Former University of Houston and NBA star Elvin Hayes enjoyed a celebrated professional career before returning to Houston and getting involved in the local business community. (Image courtesy of the Special Collections at the University of Houston.)

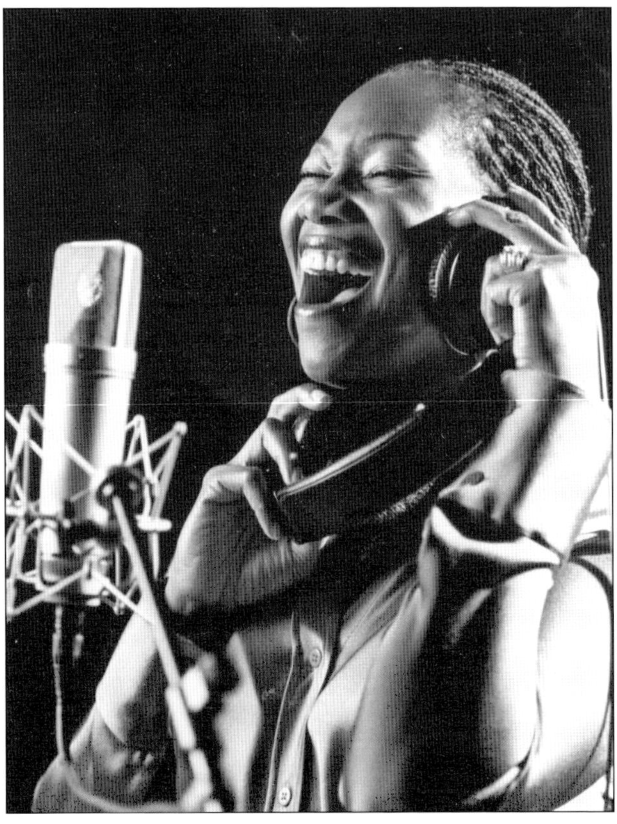

Grammy Award–winning artist Yolanda Adams, an alumna of Texas Southern University, has redefined gospel music with her voice and elegance. Her music has illuminated the spirit, and she has always credited TSU for nurturing her talent. (Image courtesy of the Heartman Collections at Texas Southern University.)

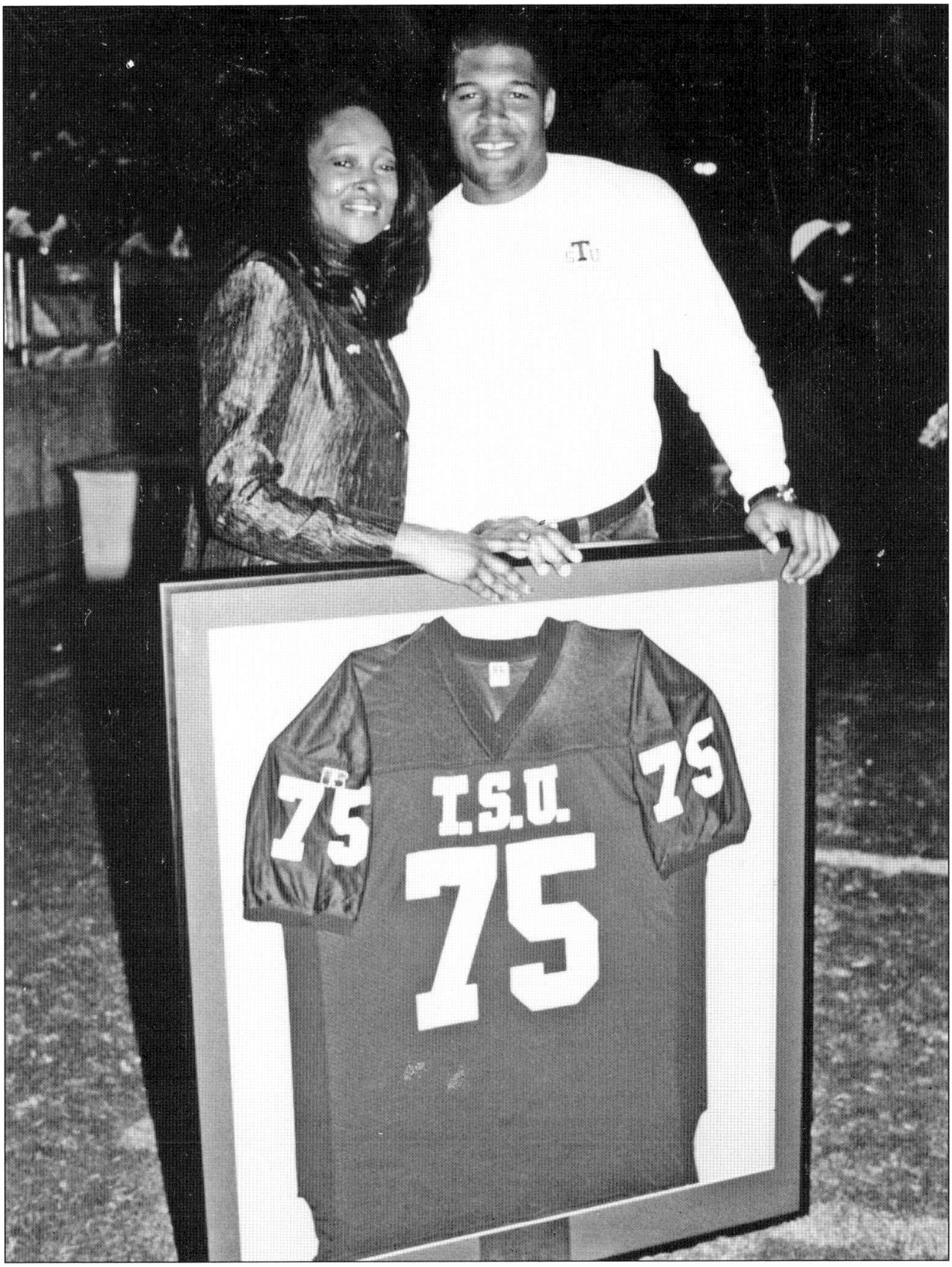

Former Texas Southern University and NFL star Michael Strahan is pictured with former university president Priscilla Slade during a ceremony retiring his No. 75 jersey. Strahan continues to excel off the football field as an analyst and morning television host. (Image courtesy of the Heartman Collections at Texas Southern University.)

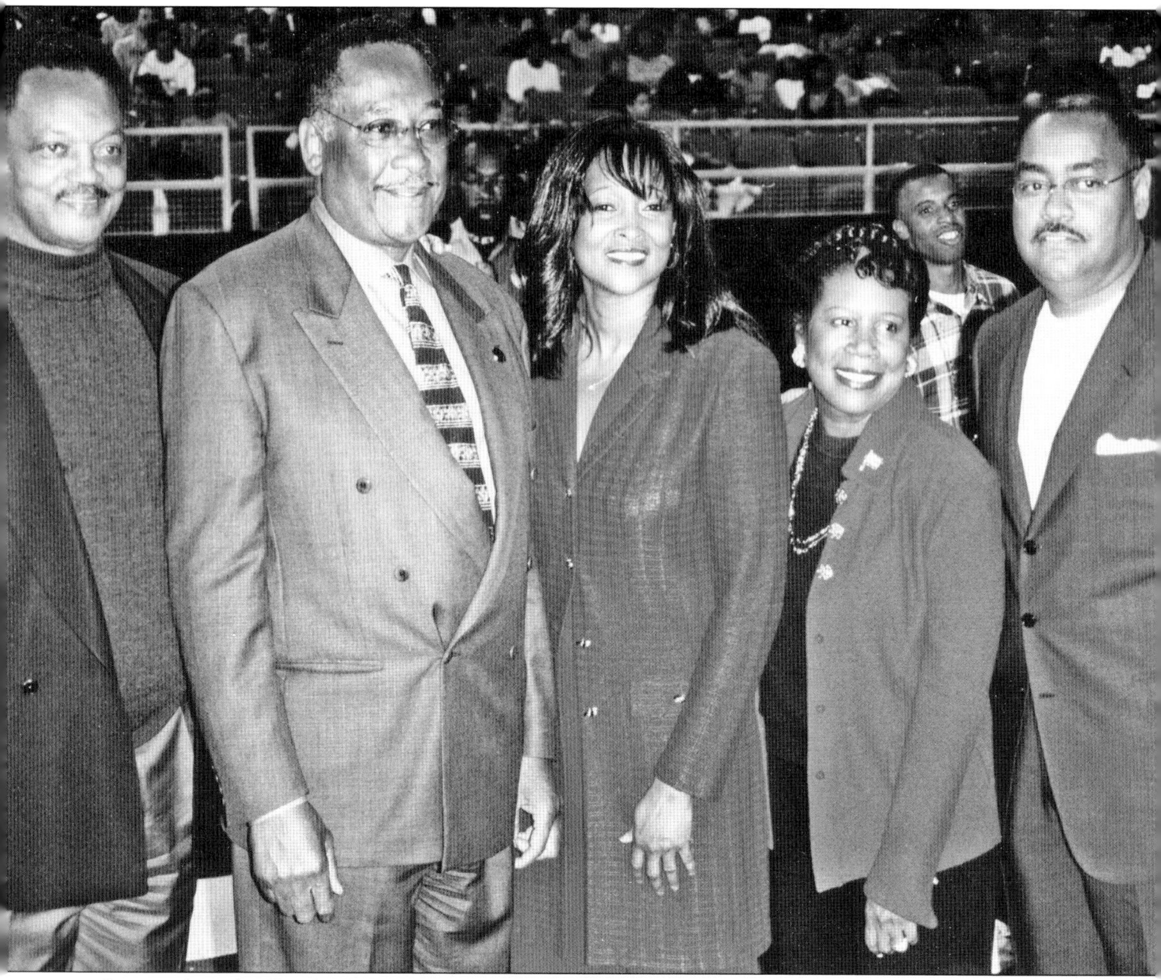

These political officials observe a TSU football game as guests of then president Priscilla Slade. Pictured are, from left to right, Jesse Jackson, Lee Brown, Slade, Sheila Jackson Lee, and Rodney Ellis. (Image courtesy of the Heartman Collections at Texas Southern University.)

In a light-hearted moment, Barbara Jordan is seen playing the guitar at a park in her native Fifth Ward community. Her ability to bring people together was obvious during her tenure in the state legislature, and she became an influential figure during the Watergate hearings in the early 1970s.

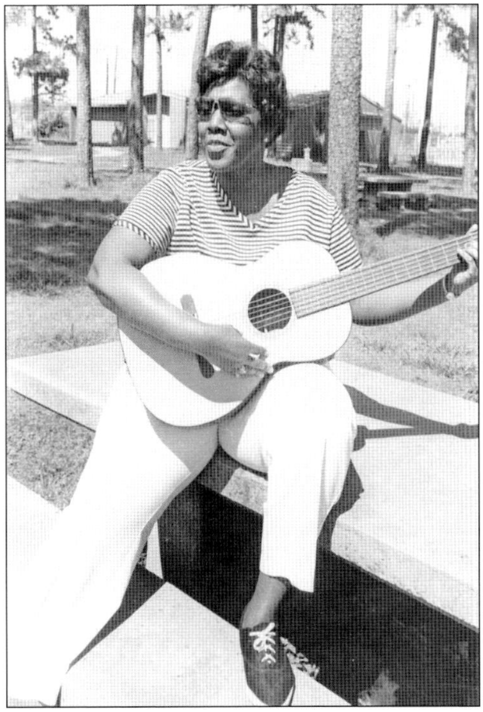

State senator Rodney Ellis, former TSU president Priscilla Slade, and civil rights activist Jesse Jackson are pictured on the campus of Texas Southern University. (Image courtesy of the Heartman Collections at Texas Southern University.)

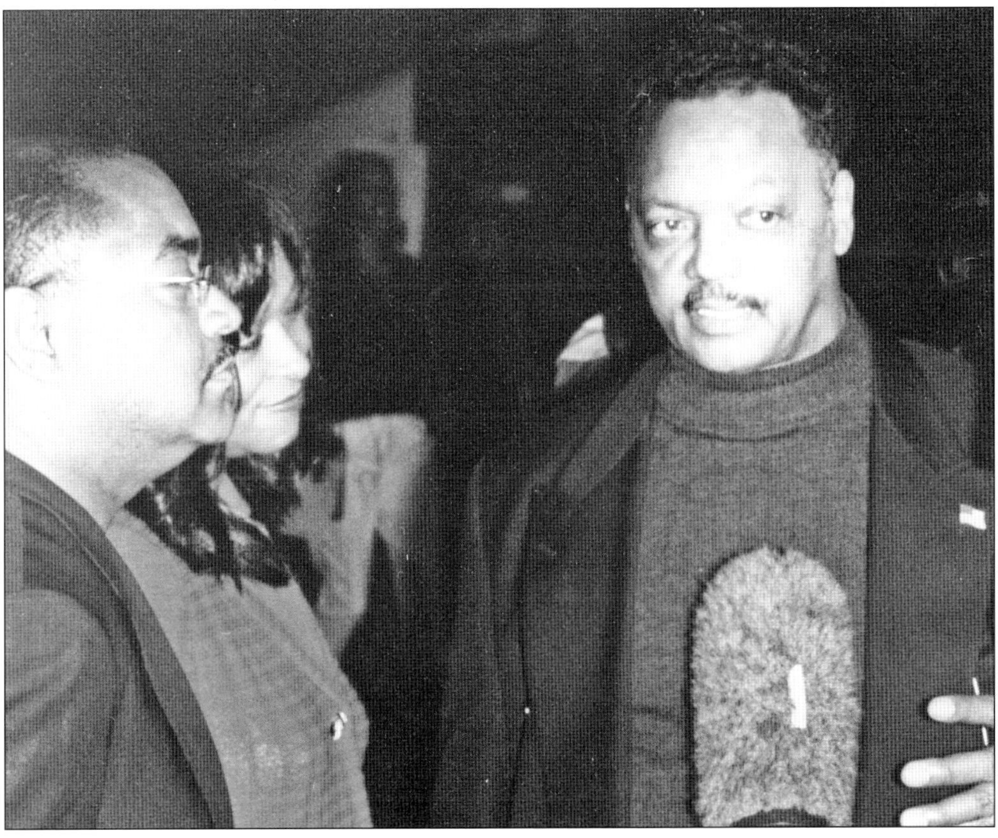

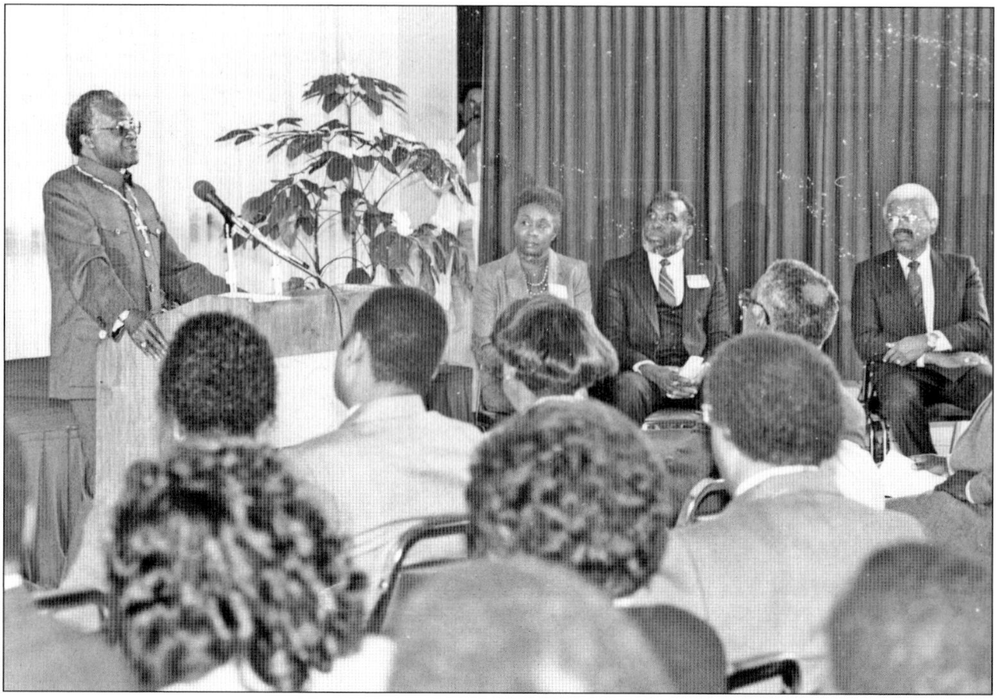

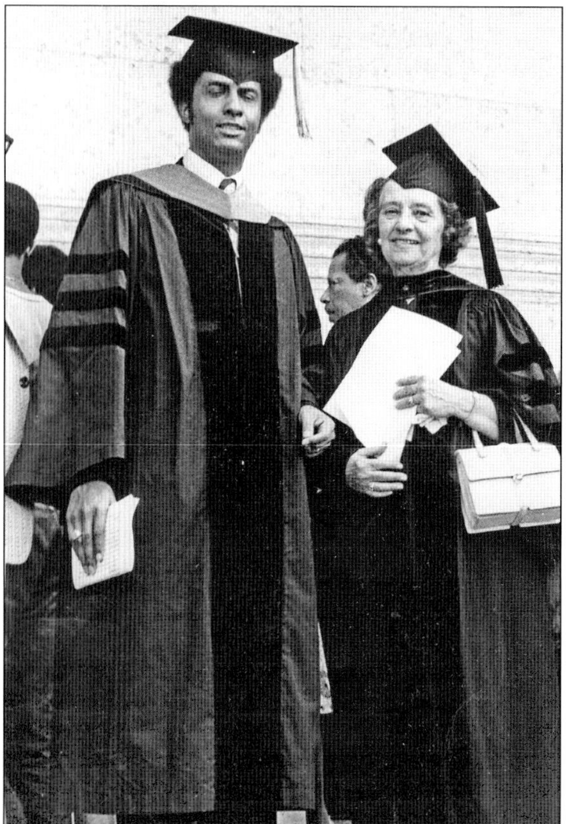

Few individuals have influenced societies across the world; Desmond Tutu, who visited the TSU campus in the 1980s, has been one of those individuals. TSU maintains a practice of inviting newsmakers to its campus, providing students and Houston's black community access to the experience and wisdom of those influential leaders.

This image shows Dr. Walter McCoy at a TSU commencement ceremony. Dr. McCoy has been one of the academic stalwarts at TSU for decades and continues to train students in public and urban affairs. His commitment to his students and the black community has earned him the respect of his peers and of the scores of students he has mentored. (Image courtesy of the Heartman Collections at Texas Southern University.)

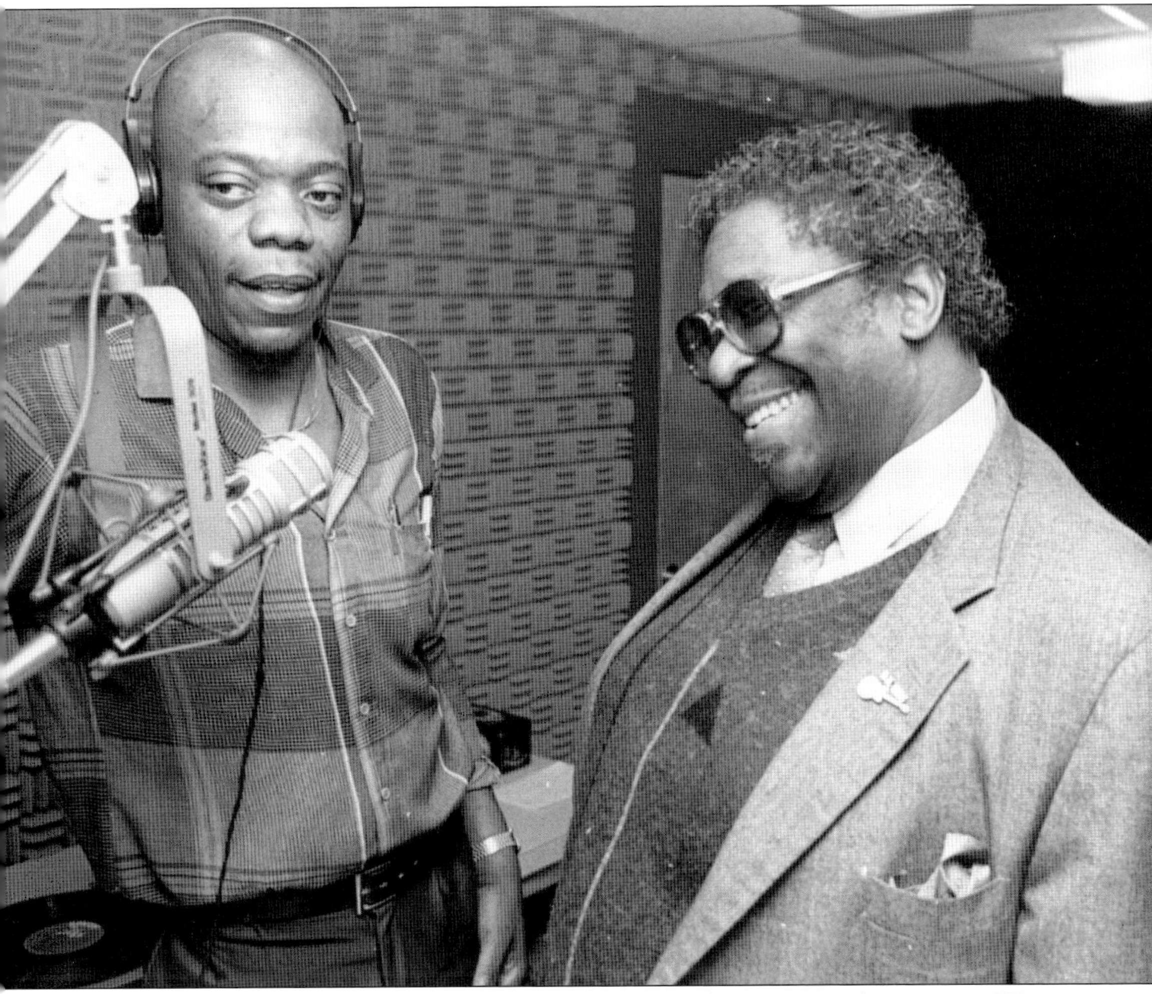

Famed R&B legend B.B. King is seen visiting the KTSU radio station on the campus of Texas Southern University. King's music career, which began in the Jim Crow South, encouraged hundreds of black musicians who played only in front of black audiences because they were not allowed to perform in predominantly white venues. (Image courtesy of the Heartman Collections at Texas Southern University.)

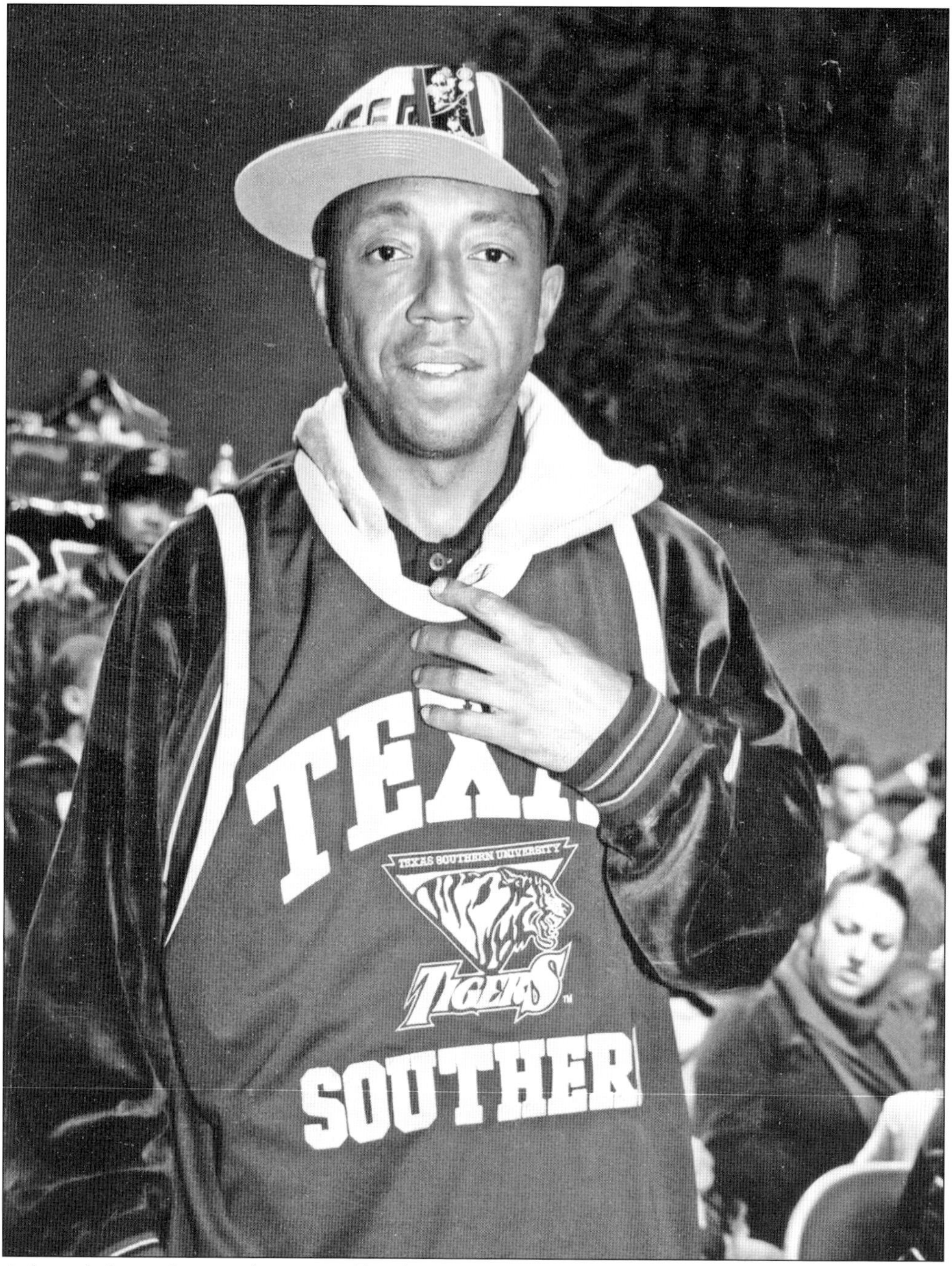

Acknowledging the social impact of hip-hop music and culture on the black community, music mogul, legend, and entrepreneur Russell Simmons visited Texas Southern University and discussed the negative influences of the genre on the black community. (Image courtesy of the Heartman Collections at Texas Southern University.)

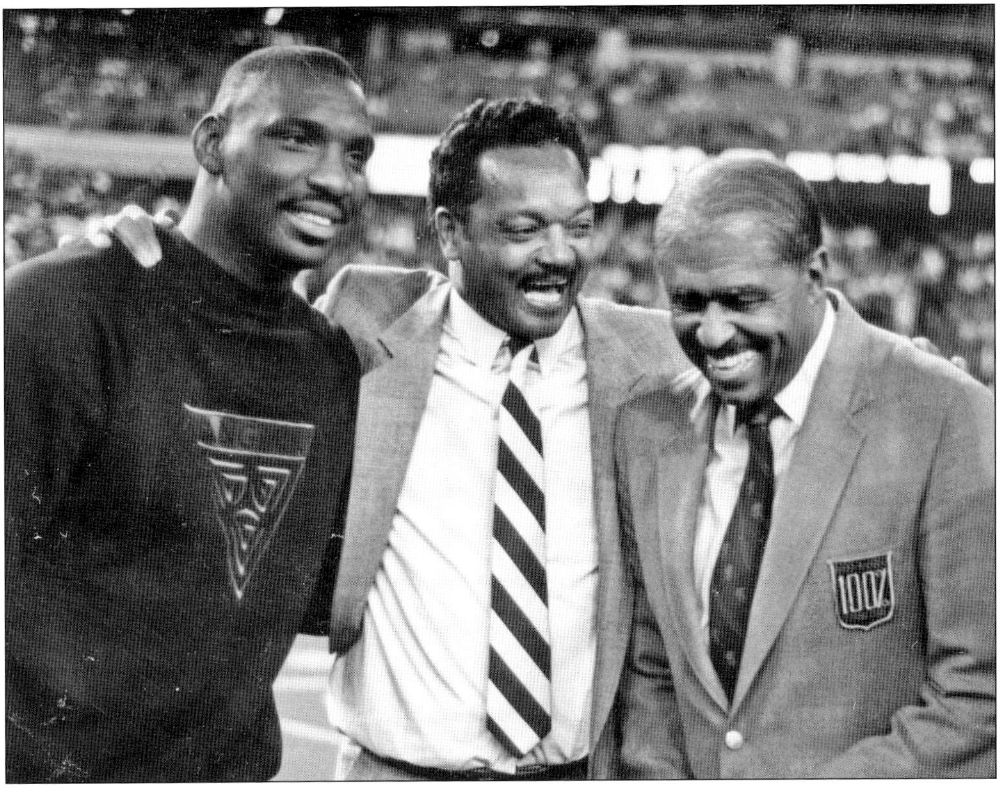

Super Bowl quarterback Doug Williams enjoys a lighthearted moment in the Astrodome with Jesse Jackson and Grambling's legendary head football coach Eddie Robinson. While black college football teams do not receive the recognition or publicity of their white counterparts, numerous alumni from HBCUs made the transition to the professional leagues, and some, like Doug Williams, Walter Payton, and Jerry Rice, dominated at their respective positions. (Image courtesy of the Heartman Collections at Texas Southern University.)

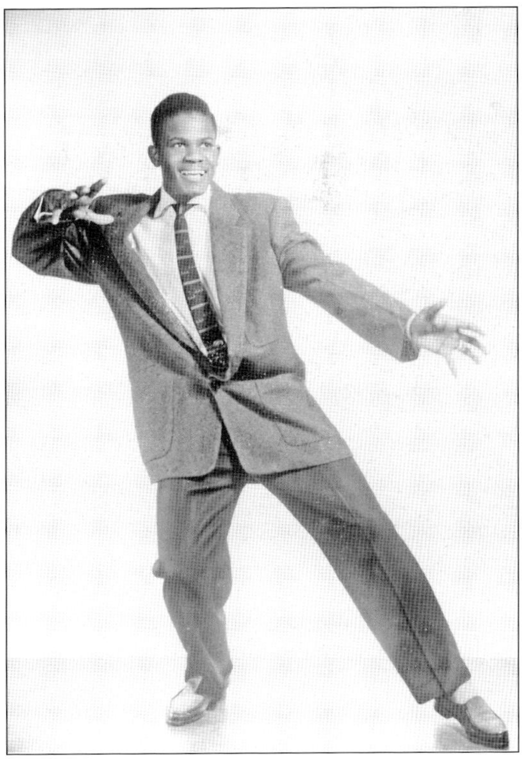

Joe Tex was one of the most popular black performers in the 1960s and 1970s. He was a fan favorite in Houston, and his shows were often sold out. Like other black performers of the era, Tex did not receive the same recognition or fortune as some less-talented performers. Nonetheless, Houston's black community embraced his blend of southern soul, blues, and country.

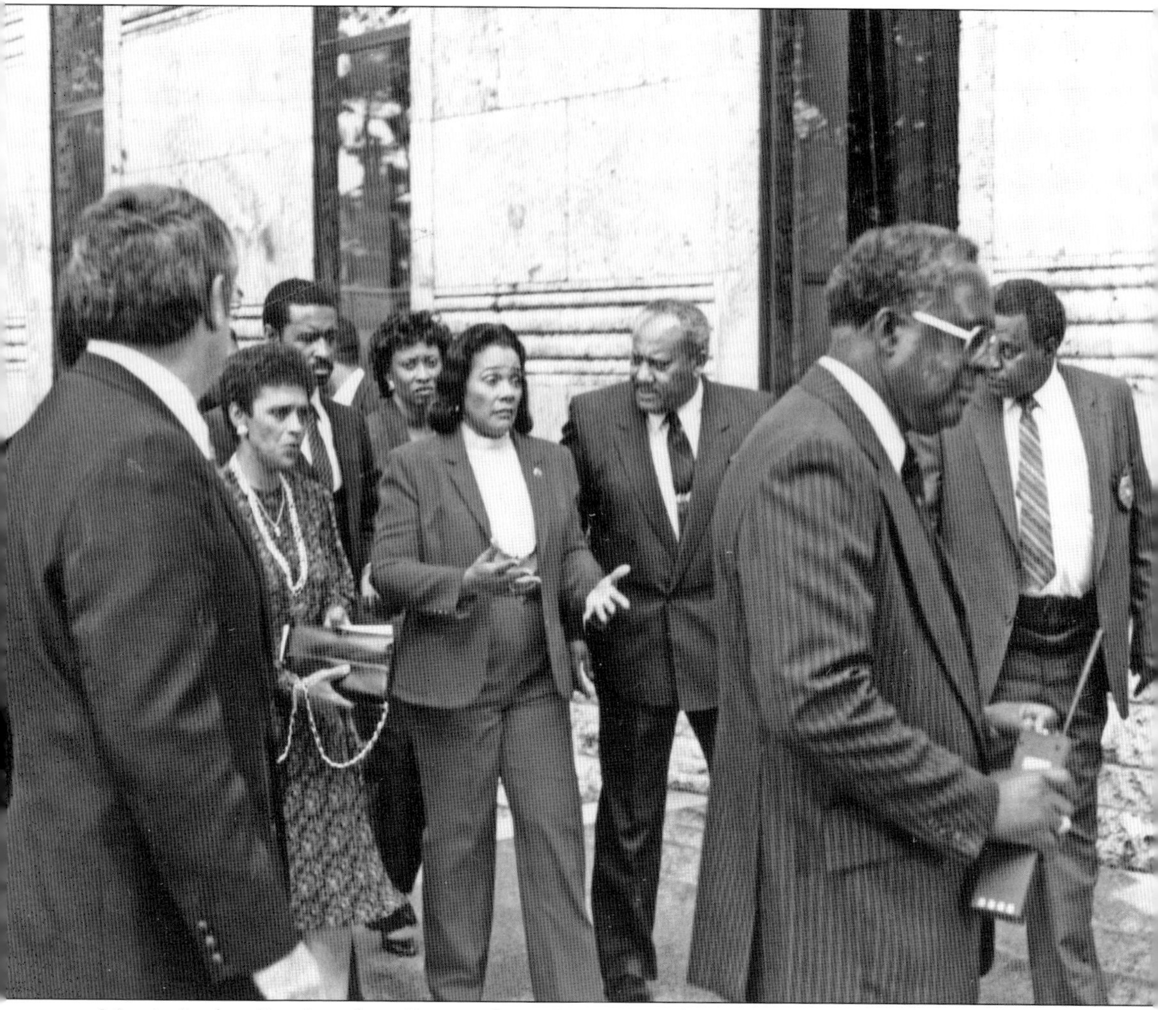

Martin Luther King's widow, Coretta Scott King, visited Texas Southern University in the late 1980s and provided a connection between the objectives of the 1960s civil rights movement and the accomplishments of the post–civil rights era. (Image courtesy of the Heartman Collections at Texas Southern University.)

Five

African American Life

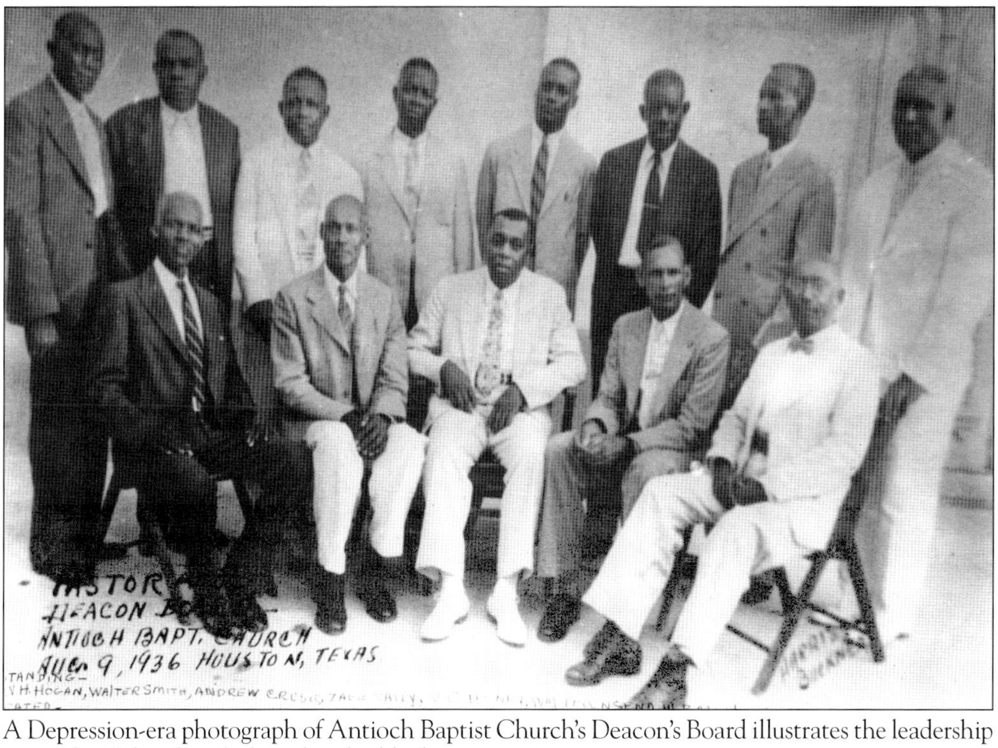

A Depression-era photograph of Antioch Baptist Church's Deacon's Board illustrates the leadership not only of the church, but also the black community.

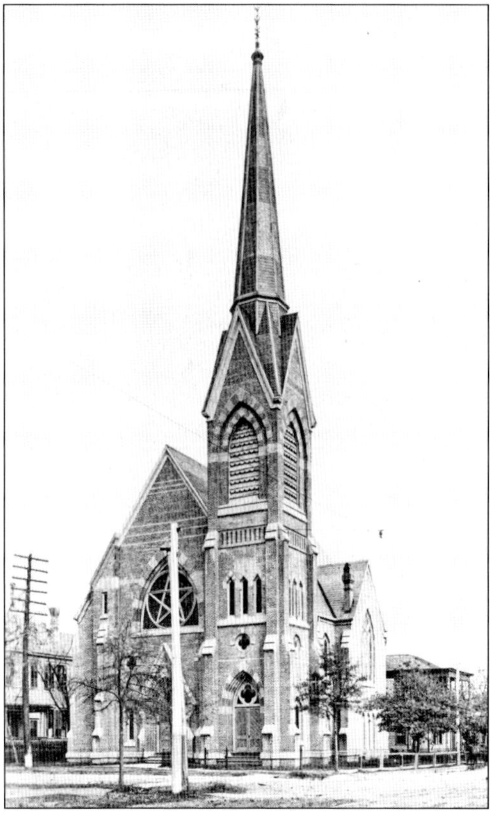

This 19th-century image of the First Baptist Church is indicative of the relationship between the church and the black community in Houston. Even though the church was a segregated institution, it provided professional and social contacts for the black community that fostered the local civil rights agenda and access to services throughout the city.

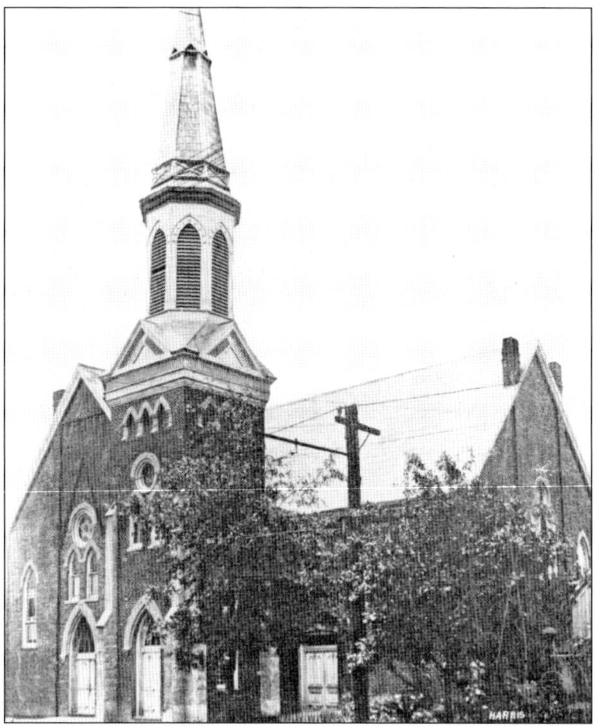

In his seminal commentary on black life, W.E.B. Du Bois wrote in *The Souls of Black Folk* that the songs sung in the black church tell of the pain of racism, separation, hardships, and violence. The black church has always been a refuge where the soul can rest and prepare for the difficulties of the coming week. Since the time of Houston's inception, black churches played a significant role in the social, economic, and political lives of the city's black community. Sadly, the integration of the 1960s and 1970s left too many parishes in the Third, Fourth, and Fifth Wards with declining membership as the black community sought refuge from the turmoil of the inner city.

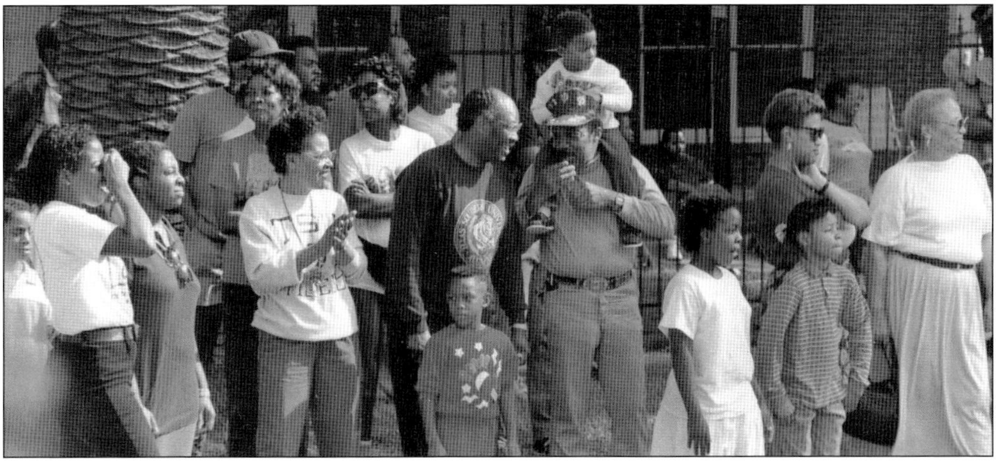

Today, society bemoans the fact that little is known about next-door neighbors. However, before PlayStations and Xboxes, neighbors often gathered outside to discuss the days' events, thus creating a true community. The image shown depicts the Third Ward community gathering to observe a homecoming parade in the 1980s. These events continue to this day, but the sense of community experienced by its observers is a pale comparison to those of years gone by. (Image courtesy of the Heartman Collection, Texas Southern University.)

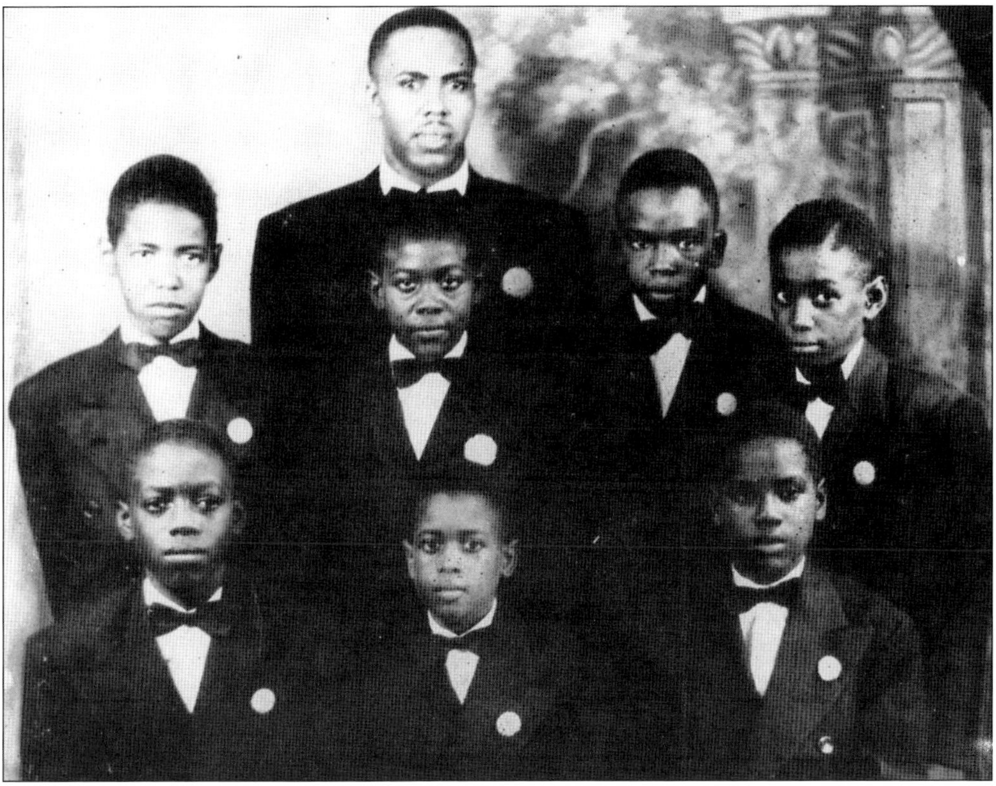

This image of the Greater Zion Junior Male Quartet dates to around the 1950s. During the Jim Crow years, the black church not only provided spiritual support, but also nurtured the community's singing talents. Many of the R&B stars of the 1950s and 1960s began singing in their churches, and this cultivation of musical talent was also present in Houston's black community.

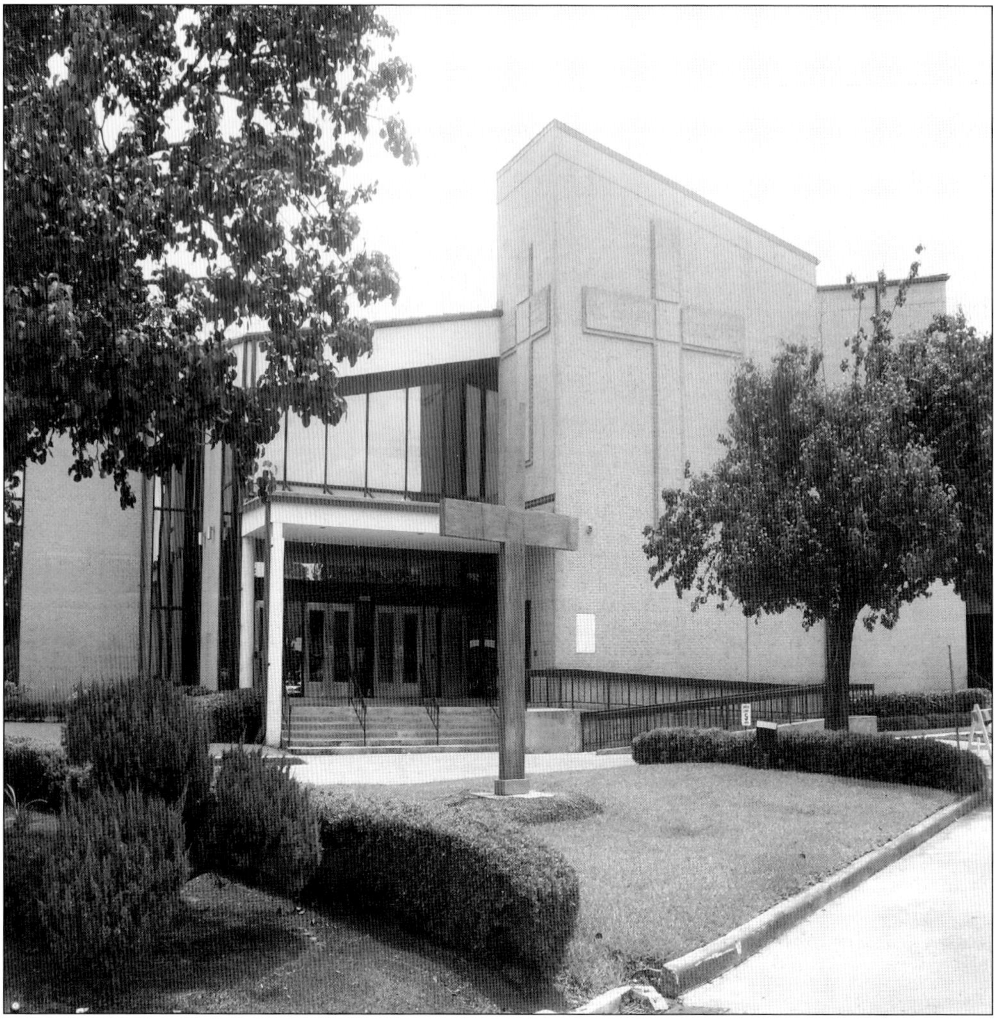

Founded by Rev. William Lawson in the Third Ward, Wheeler Avenue Baptist Church was the pivotal location in the black community's efforts to integrate the city's segregated facilities during the 1950s and 1960s. (Author's collection.)

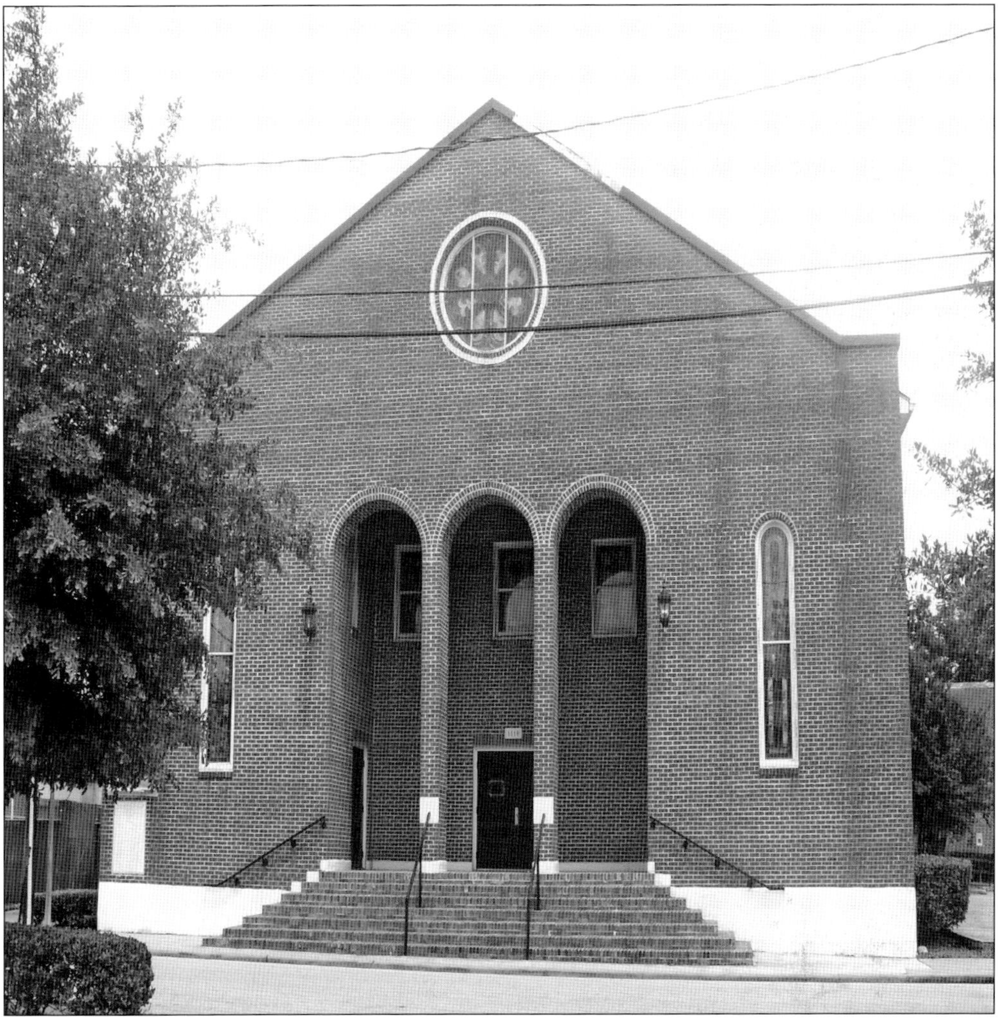

Pleasant Hill Baptist Church was a religious cornerstone in the Fifth Ward. The Reverend L.H. Simpson was a local giant in the religious community. The exodus of blacks from the Fifth Ward negatively affected Pleasant Hill as those in the community that could left for suburban housing. By the 1980s, however, a new generation, led by Rev. Harvey Clemons, believed the Fifth Ward could be revived with renewed emphasis on housing and businesses. (Author's collection.)

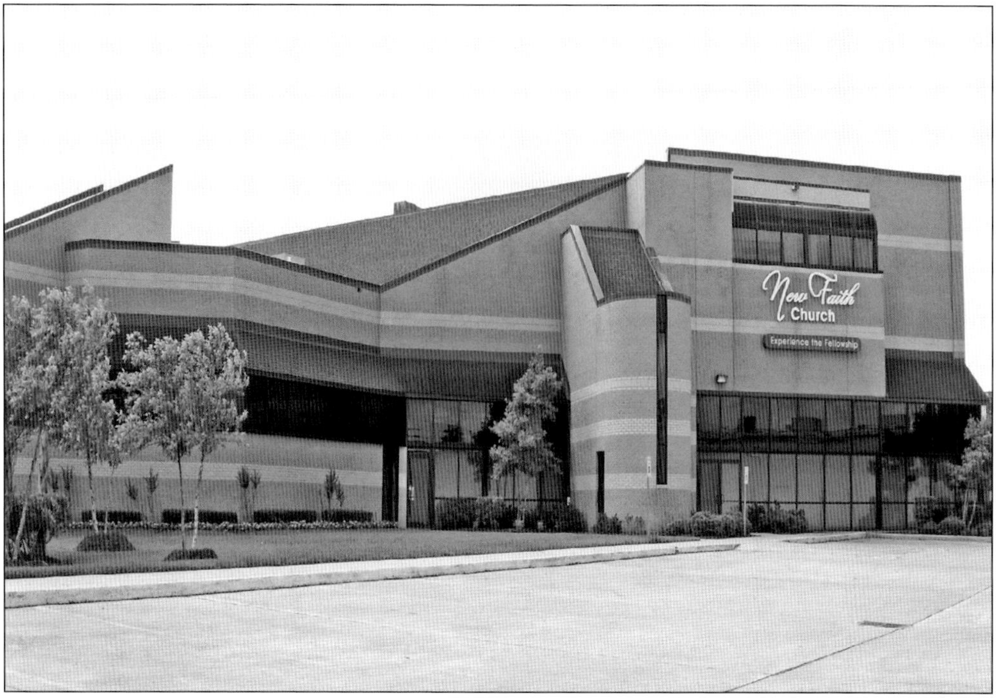

Dr. T.R. Williams is the pastor and founder of the New Faith Church. His emphasis on adherence to the Bible and on numerous programs to strengthen the family has allowed New Faith to become an influential congregation in Houston's black community. (Image courtesy of New Faith Church.)

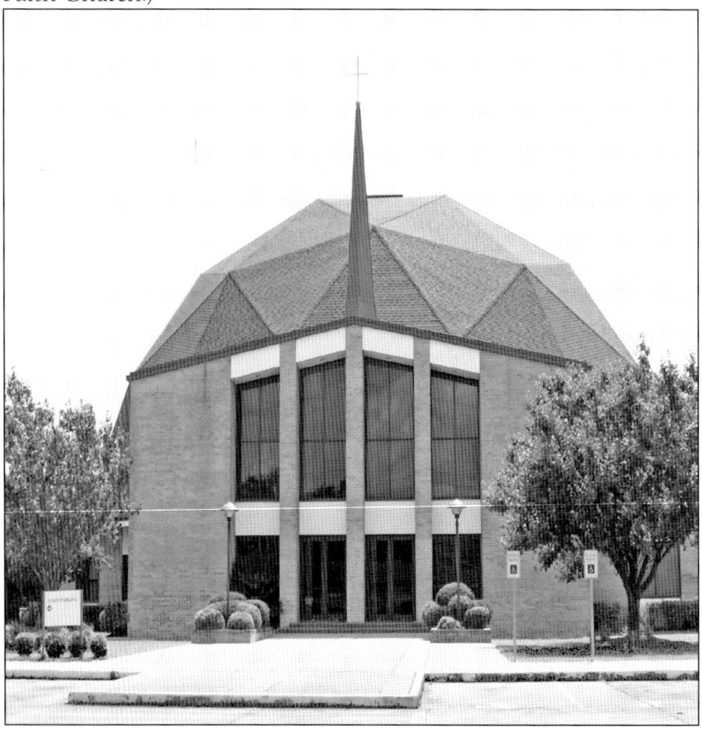

Brentwood Baptist Church was once a suburban parish, but with the dispersal of the black community, it found itself in a predominantly minority community by the 1970s. Its pastor, Dr. Joe Ratliff, is a dynamic personality in the black community.

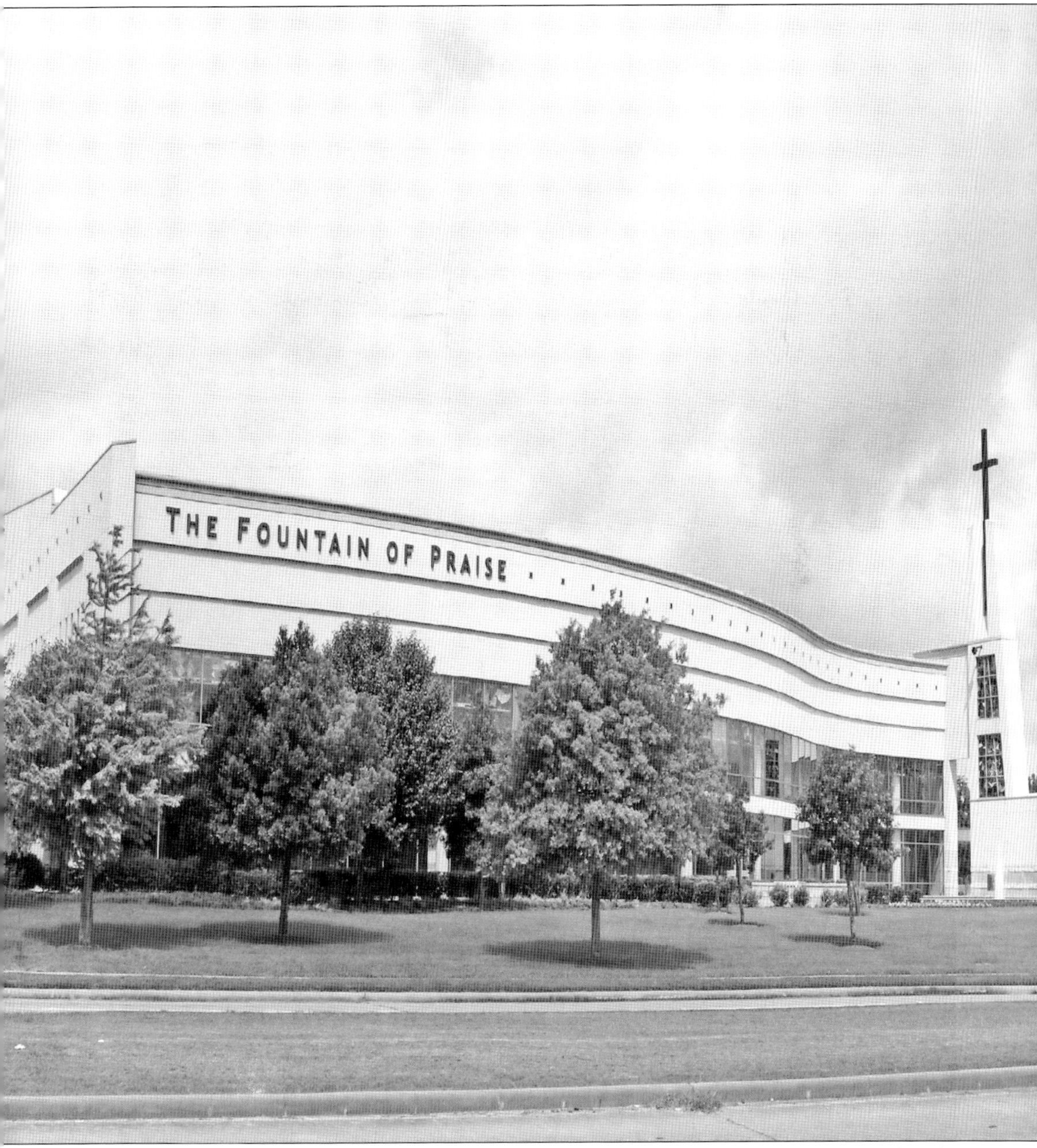

The Fountain of Praise Baptist Church was initially known as South Post Oak Baptist Church. When Rev. Remus Wright assumed the pastorate, he built a new campus on Houston's south side and changed the name to better reflect the congregation's new emphasis on praise and worship. (Author's collection.)

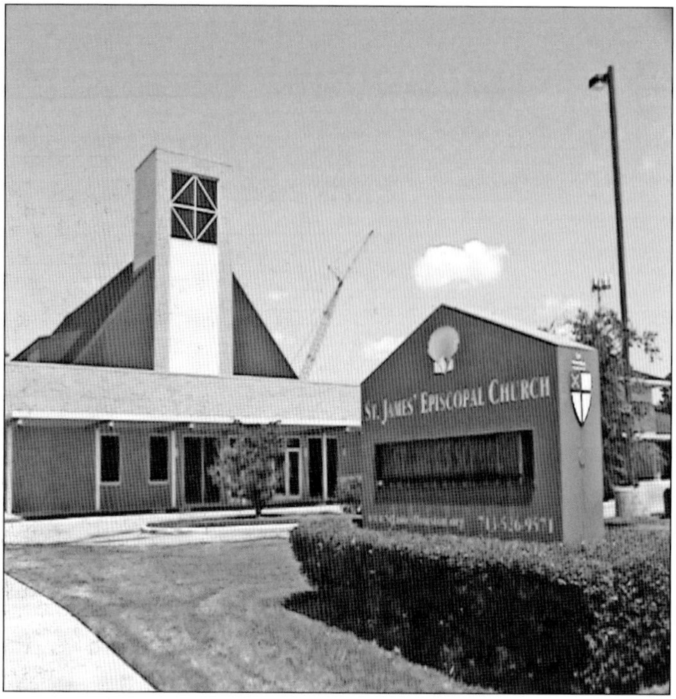

St. James Episcopal Church is one of the key religious institutions in the Third Ward. Not only has it provided religious instruction, its associated schools have educated area children for decades. (Author's collection.)

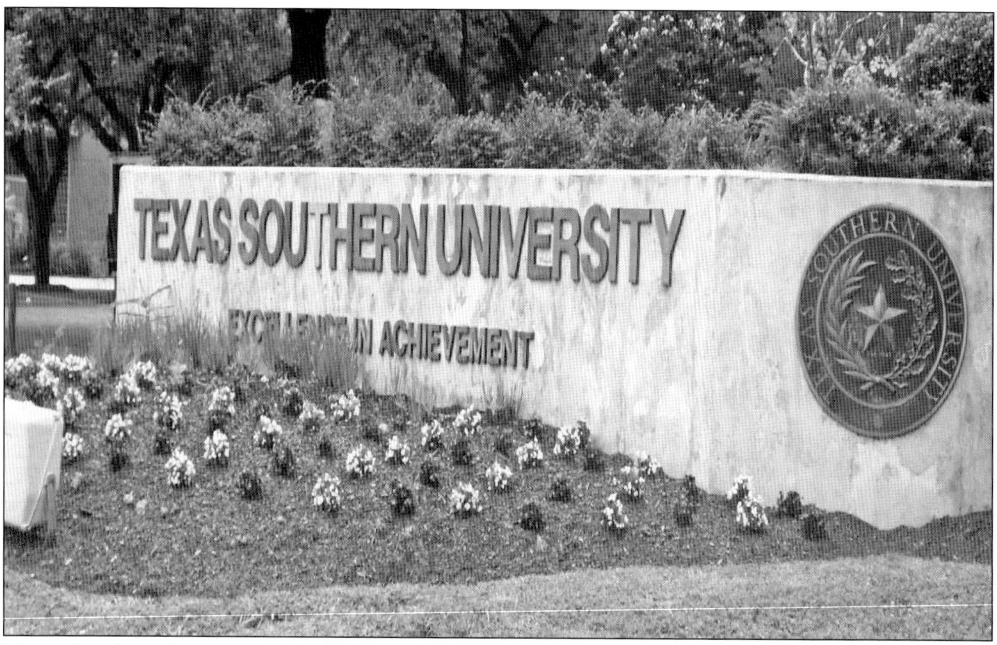

Texas Southern University was born out of the US Supreme Court's decision in *Sweatt v. Painter.* University of Texas officials wanted so vehemently to maintain their law school as a "whites only" institution that they allowed the creation of a school to provide law instruction to blacks. Before successfully arguing for the reversal of *Plessy v. Ferguson*, Thurgood Marshall accepted the gesture of a black school in Houston but maintained that it was not equal. Therefore, University of Austin officials could not deny admission to a black applicant without violating the essence of the *Plessy* decision. (Author's collection.)

This painted wall is a celebration of the Fifth Ward community. Local community leaders have fought for generations to maintain and preserve the history of the Fifth Ward, its residents, and its role in the history of Houston. (Author's collection.)

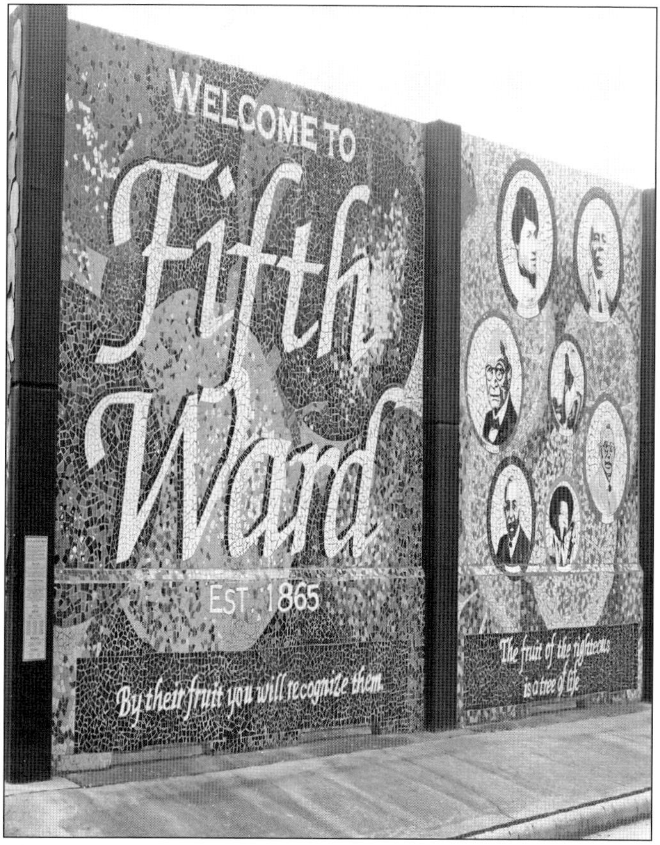

Pictured is a local chapter of the Alpha Kappa Alpha sorority. Black fraternities and sororities provided a social outlet that shaped and influenced the black community through the support of education initiatives and community service projects.

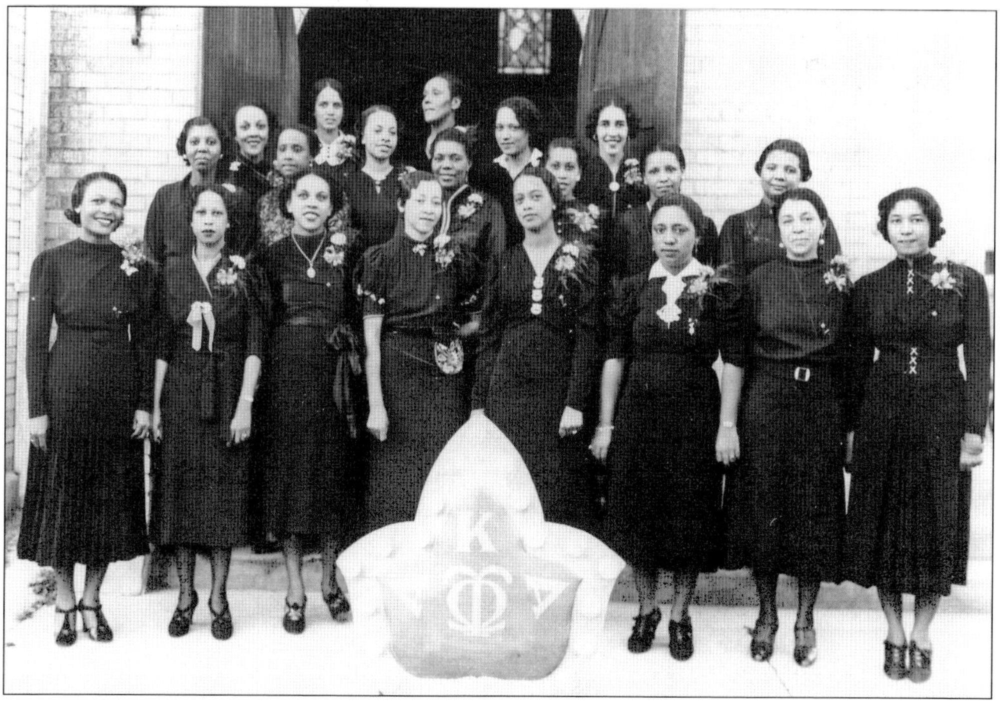

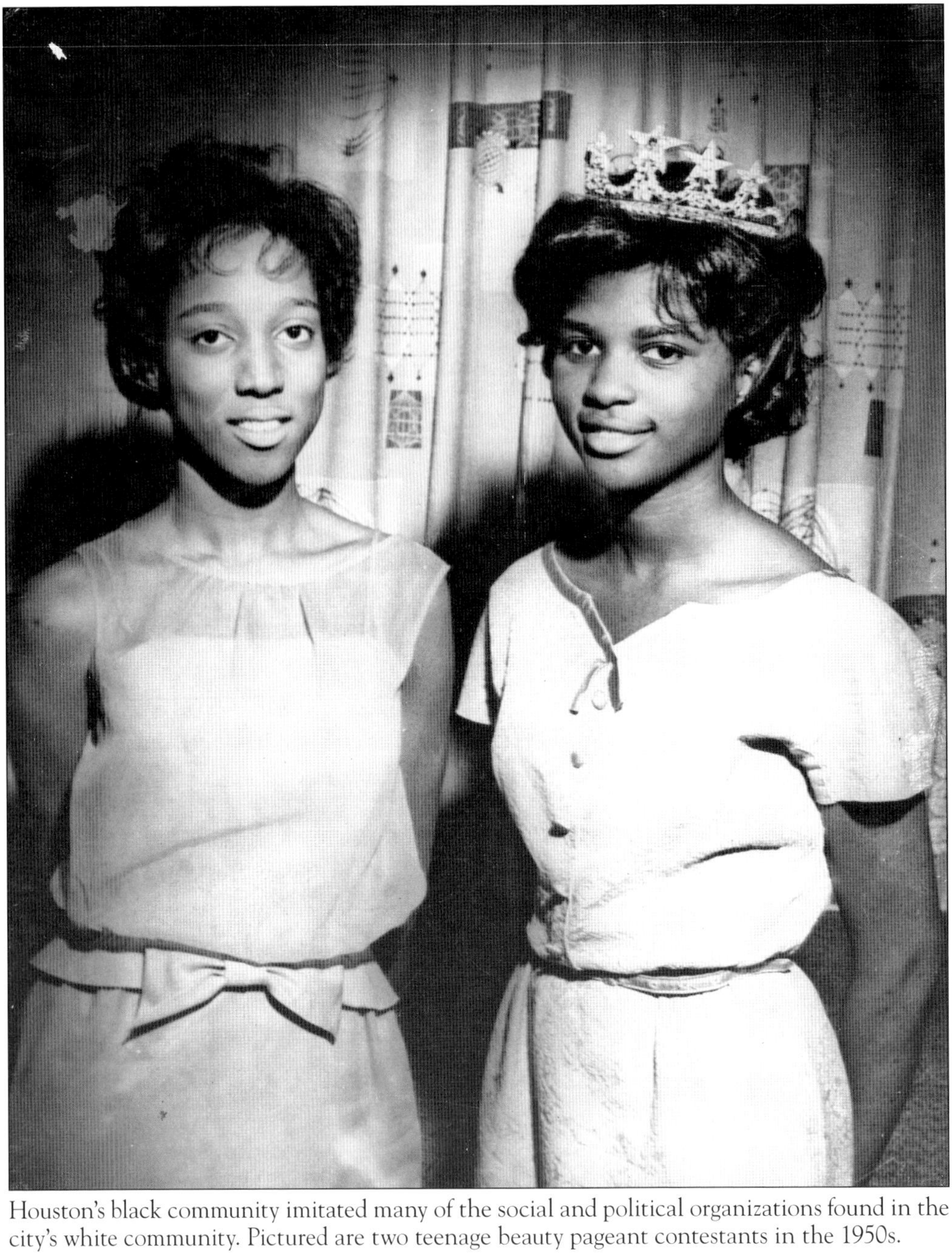

Houston's black community imitated many of the social and political organizations found in the city's white community. Pictured are two teenage beauty pageant contestants in the 1950s.

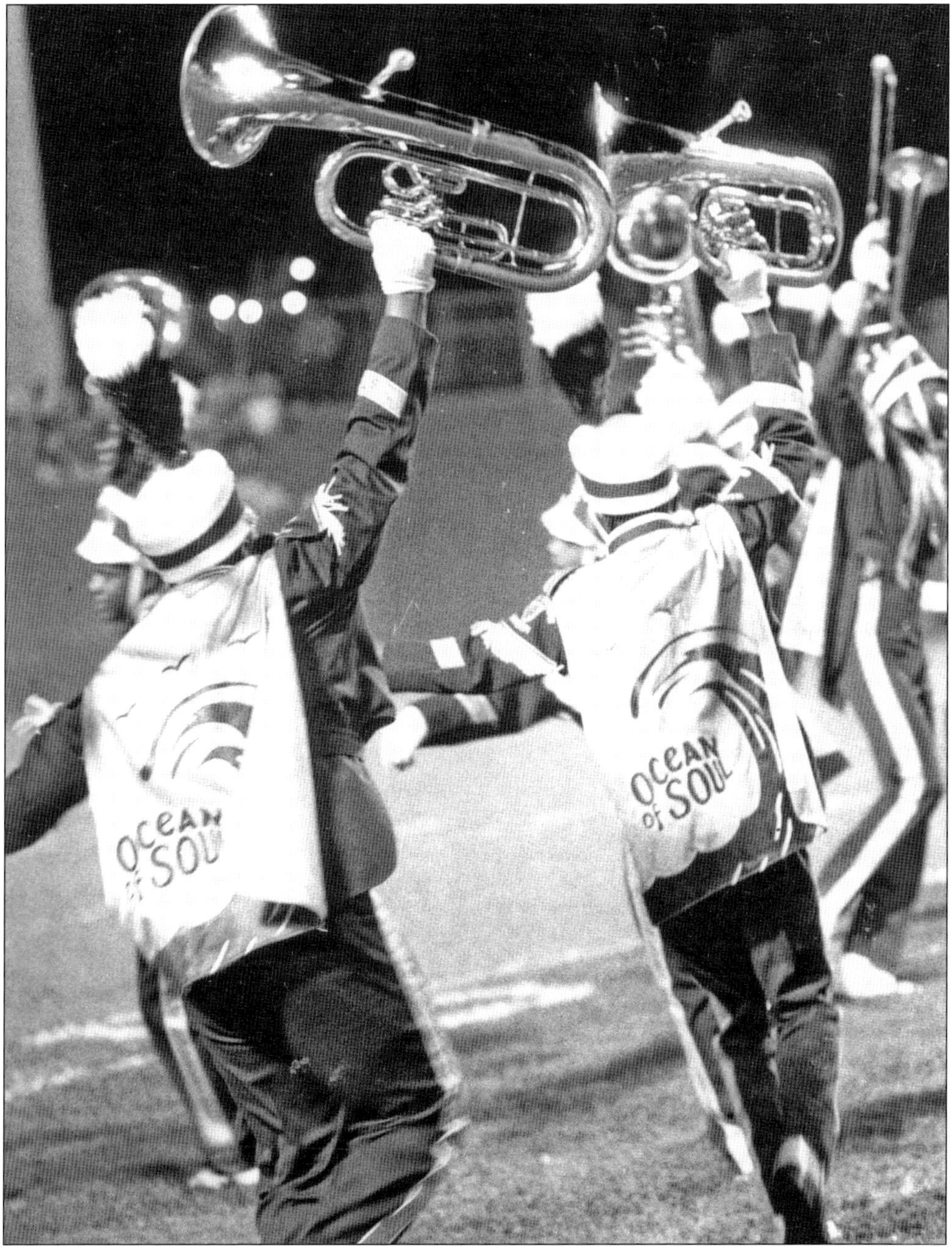

The Texas Southern University's Ocean of Soul band is pictured performing during halftime at a home football game. Over the years, the band has received numerous awards and recognition for its performances and showmanship. In the black community throughout the South, the highlight of any HBCU football game is the halftime performance of the band. (Image courtesy of the Heartman Collections at Texas Southern University.)

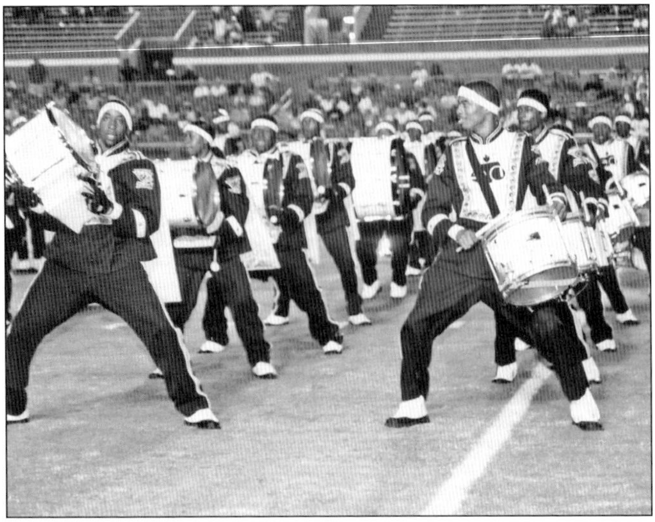

The drum line of the Ocean of Soul is often the focal point of halftime performances. The driving rhythms, which are reminiscent of R&B, rap, and hip-hop music, make the drum lines fan favorites at football games. On campus, members of the drum line hold similar positions of status similar to that of the quarterback or other football players. (Image courtesy of the Heartman Collections at Texas Southern University.)

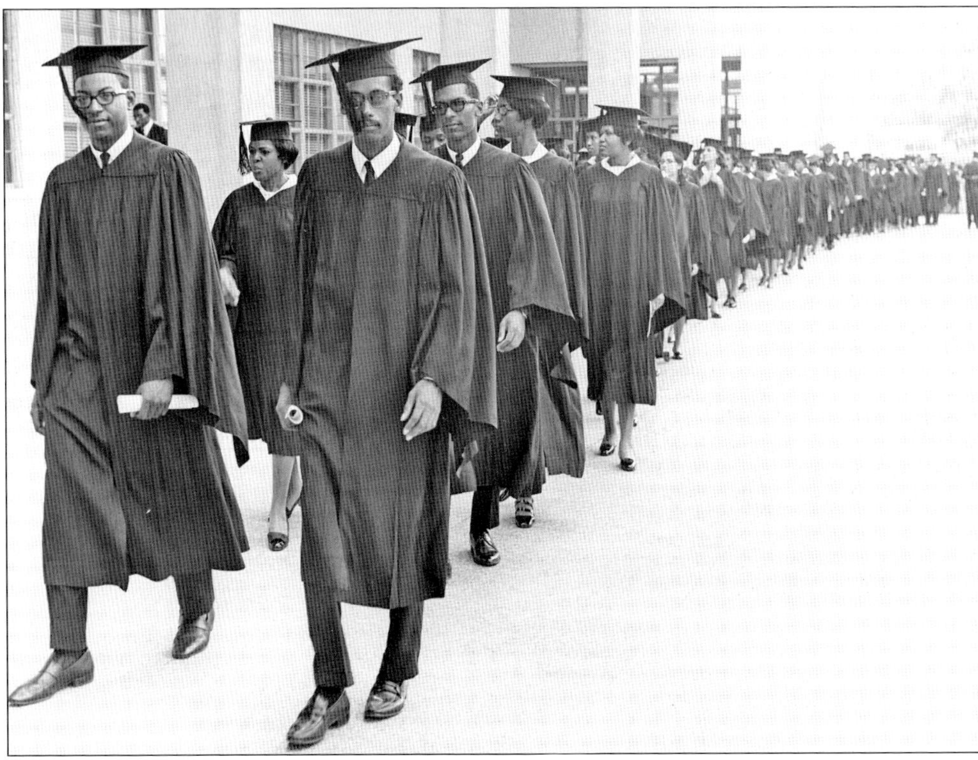

In his famed Atlanta Compromise, former slave and educator Booker T. Washington urged the black community to achieve some form of education, be it a traditional liberal arts training or an education in the skills and trades. The desire to achieve beyond a high school education was virtually unattainable for Houston's black community before Heman Sweatt and Thurgood Marshall challenged the University of Texas and the constitutionality of a "separate but equal" society. Texas Southern University became the avenue for many blacks to gain a higher education when the doors to a majority of institutions remained stumbling blocks not only to education, but also to a greater social, political, and economic standing. (Image courtesy of the Heartman Collections at Texas Southern University.)

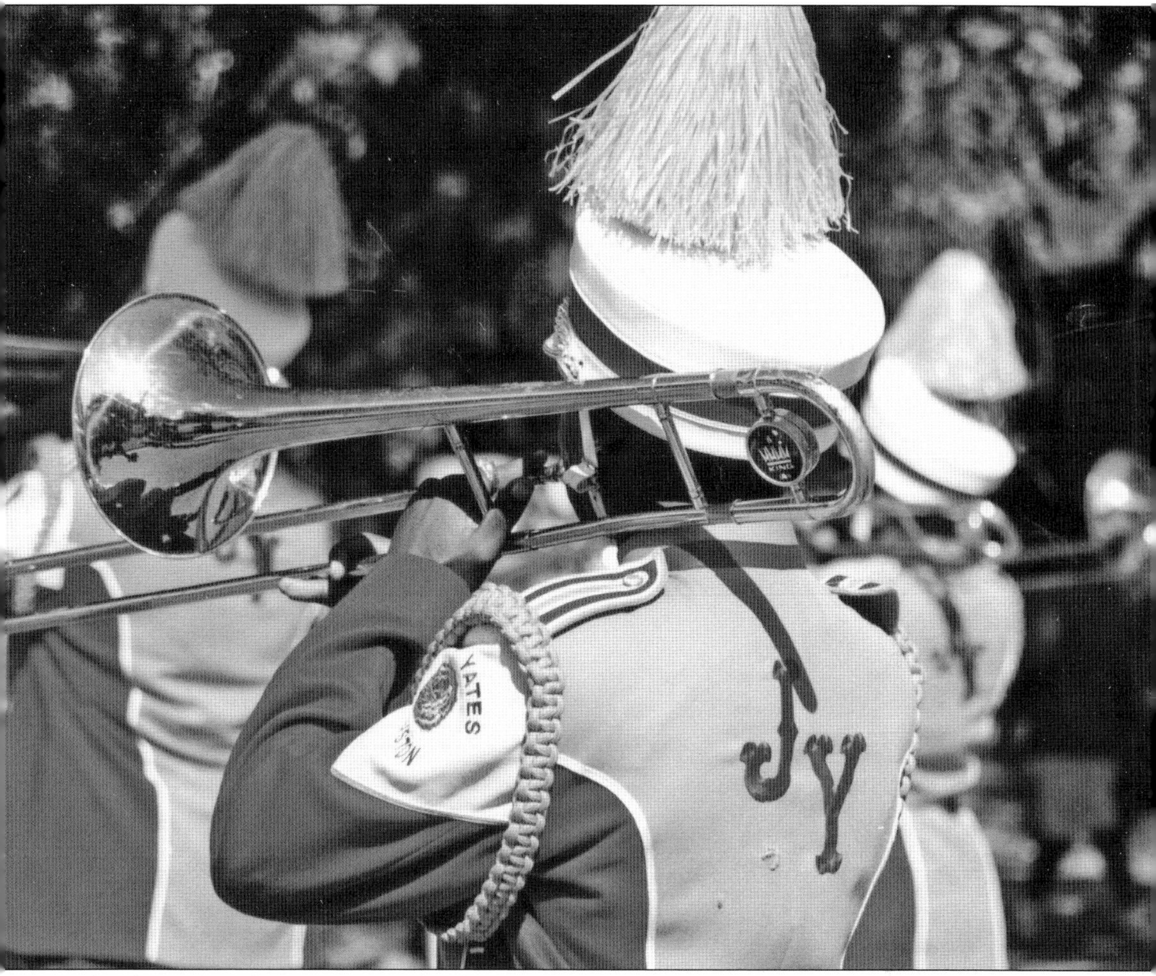

Third Ward's Jack Yates High School, named after former slave Jack Yates, is one of the oldest schools in Houston's black community. The high school band is a show band that performs in parades and at halftime during high school and college football games. Like the show bands at HBCUs, the Yates drum line entertains the audience with skillful drumbeats. (Image courtesy of the Heartman Collections at Texas Southern University.)

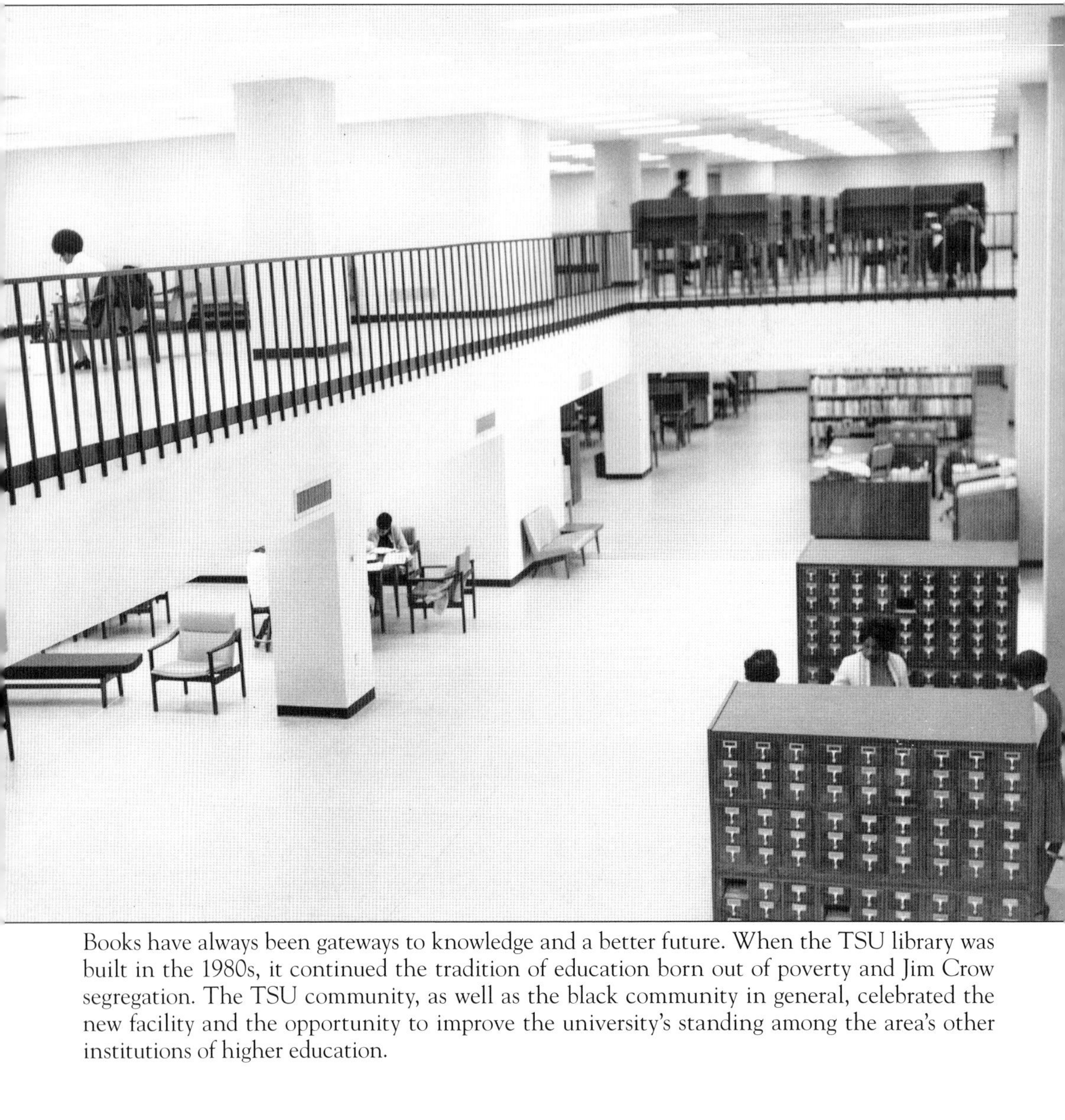

Books have always been gateways to knowledge and a better future. When the TSU library was built in the 1980s, it continued the tradition of education born out of poverty and Jim Crow segregation. The TSU community, as well as the black community in general, celebrated the new facility and the opportunity to improve the university's standing among the area's other institutions of higher education.

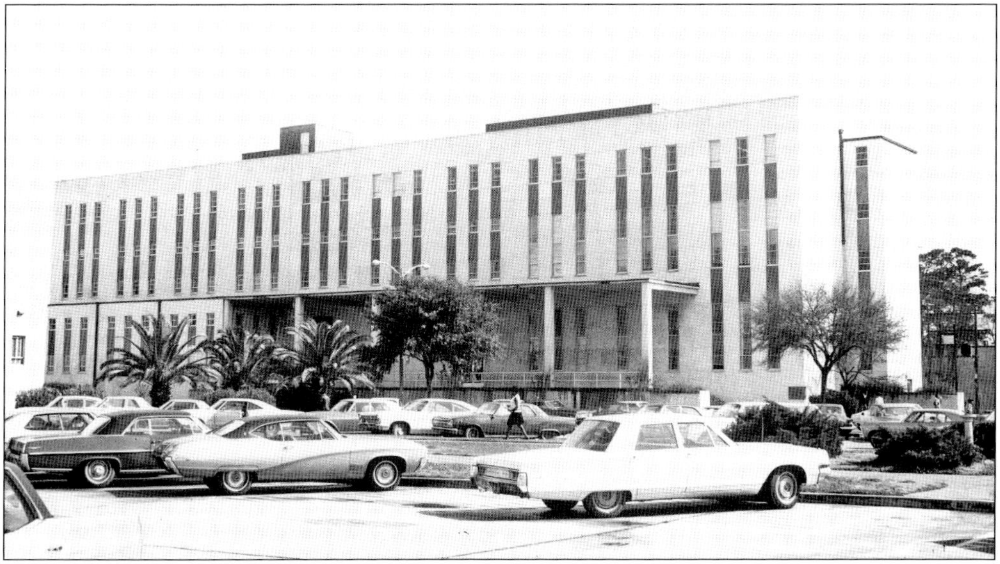

By the 1970s, TSU officials celebrated the school's objective of providing an education to those who had few, if any, opportunities elsewhere. Having been influential in desegregating Houston's downtown facilities, campus officials believed that the last quarter of the 20th century would see more students achieving a college education and more alumni contributing to the shaping of the local community and the country as a whole.

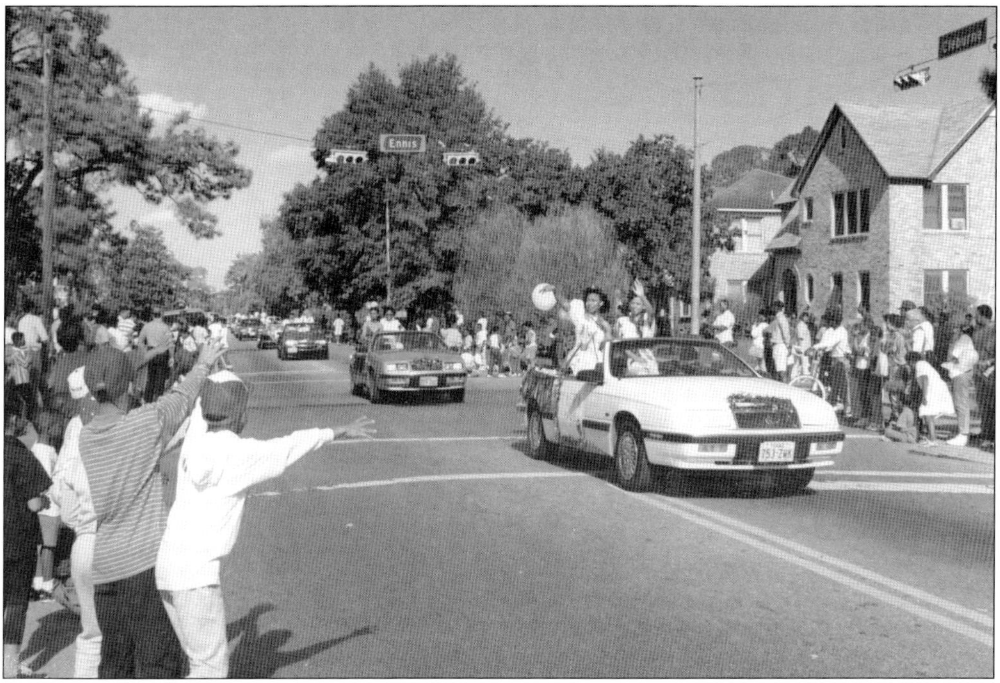

Local parades were opportunities to build up the camaraderie of the black community as a reinforcement of common values and ethos. This was especially true by the 1970s, as Houston's black community celebrated the local dissolution of Jim Crow and the prominent role played by Houstonian Barbara Jordan during the Watergate hearings. (Image courtesy of the Heartman Collections at Texas Southern University.)

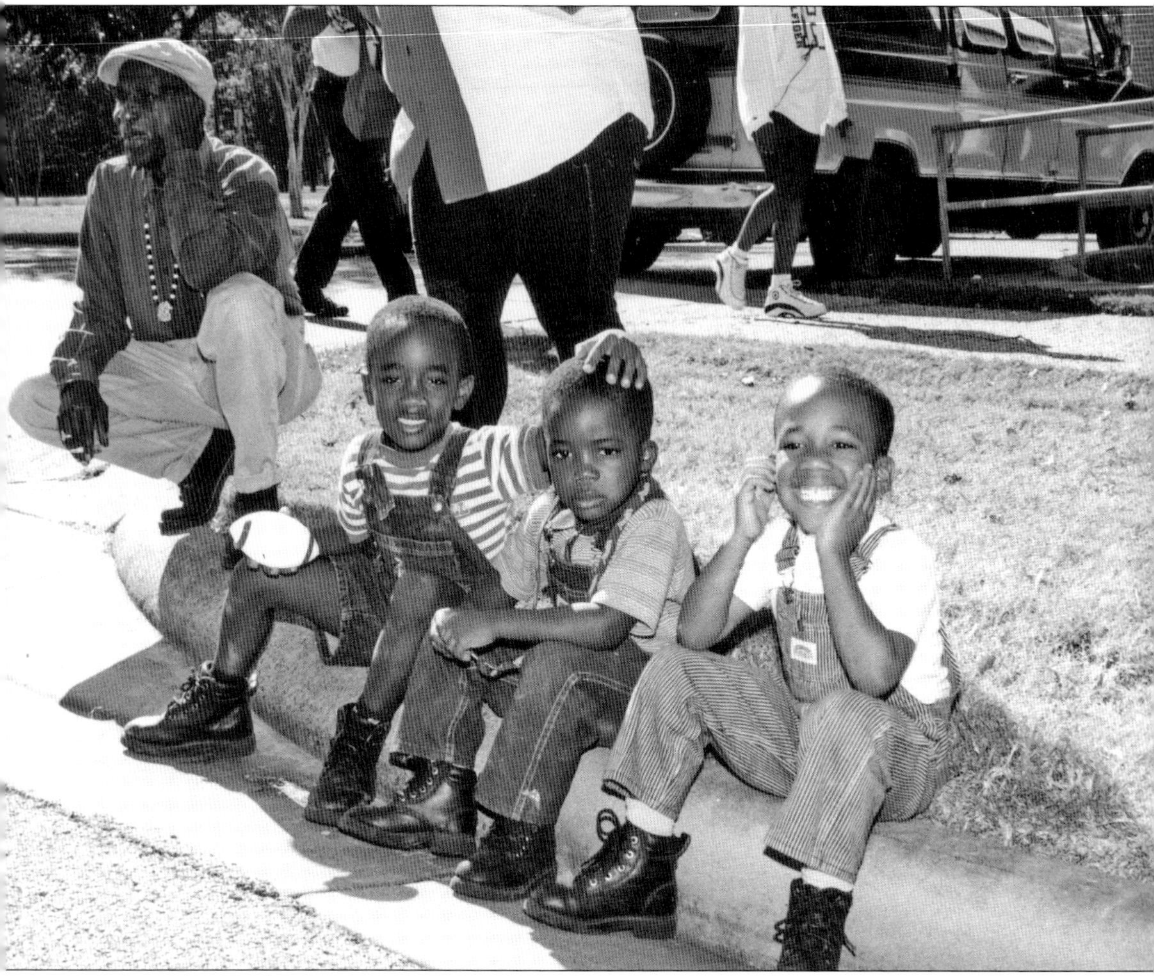

The children in this image are observing a homecoming parade in Houston's Third Ward. Such events solidified TSU's vital importance to the essence of Houston's black community. Local black officials often appeared on campus in city hall events and to commemorate the institution's achievements. (Image courtesy of the Heartman Collections at Texas Southern University.)

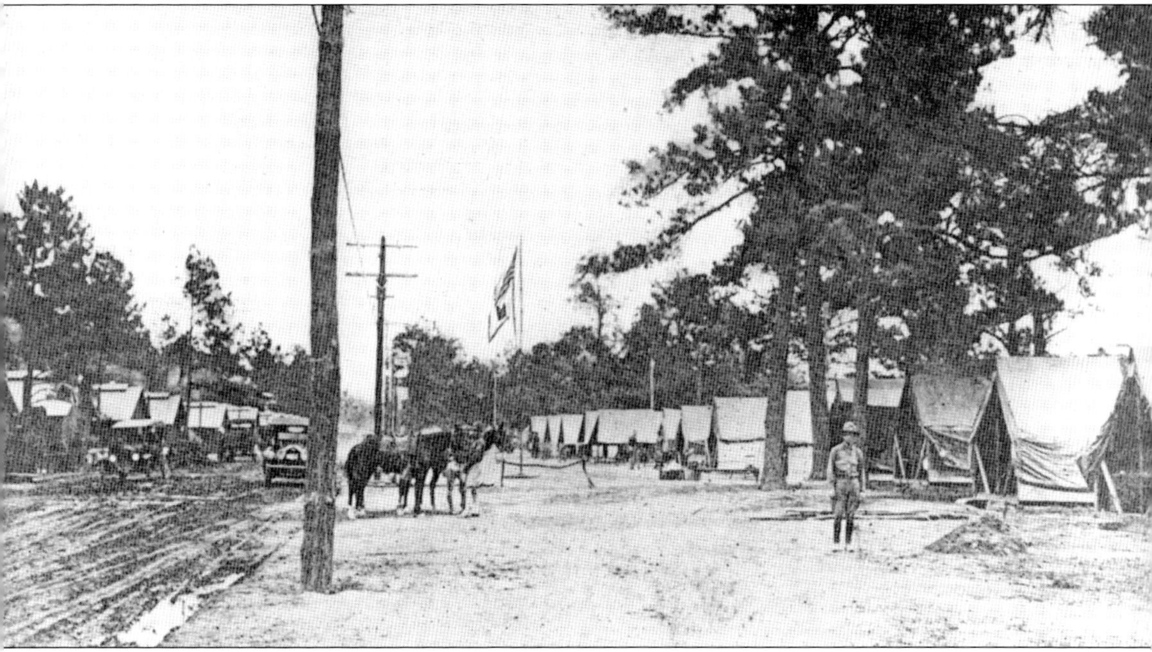

Camp Logan was home to black soldiers, many of whom were not originally from the South. As a result, the atmosphere of Jim Crow racism would eventually prove too humiliating and lead to a conflict between black soldiers and local police. Sadly, many of the soldiers involved in the insurrection would be executed, and the black community was faced with the ramifications of increased hatred and fear.

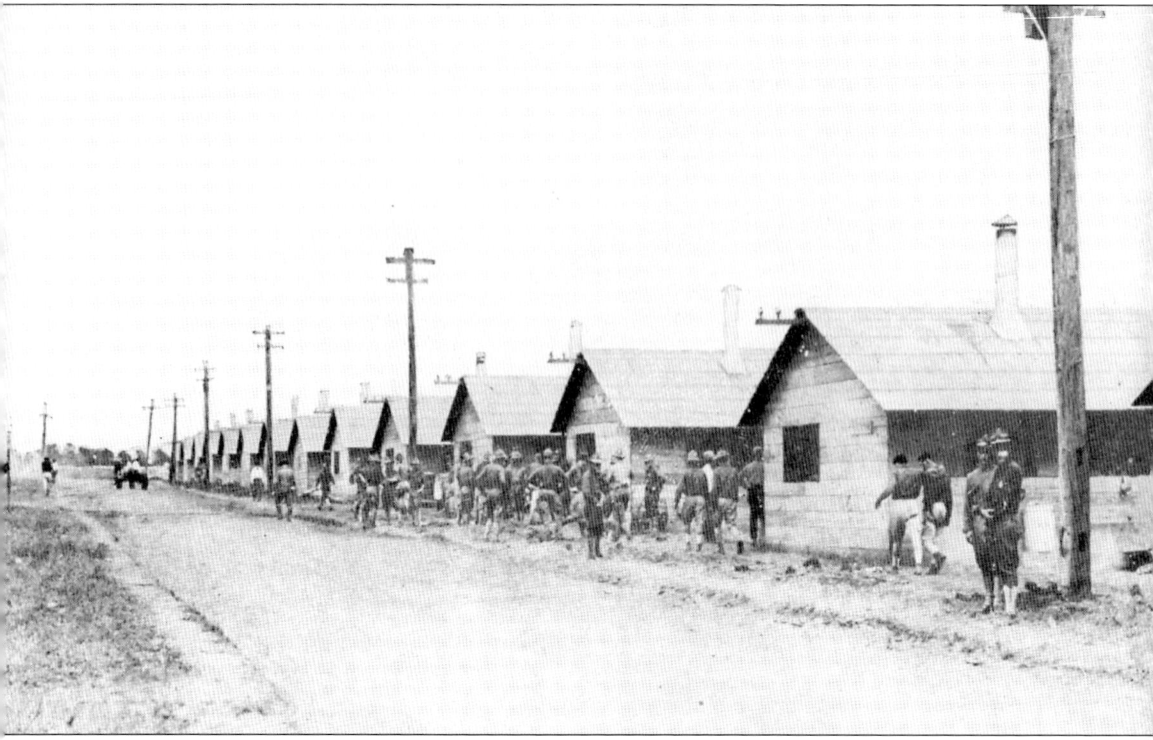

African Americans have participated in every conflict in this country's history. From the American Revolution to today's peacekeeping activities in Afghanistan and Iraq, blacks have fought for the principles of liberty and democracy. However, those same principles were denied the countless thousands who sacrificed their lives for this country during the Jim Crow era. This image depicts the barracks of Camp Logan during World War I before the black soldiers armed themselves and marched toward Houston's downtown in protest of their treatment by police officers. (Image courtesy of the Houston Public Library.)

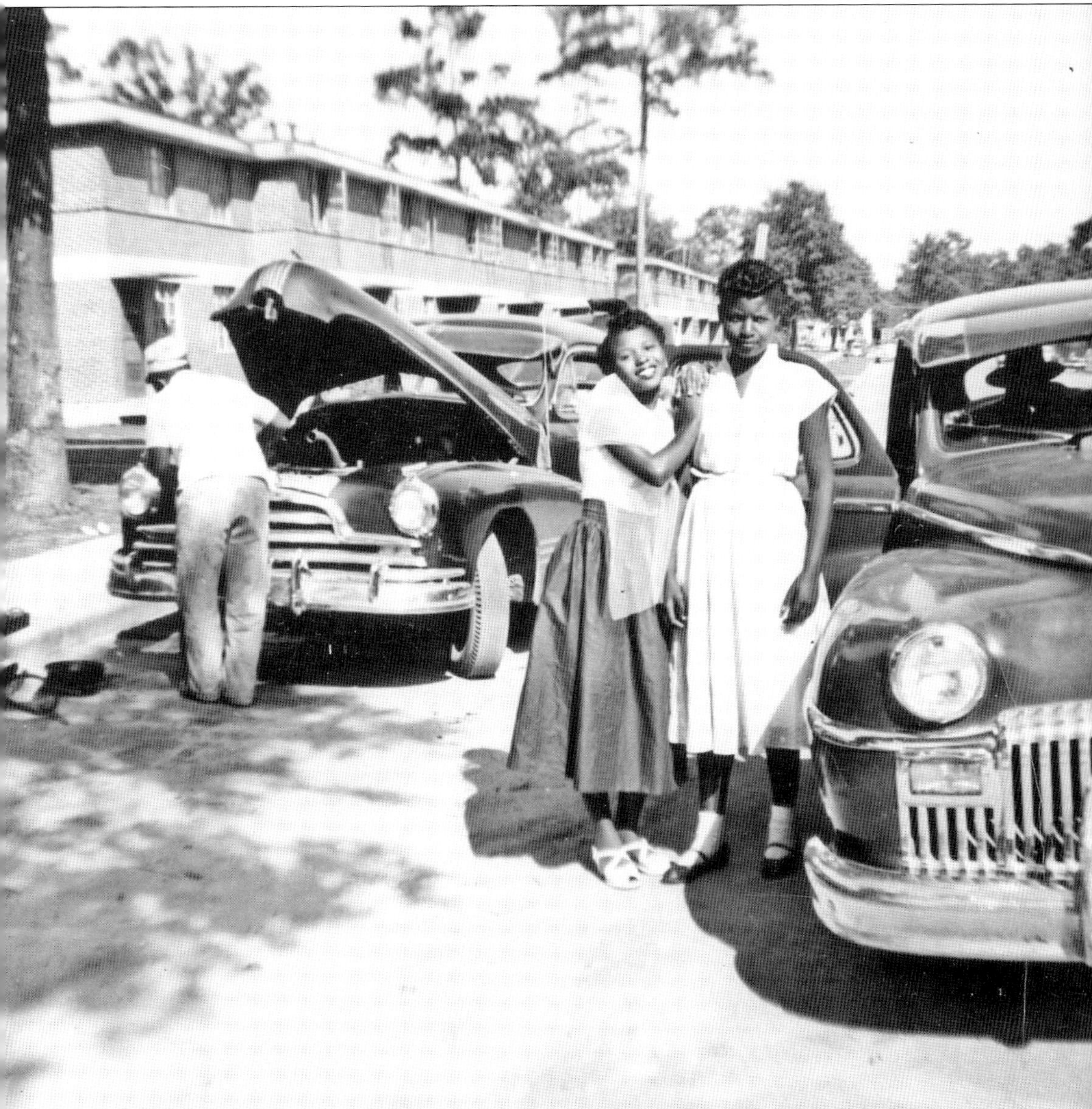

Between the 1930s and 1970s, the federal government initiated the development of housing projects for the inner-city poor. In places like Chicago and Philadelphia, these facilities were once examples of government investments in inner-city housing. However, as the structures aged, they became eyesores and bastions of crime, poverty, and despair. Third Ward's Cuney Homes government housing project (around the 1950s) was no different than those in other cities with large black populations.

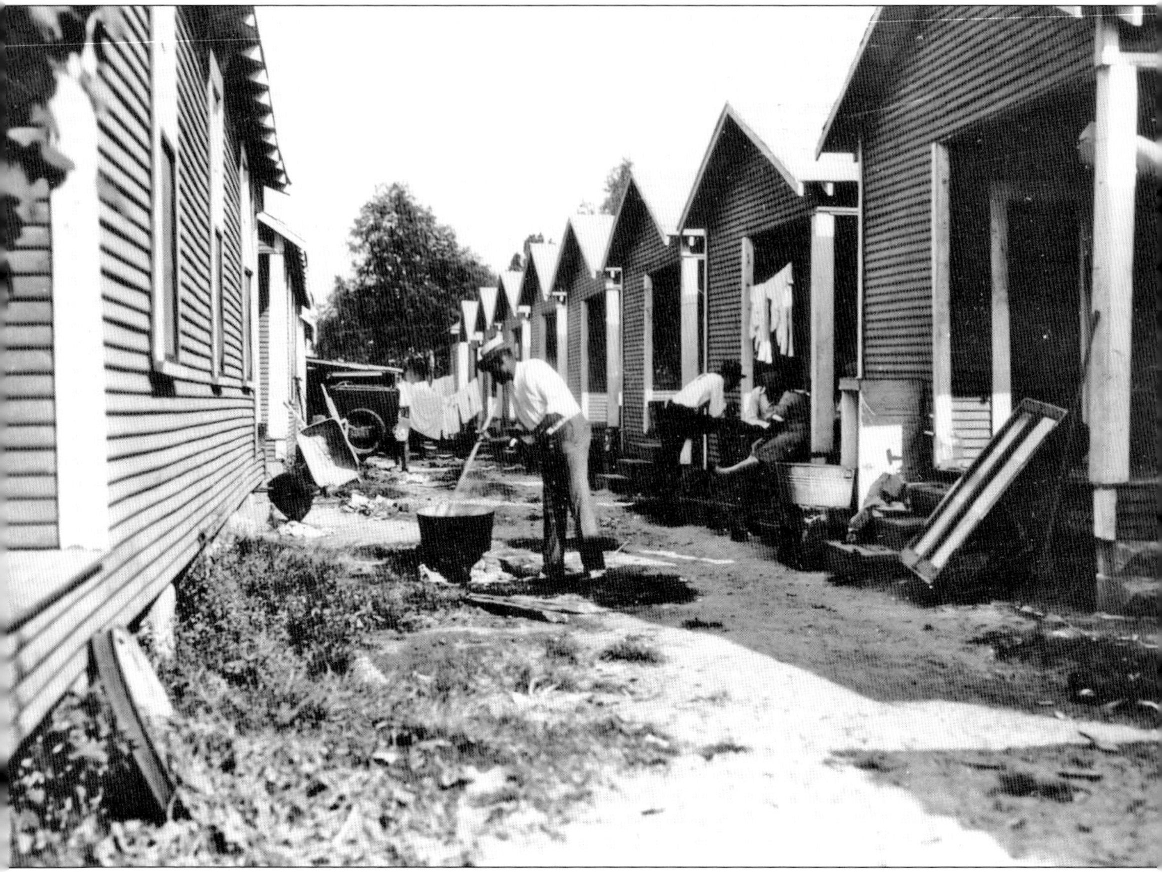

Row houses were common in Houston's black community. The design fostered a community that would serve as an extended family. Neighbors often assisted in caring for children when parents worked long or irregular hours.

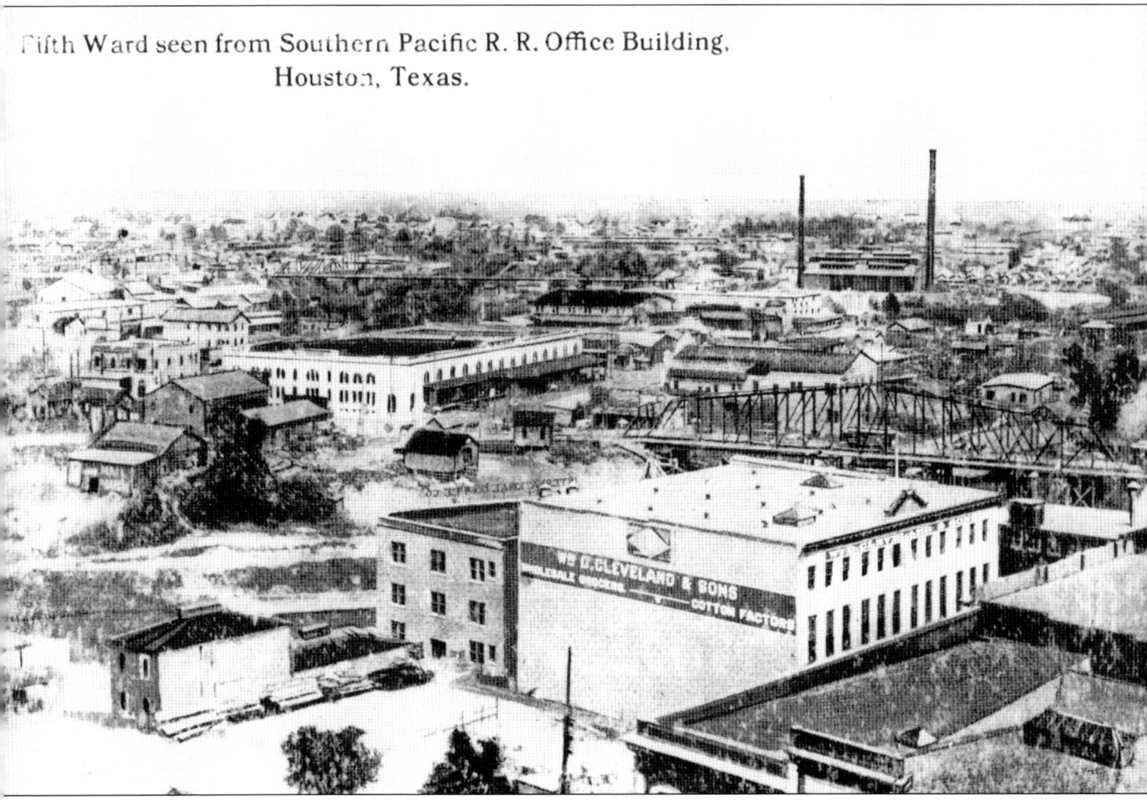

Fifth Ward in the late 19th century was not initially a segregated black community. However, as in the city's Third Ward, its initial inhabitants would leave the area as blacks moved in to be near employment centers.

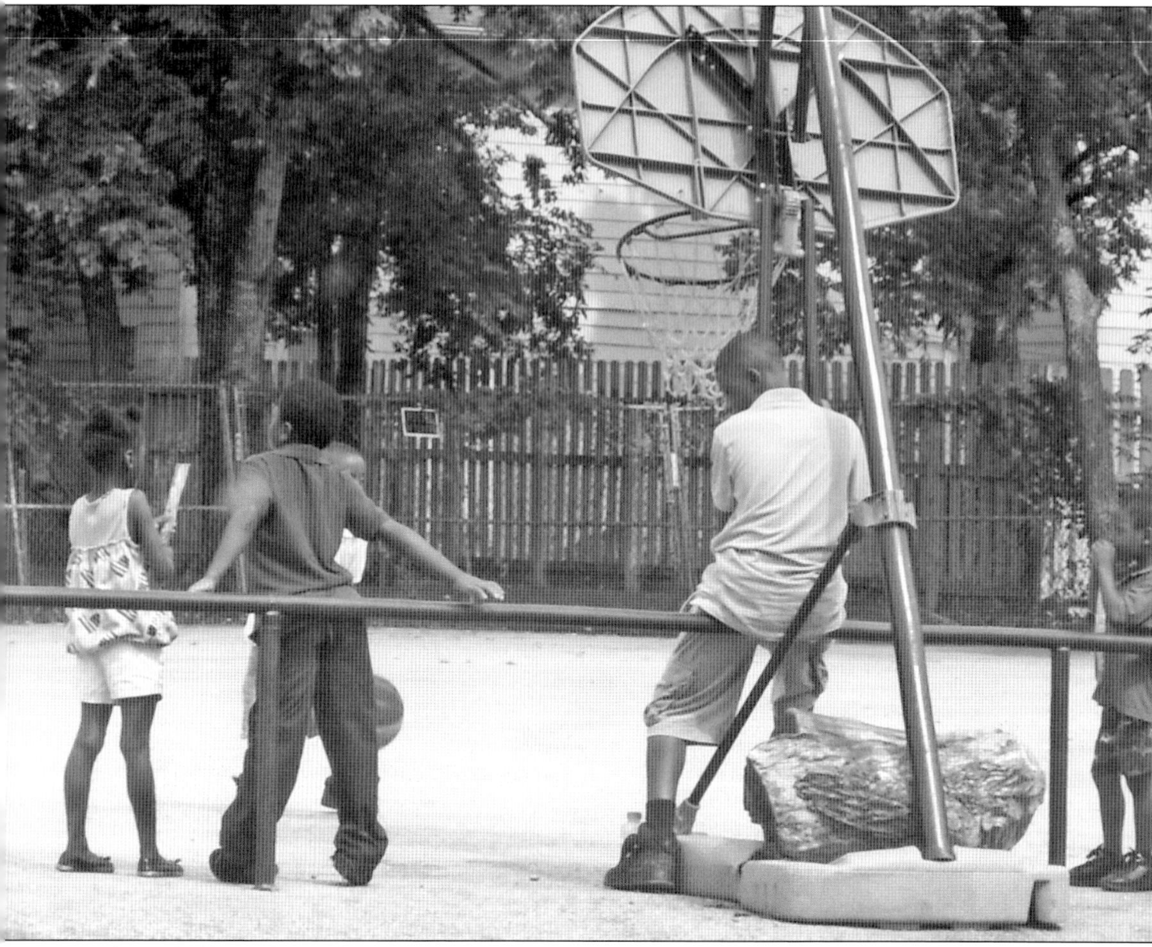

These children play in the Fourth Ward in the shadows of Houston's downtown skyscrapers. For generations, children have played in this neighborhood, even as it continues to undergo change. Whereas whites moved out, allowing former slaves to move in more than 100 years ago, the white population is now returning to be closer to downtown employment. (Author's collection.)

A professional stage band in the 1950s often performed in the segregated venues of Houston and the surrounding areas. Even though they seldom (if ever) performed in front of white audiences, they nonetheless enjoyed immense popularity among the black community.

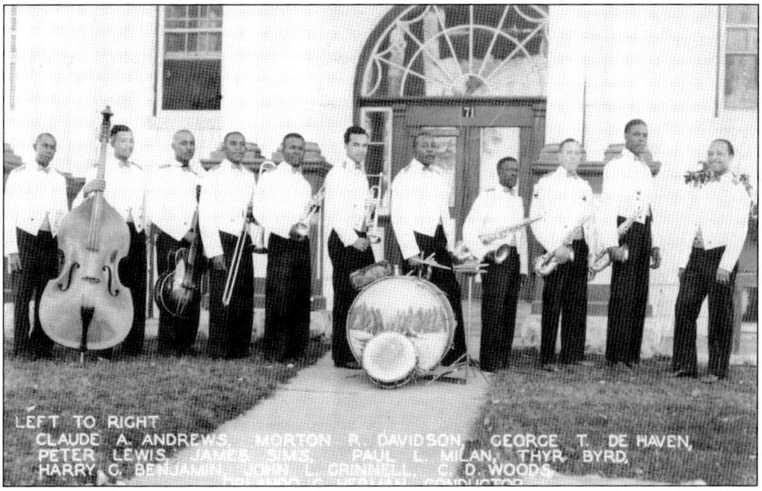

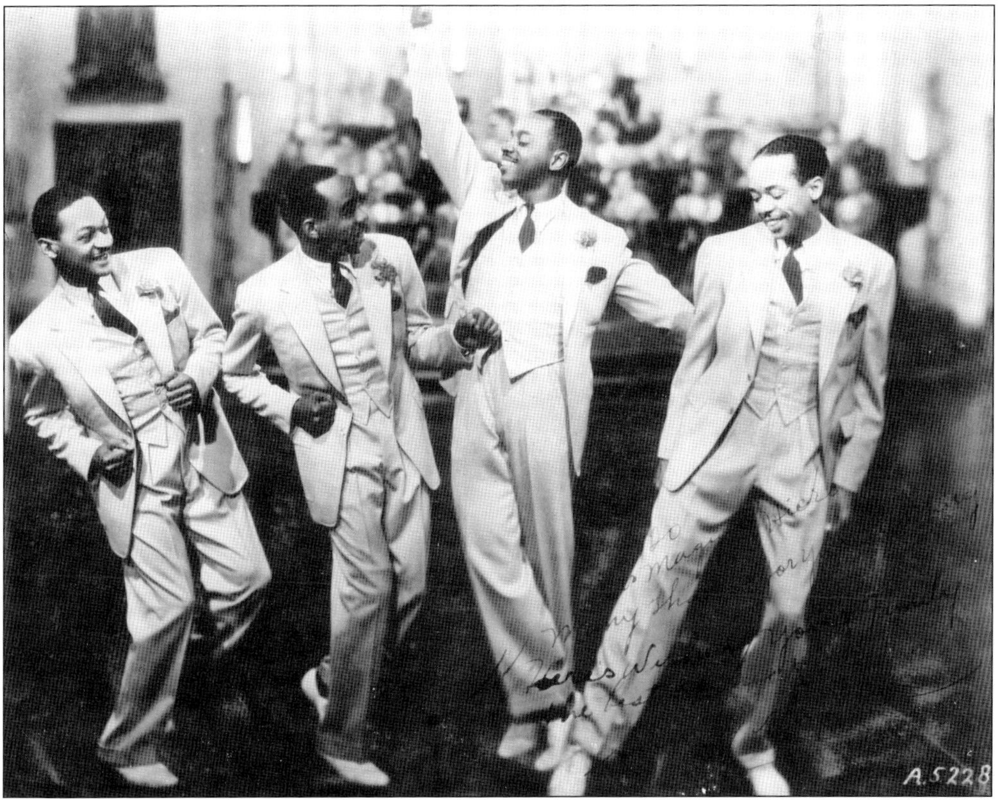

The genre of music performed by black singers from the 1940s through the 1960s changed before its eventual acceptance by white audiences. Nationally, black singers and groups provided the sound track of the civil rights generation as they sought the inclusion in a society that was promised at the end of the Civil War. Artists like James Brown performed in-your-face music that helped lead to the end of Jim Crow.

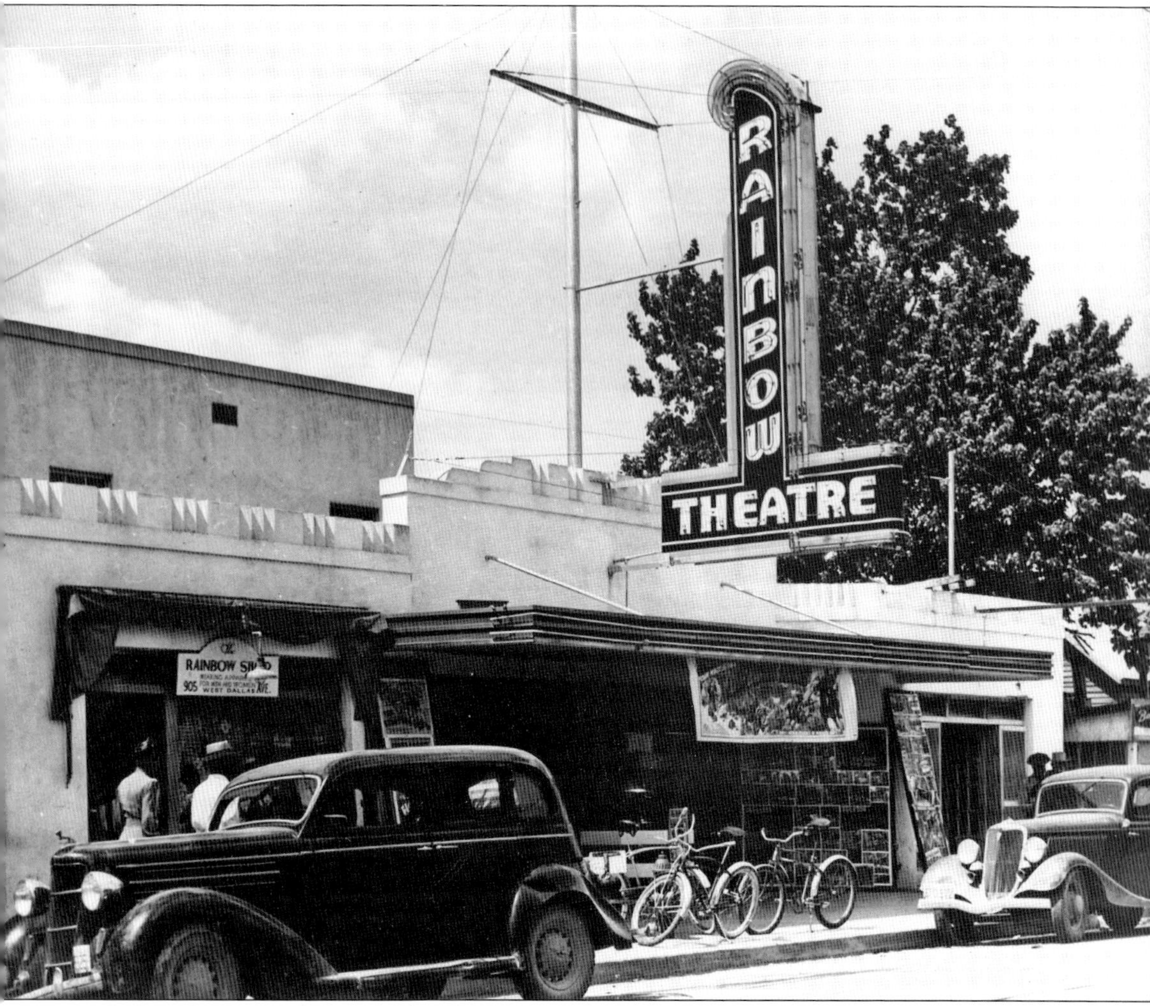

Black performers used segregated facilities like the Rainbow Theatre to perform in front of Houston's black community. Even though these facilities were segregated, the black community fiercely defended them as places where they could enjoy themselves outside the view of white authorities.

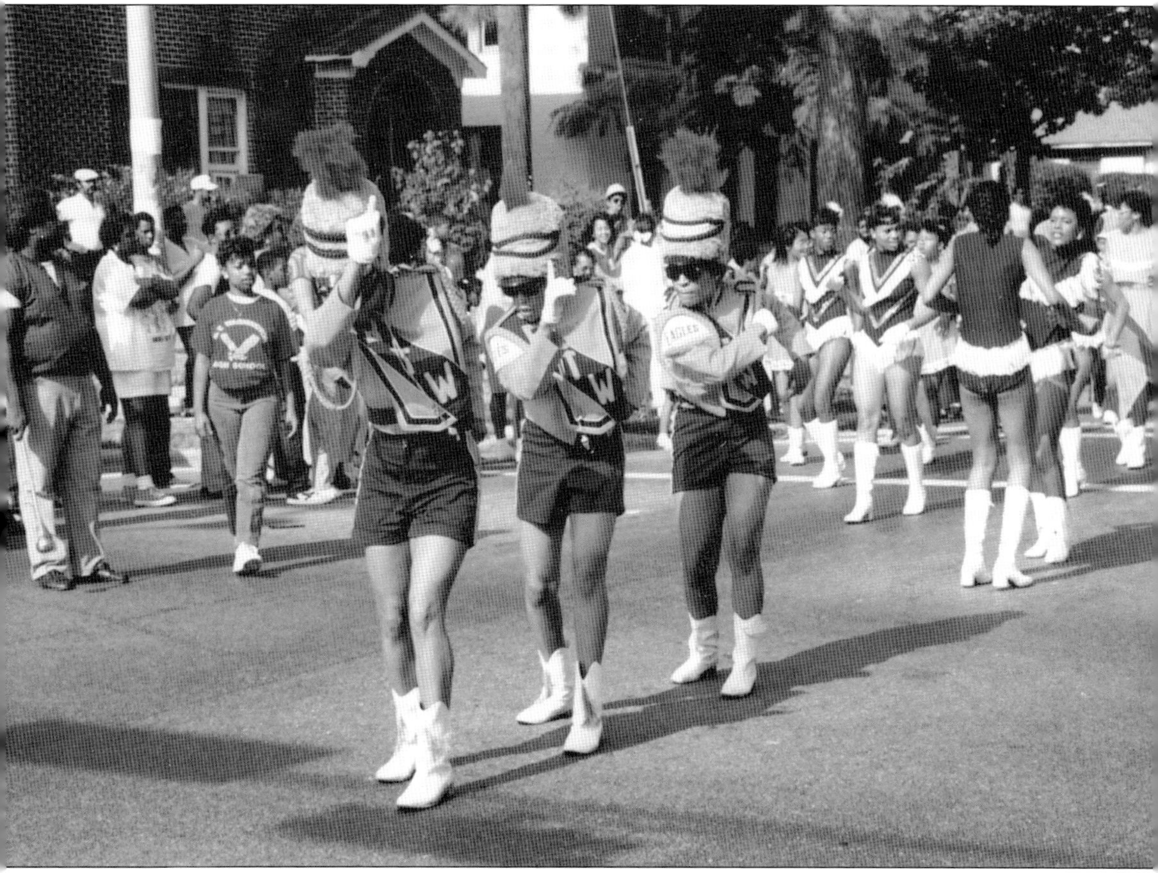

The Booker T. Washington High School band entertains the crowd during a parade in the 1980s. The community not only supported the school, but perhaps more importantly came out in support of local area children. Such events as parades and sporting events galvanized the black community and fostered the sense of togetherness that was prevalent during the time of Jim Crow and continued afterwards.

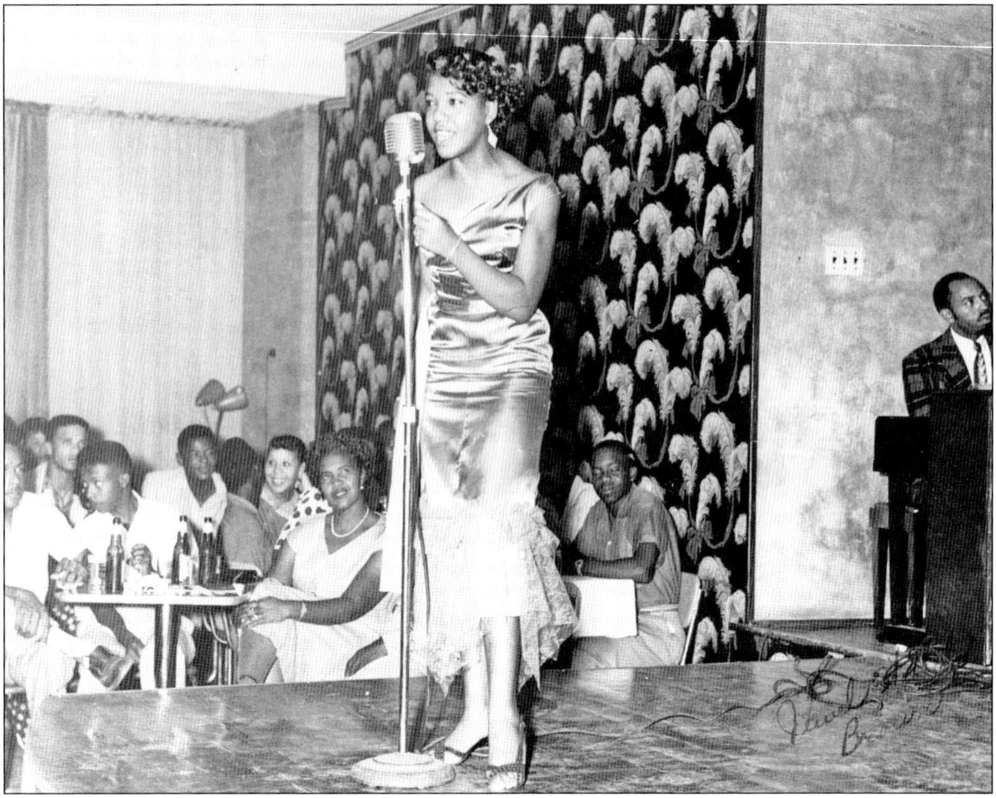

Singer Jewel Brown is pictured performing in front of a black audience in Houston.

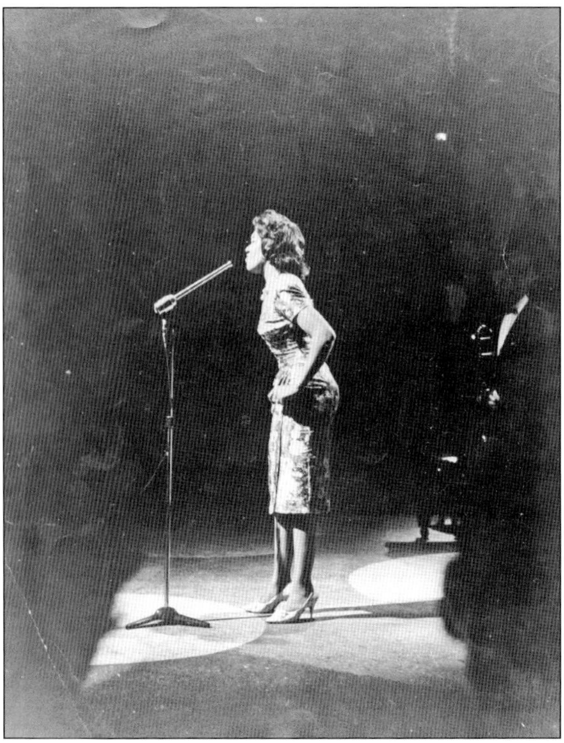

Singers like Jewel Brown would perform at a Houston's black nightclubs. Like other black entertainers, Brown recognized that her audience was the black community even after blacks were able to frequent previously segregated venues.

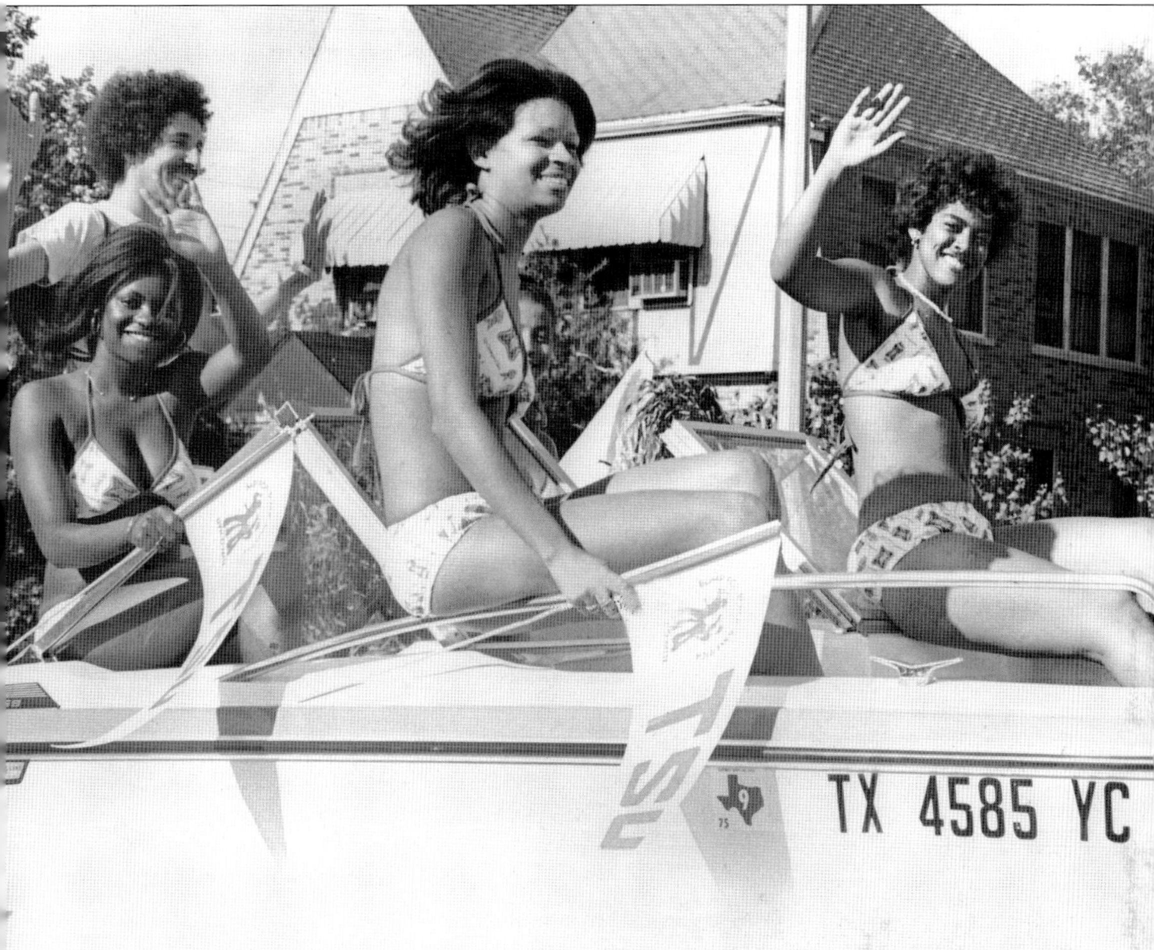

Homecoming and Juneteenth parades provided Houston's black community the opportunity to celebrate its past accomplishments while simultaneously supporting their children. These events became a symbolic link to the past when the black community had few events worth celebrating. By keeping the legacy of the past alive in the present, the community preserved its rich legacy of achievement and survival. (Image courtesy of the Heartman Collection, Texas Southern University.)

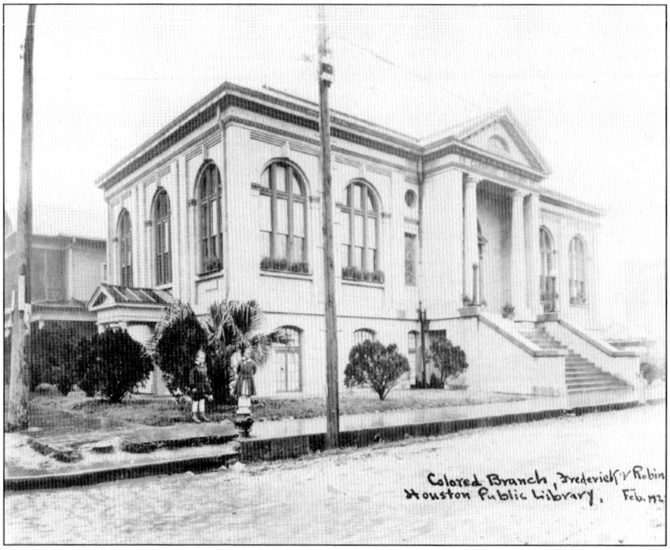

The segregated Negro Carnegie Library was constructed in Houston to facilitate the education of the black community. Throughout the country, blacks were agitating for the right to attend white institutions and end the practice of "separate but equal." Coincidently, it would be issues of equal education that would eventually overturn the ruling in *Plessy v. Ferguson*.

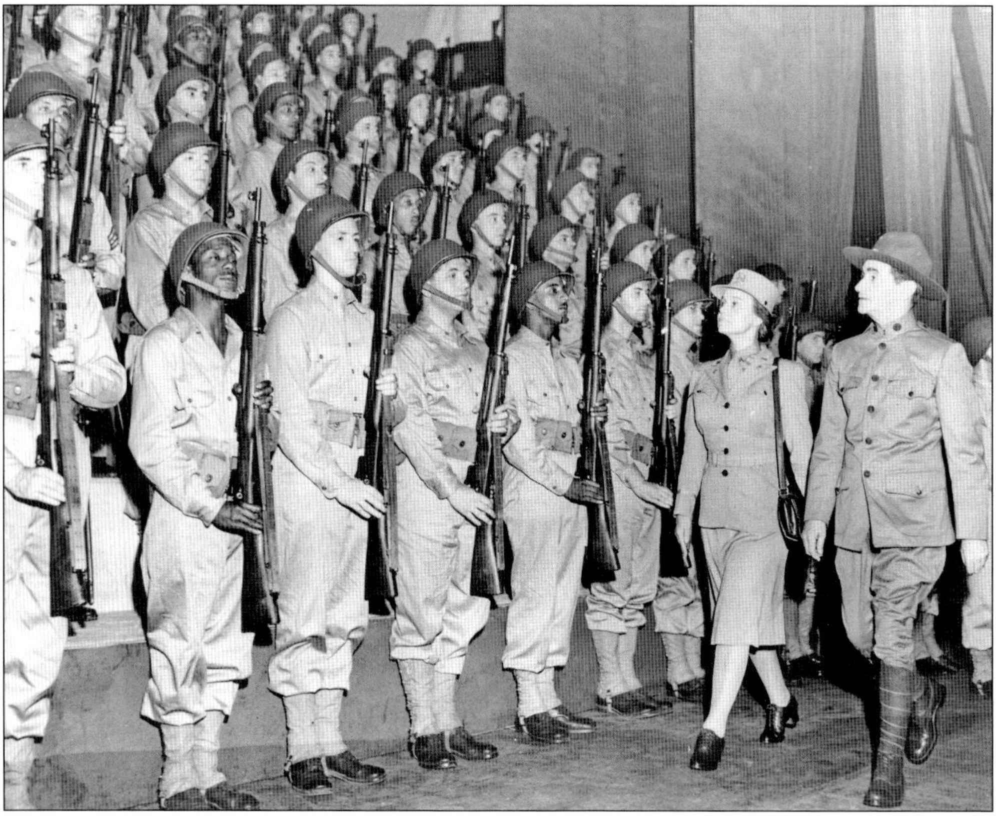

Seen here is a review of an integrated US Army unit in Houston. There is no question that military service contributed to the development of this country's black middle class in the 1950s and 1960s. Those in Houston's black community that either were drafted or voluntarily served in the military did so with pride and honor. Unfortunately, their sacrifices were not always recognized by the very public whose rights they swore an oath to protect. Still, history will show that blacks have served with valor and grace despite the history and presence of Jim Crow.

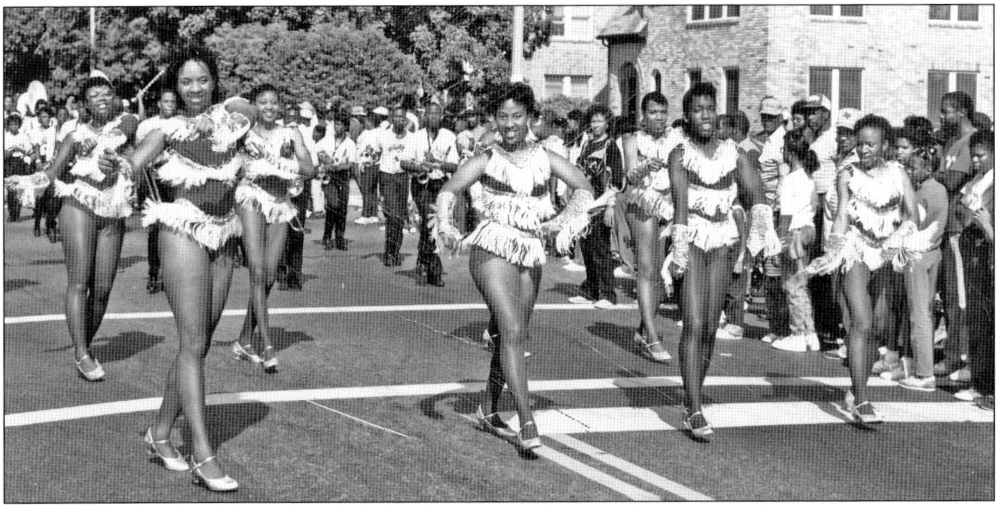

During the years of Jim Crow in Houston, the black community created its own celebrations and festivals under the banner of "NoTsu Oh," which is Houston spelled backwards. Many mirrored those of the Houston's white community, but some were unique to the city's black citizenry. Local parades were celebrations that involved local clubs, high school and college pep squads, and bands. Homecoming celebrations were often the most festive parades, generating much participation and serving as a galvanizing element for black Houstonians. (Image courtesy of the Heartman Collections at Texas Southern University.)

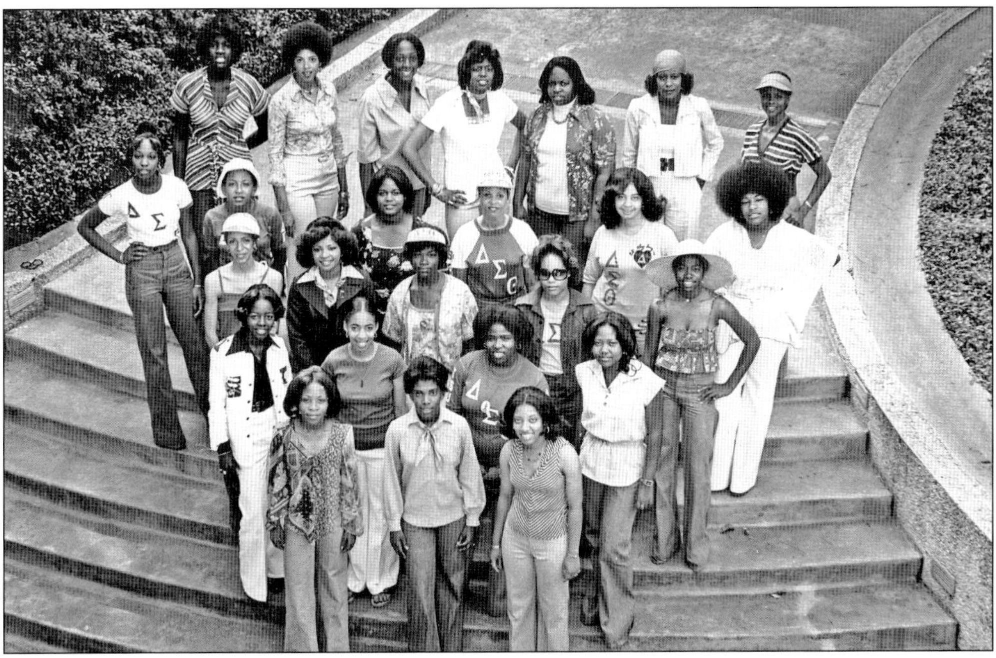

Black sororities have played a prominent role not only in the academic lives of black students, but also in the efforts to gain recognition for women throughout this country. The founding members of Delta Sigma Theta were active participants in the Progressive Era demonstrations for women's suffrage. Today, the Texas Southern University chapter of Delta Sigma Theta continues the legacy of activism for the economic betterment of the black community. (Image courtesy of the Heartman Collections at Texas Southern University.)

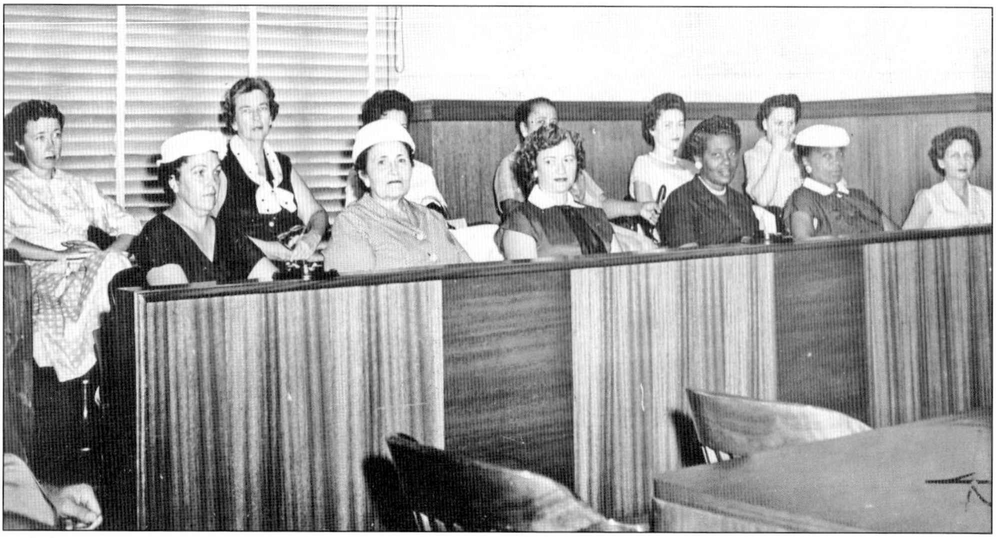

While women were granted the right to vote under the 19th Amendment, they still found themselves relegated to the second tier of American society. This image shows an all-female jury with one African American juror.

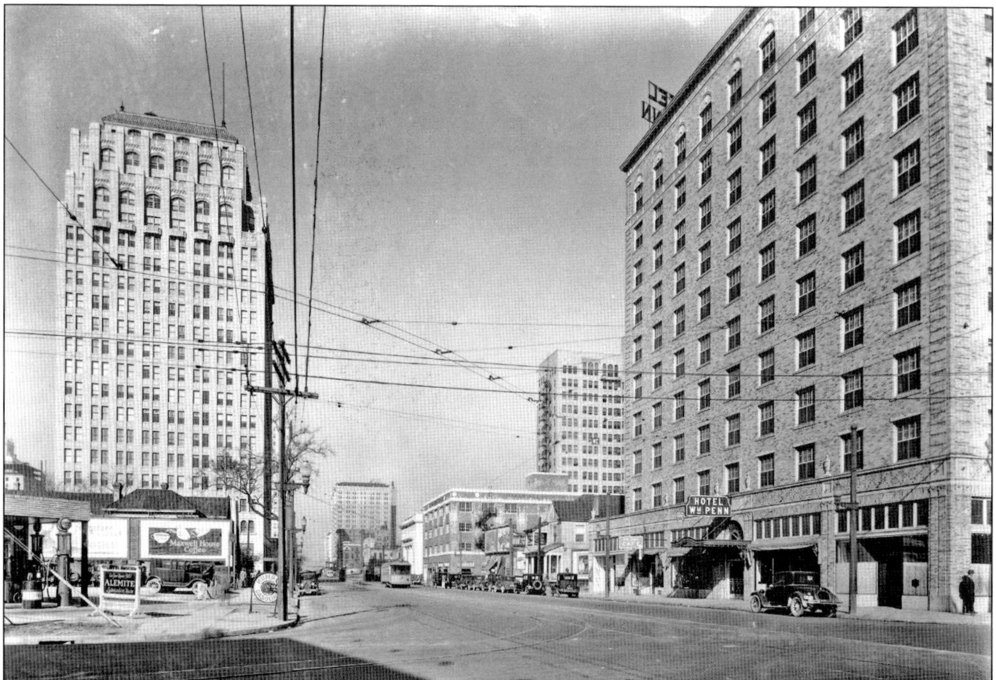

This street scene outside downtown Houston during the World War I era shows the overheard electric wires used for public transportation vehicles. The electric public transportation vehicles were technologically advanced for the day. However, by the onset of the Great Depression, the bus with its combustion engine would lead to the disappearance of electric streetcars from Houston's city streets. Buses were seen as being more flexible and responsive to the demographic movements of Houstonians. Sadly, the bus routes in Houston's black community were segregated, and reports indicated that service was lesser than that found in white communities.

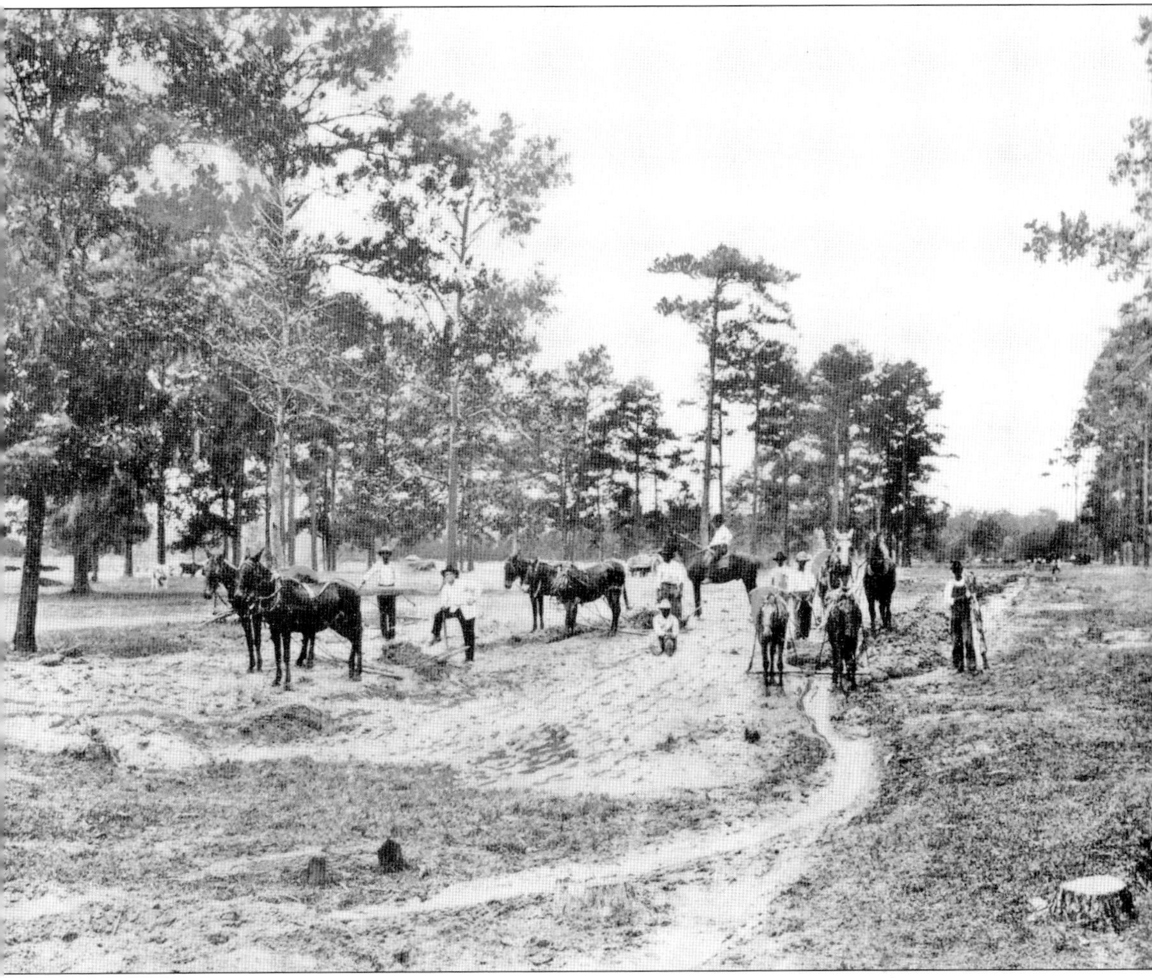

This image depicts black workers at a construction site around 1907. During the early days of the 20th century, blacks throughout the country were generally restricted to the most menial jobs available. Houston was no different, as the black community was generally found along the port areas of Fifth Ward and in the agricultural fields of nearby Fort Bend County.

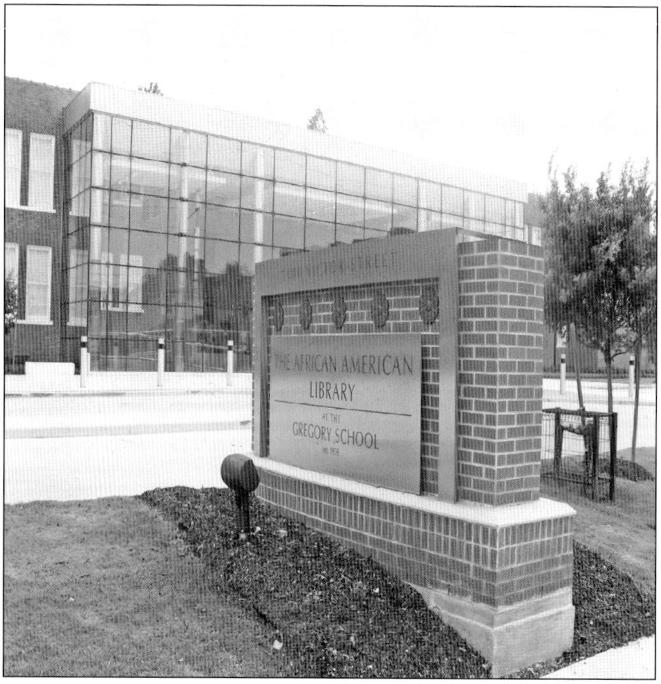

The rebuilt Gregory School in Houston's Fourth Ward became the African American library to preserve the history of the city's black community. (Author's collection.)

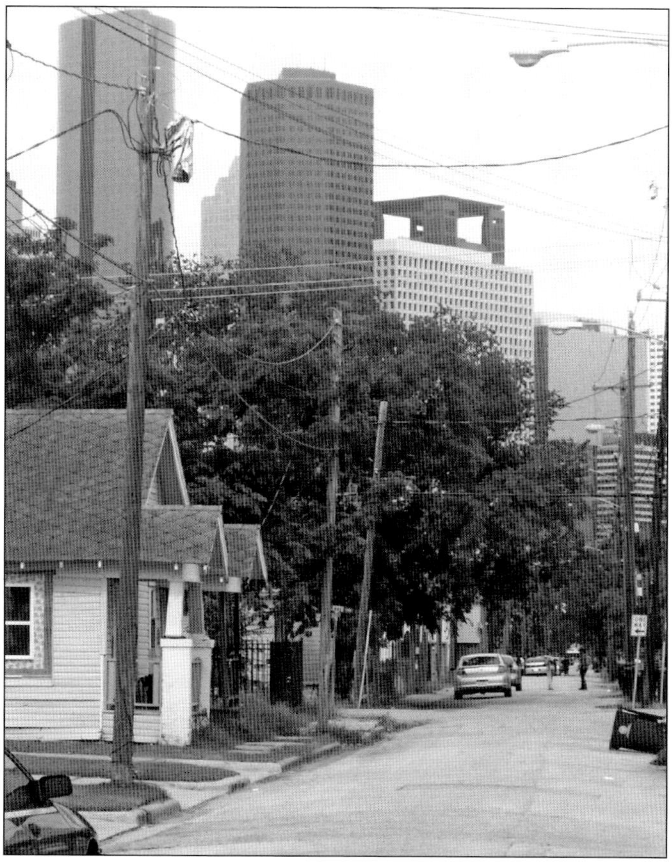

The Fourth Ward row houses are pictured in the late 20th century with the Houston downtown skyline in the background. (Author's collection.)

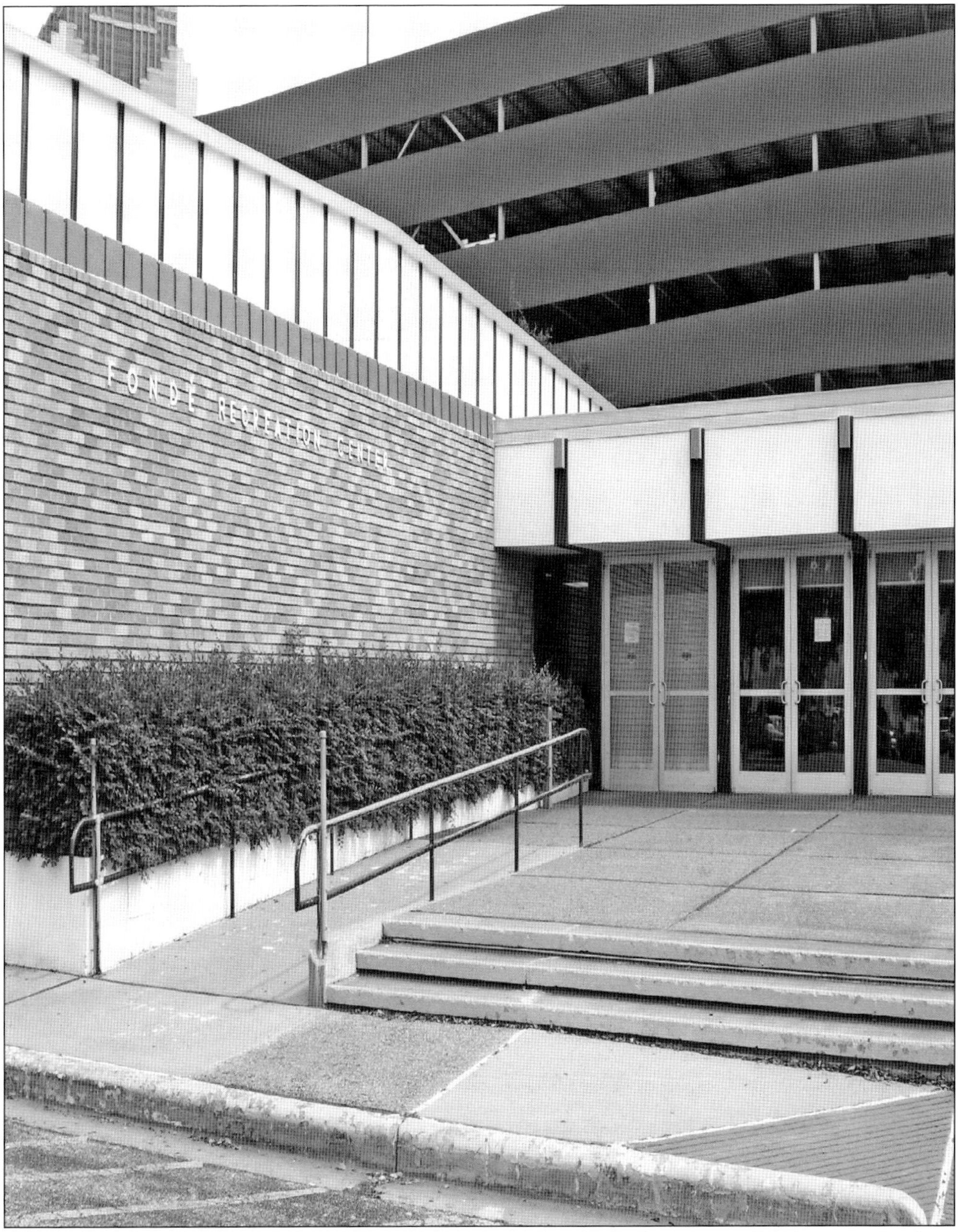

The Fonde Recreation Center is where many National Basketball Association players and others who dream of NBA stardom hone their skills.

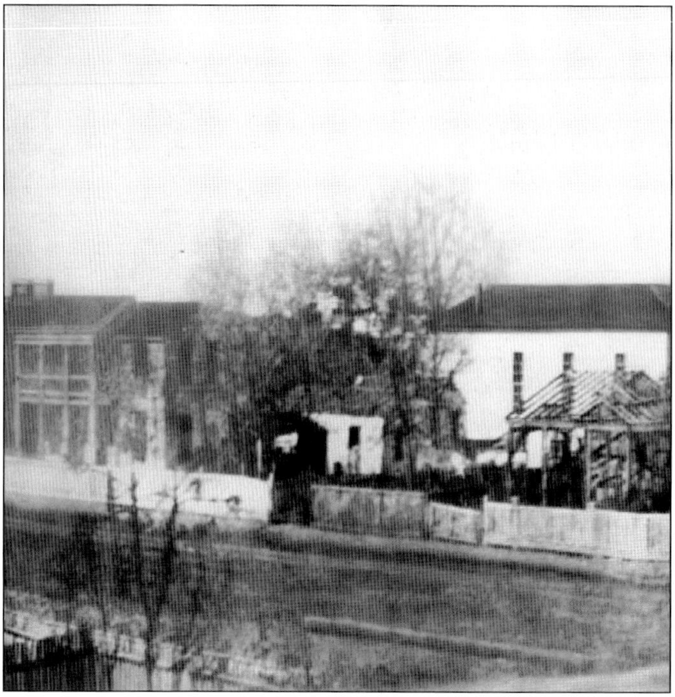

This image shows downtown Houston in the late 19th century when the city was economically subordinate to the port city of Galveston. It was only after Galveston was damaged by a hurricane that Houston's city leaders took advantage of the opportunity to extend the seaport. This eventually elevated Houston's economic status while at the same time turning Galveston into basically a tourism-based town.

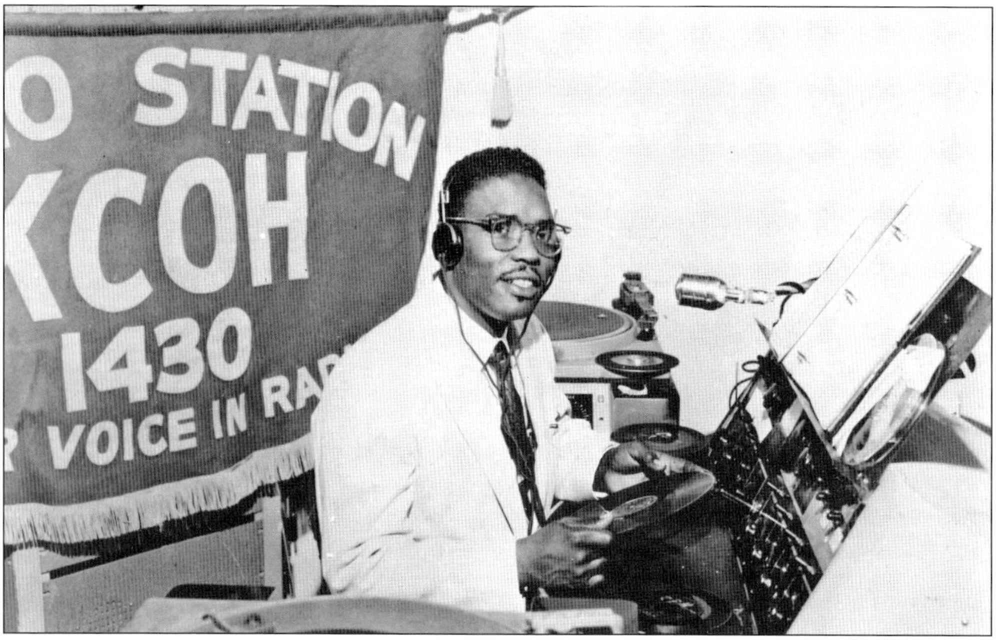

Seen here is a DJ at radio station KCOH, one of the first urban-themed AM radio stations in the country. Before black musicians were given the opportunity to be heard by white audiences, they survived by performing on the Chitlin' Circuit. The black community in Houston and elsewhere supported black artists during the days of Jim Crow segregation. Radio stations like KCOH were invaluable to the dissemination of black music to a community that related to not only the songs, but also to the individuals who performed them. (Image courtesy of the Heartman Collections at Texas Southern University.)

TSU students are seen participating in a Greek step show on campus. Such shows play a part in connecting the current generation of fraternities and sororities with their predecessors. Step shows allow friendly competition while entertaining audiences in a form of camaraderie. (Image courtesy of the Heartman Collections at Texas Southern University.)

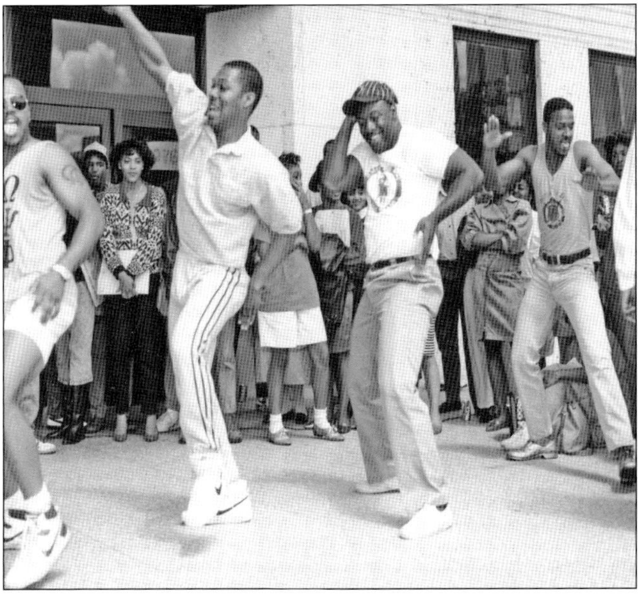

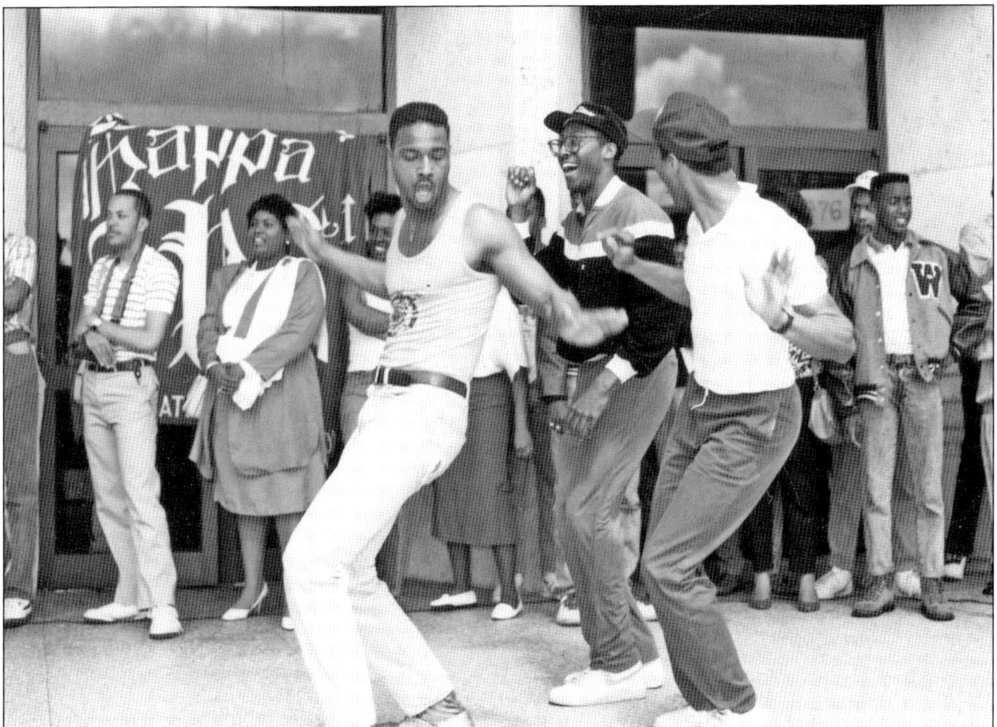

The tradition of fraternities and sororities on the campuses of historically black colleges honors the aspirations of those who fought for the education of the black community. Created in the early 1900s, black fraternities and sororities provided organizations where the "talented tenth" could be trained to assume positions of leadership and influence in the black community. (Image courtesy of the Heartman Collections at Texas Southern University.)

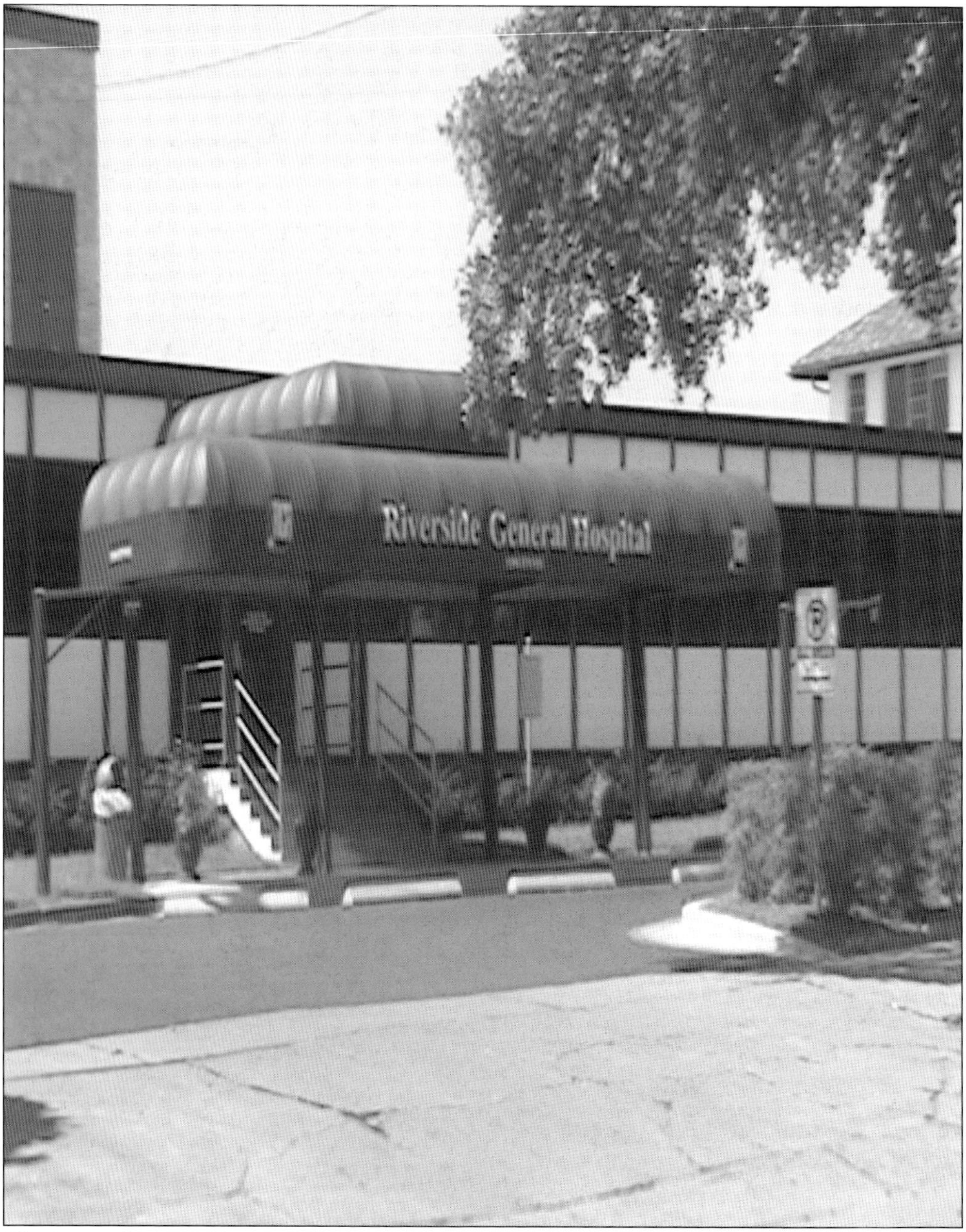

The Riverside General Hospital began serving Houston's black community as the Houston Negro Hospital in 1927. By the 1940s, the facilities were modernized and expanded to meet the needs of Houston's growing black population. In 1961, a $1.2-million expansion led to the renaming of the hospital to Riverside General. Today, the hospital continues providing health care services to a community that has become increasingly diverse after the exodus of the black middle class during the 1980s and 1990s.

This horse-drawn car from the turn of the 20th century illustrates the primary source of urban mobility. Unfortunately, those in Houston's black community were prohibited from accessing most forms of transportation during this period. While there were segregated options that served the black community, those vehicles were often less serviceable than the ones used in white communities.

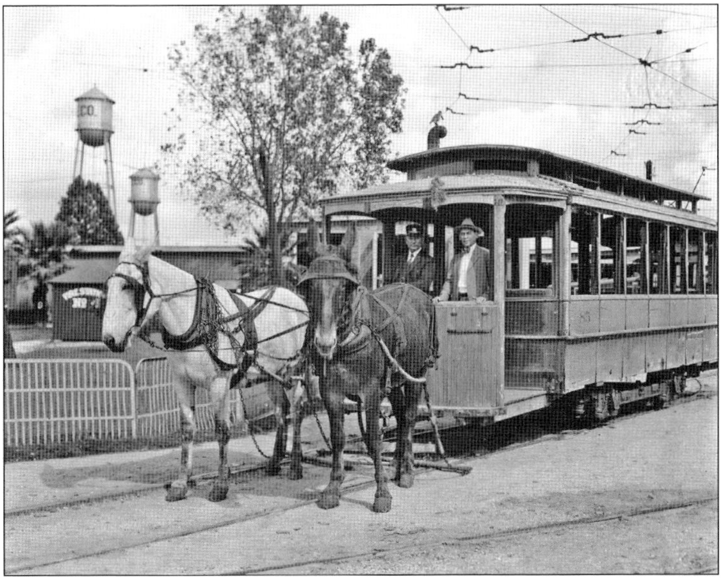

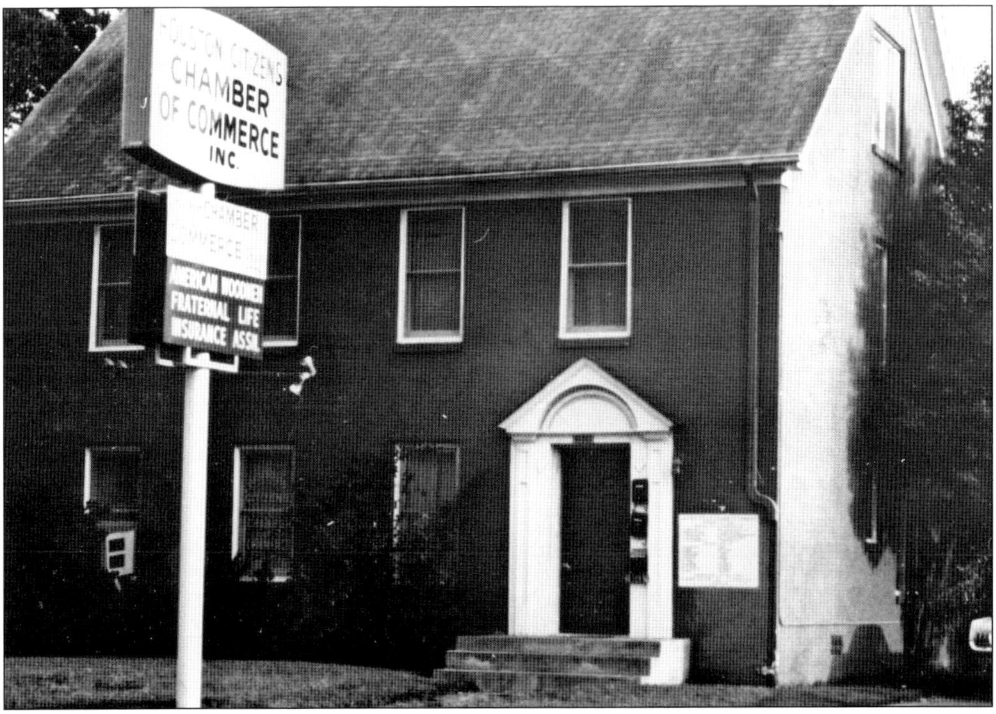

The Houston Citizens Chamber of Commerce (HCCC) in the Third Ward has been a consistent source of business development in the black community. Like any other chamber of commerce, the HCCC promotes black businesses and professionals to a clientele located throughout the city. However, in the era of segregation, black businesses flourished as the black community were geographically restricted. Sadly, integration has meant the decline of black businesses as their traditional customers have been scattered throughout the region. (Image courtesy of the Greater Houston Black Chamber of Commerce.)

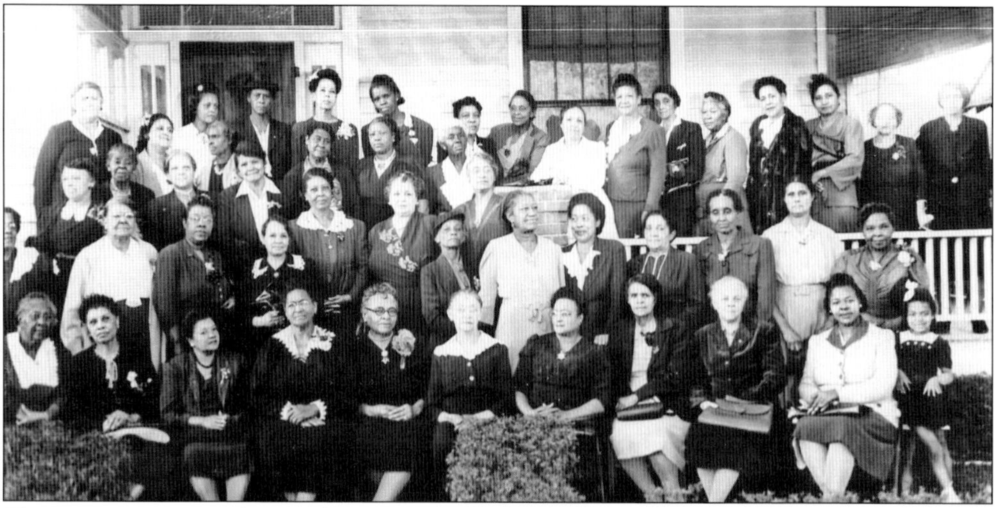

These women are members of the Delta Sigma Theta Sorority, one of the oldest black sororities in the country. Founded in 1913, Delta Sigma Theta endeavored to provide an organization that empowered black women to better serve their communities and families. Its members were among the first participants in the movement for women's suffrage and continue to be politically involved in the present day.

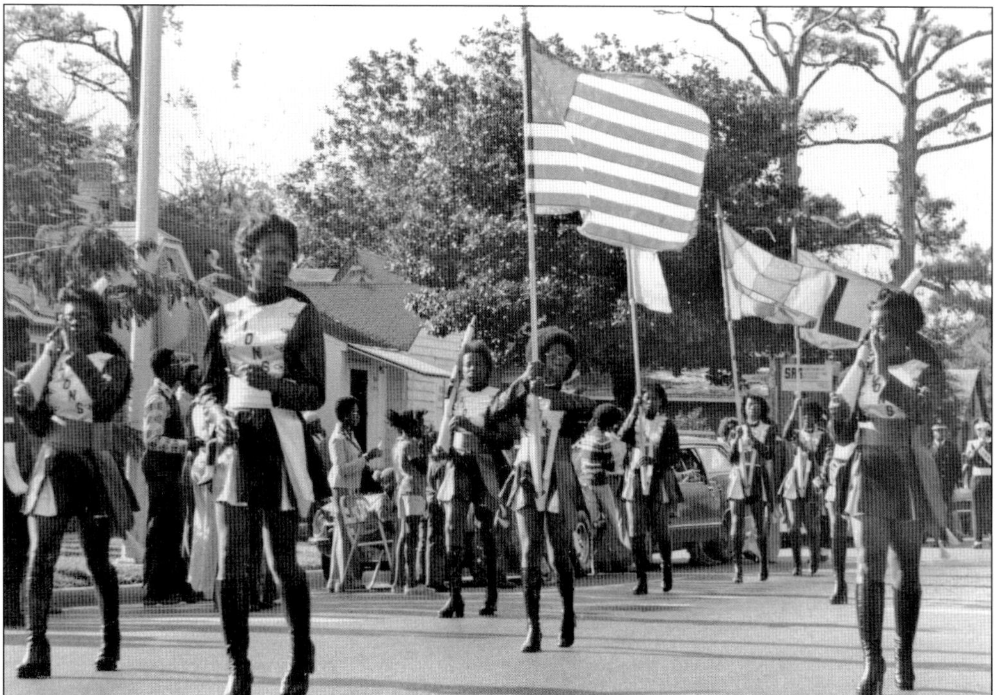

In Houston's black community, parades are celebrations of holidays and other special occasions. This image shows the Yates High School band as they march along the streets of Houston's Third Ward. (Image courtesy of the Heartman Collections at Texas Southern University.)

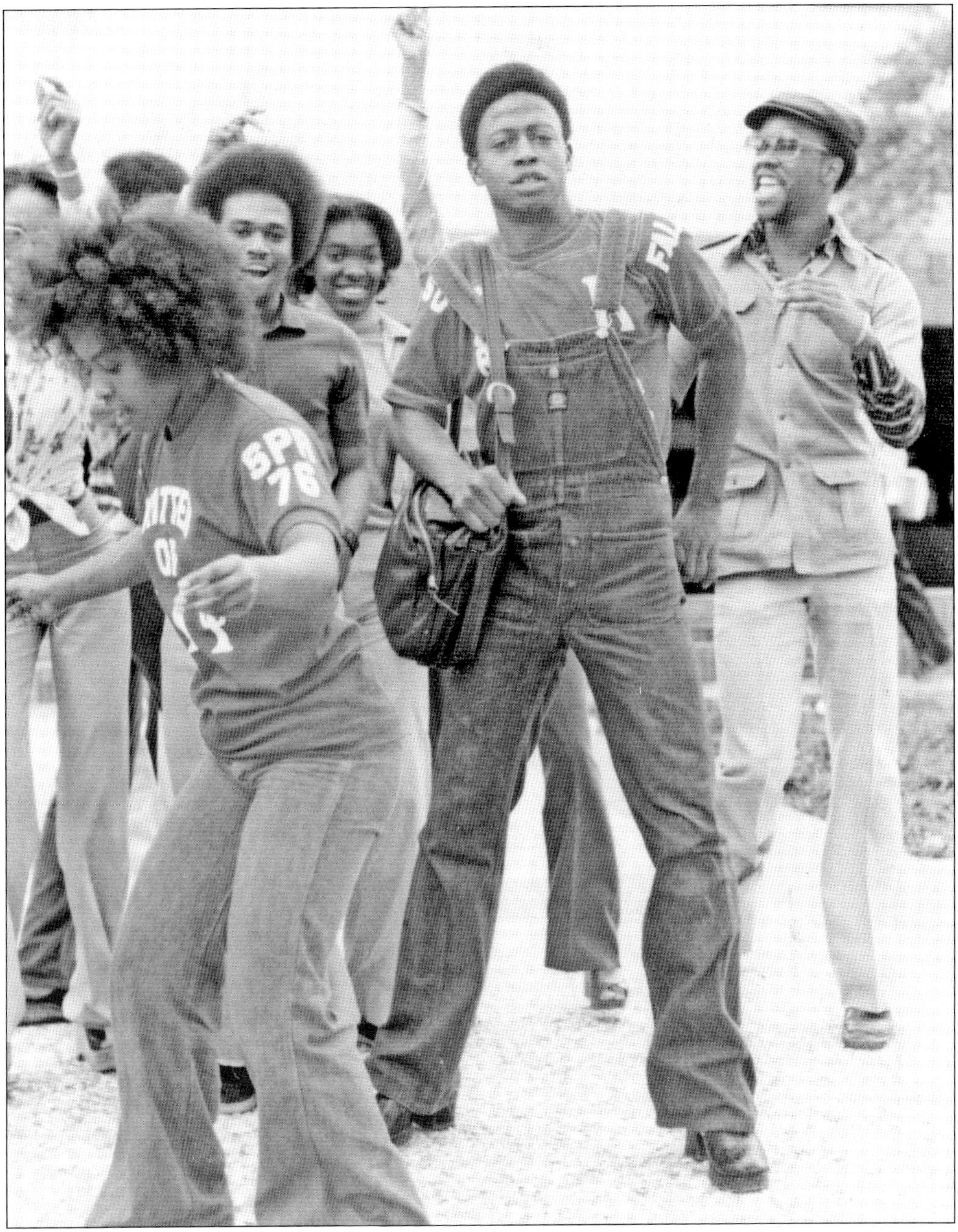

TSU students celebrate homecoming in the late 1970s. Homecoming activities were designed to encourage alumni to return to the campus. At historically black schools, homecoming holds a special meaning as alumni return to celebrate the institution that not only educated them when other colleges and universities refused them admission, but to also remember their own transformation from wide-eyed student to educated professional.